Also by Mark Rotella

Stolen Figs: And Other Adventures in Calabria

Amore

Amore

THE STORY OF

Italian American Song

Mark Rotella

FARRAR, STRAUS AND GIROUX

NEW YORK

♪

FARRAR, STRAUS AND GIROUX
18 West 18th Street, New York 10011

Distributed in Canada by D&M Publishers, Inc.
Printed in the United States of America
First edition, 2010

Library of Congress Cataloging-in-Publication Data
Rotella, Mark, 1967–
    Amore : the story of Italian American song / Mark Rotella. — 1st ed.
        p. cm.
    Includes bibliographical references and index.
    ISBN 978-0-86547-698-1 (hardcover : alk. paper)
    1. Popular music—United States—History and criticism.   2. Italian American singers.
3. Italian Americans—Music—History and criticism.   I. Title.

ML3477.R67 2010
782.42164089'51073—dc22

                                                                    2010010284

Designed by Abby Kagan

www.fsgbooks.com

1   3   5   7   9   10   8   6   4   2

For Martha, Sam, and Lulu

Contents

Contents ix

The Verse

You stand in front of an unassuming eleven-story yellow-brick building on the corner of Flatbush and DeKalb avenues in downtown Brooklyn. A green iron and glass awning fans over what must once have been a grand entrance. Many of the doorways have now been filled in by brick, and people file in through a revolving door set off to one side. Once the Brooklyn Paramount Theatre—an entertainment mecca for three decades—the building now houses the Brooklyn campus of Long Island University. Where once there were brightly lit marquees advertising the theater's name—along with the day's shows—red, blue, and yellow university banners now flap in the wind.

You follow the flow of students entering the building. To the left is a security desk; to the right is a coffee stand that doubles as a university souvenir store. You look down to notice that you have been walking on marble floors, then see that you are surrounded by veined red-marble walls.

You then realize that what at first appeared to be a large office building just at the mouth of the Manhattan Bridge was indeed one of the grand old theaters of Brooklyn. The reception room, also with its marble floors and mirrored walls, now serves as a student cafeteria. The glorious balustraded staircase winds up to a balcony with wrought-iron railings.

You follow the curve to a point where the floor slopes downward, which would have been one of the entrances to the orchestra seats. You push your way through two heavy metal doors with "Gym" stenciled in black paint. The hollow sound of basketballs bouncing echoes throughout. You walk beyond the bleachers to see the ornate gilded stage. On each side of the rococo proscenium are statues of women supporting a fountain. Below them, basketball hoops and banners hang almost lifelessly.

The athletes of Long Island University practice jump shots, oblivious to the gold detail above them. Sheetrock has filled the gaps between the columns—once box seats, now offices for various student organizations. A couple of floors below lies the Wurlitzer organ; on game days, it's elevated to the stage floor. Built in 1928, it is second in size, of those actively used, only to the Wurlitzer at Radio City Music Hall.

An intricate latticework of gilded wood frames the ceiling, upon which stars and blue clouds are painted. At one time, a Wilfred color organ player, accompanying the music of the Wurlitzer, put on a light show on the ceiling. Each key corresponded to a different light sequence.

This area of downtown was once the theater district of Brooklyn. Across the street were the Strand and Majestic theaters. Each one was built around the time of the Depression. And each was an escape.

But these theaters have now been converted to office buildings, and their stages have been torn down. The singers who performed there have long since died. One singer in particular—the Italian American Russ Columbo, who sang to audiences at the darkest moments of the Depression—is all but forgotten.

The Brooklyn Paramount would continue to be the stage for young acts up through the 1950s, when the disc jockey Alan Freed, who coined the term "rock and roll," promoted his shows. Nowadays, you'd have to ask around quite a bit to find anyone who's heard of Russ Columbo or even Alan Freed. Like Columbo and Freed, the Brooklyn Paramount has gotten lost within the constant flux of newcomers and development. After all, Brooklyn is a part of New York, a city of opportunity and disappointment, evolution and disintegration, celebration and heartbreak.

For my wife and me, Brooklyn was also a place of transformation. From the late nineteenth century to the present, thousands of immigrants poured into Brooklyn from Ireland, Italy, Eastern Europe, and, more recently, China, Russia, and the Caribbean. In the 1990s, Martha and I joined the exodus to Brooklyn from Manhattan in search of cheaper, more spacious housing. It was in the Botanic Garden there that I proposed to her; it was in a ground-floor garden apartment in Park Slope that we first lived together as a married couple. We lived within a mile of that Brooklyn Paramount Theatre, unknowingly passing it with every late-night cab ride over the bridge.

And it was while we were living in Brooklyn, in 1998, just two years after we were married, that Martha was diagnosed with breast cancer at the age of thirty-two. The next two years were harrowing for us both, but that's another story. The cancer was in an early stage and Martha survived it, but I came to know her mortality, and my own.

That emotionally wrought time is when I first became fascinated with the singers from an earlier era. A year before our lives took that sharp dip, we had seen *Big Night*, an independent film about first-generation Italians as they settle in New Jersey. Two brothers decide to open a restaurant—one brother is social and outgoing, the other an introspective artist, the chef. The opening of their restaurant is to be highlighted by the appearance of Louis Prima, who has accepted their invitation to the opening-night dinner. The brothers invite all of their friends, spend all of their money, and prepare what—even to a large Italian family—is to be a huge feast. They drink and eat as the records of Prima, his wife, Keely Smith, and Rosemary Clooney play throughout. By the early-morning hours it becomes apparent that Prima is not going to show up, casting doubt on the success of their venture. But the brothers and their friends have celebrated anyway—digging into courses of antipasti, grilled fish, roasted pig, and the finale, the *timpano*, a pastry drum of pasta, meatballs, salami, and mozzarella and Parmesan cheeses.

Those songs were familiar to me, but I had not heard them in a long time.

I bought the soundtrack on a CD. Complementing those upbeat favorites were more somber, ruminative songs performed by a 1950s Italian pop singer from Rome, Claudio Villa, and by Matteo Salvatore, a folk guitarist and singer from Apulia, the arid, flat heel of Italy's boot jutting into the Adriatic across from Albania and Greece.

When Martha's cancer diagnosis came, I reached for these songs. On one track, Louis Prima sang a jazzy "Oh, Marie," which was followed by Rosemary Clooney's whimsical "Mambo Italiano." In her smooth, clear voice, Keely Smith sang "Don't Take Your Love from Me." Matteo Salvatore strummed a tarantella on his guitar as he sang "Il Pescivendolo" (The Fishmonger). Then Claudio Villa sang, in a romantically cheerful tempo with sweet violins, about driving through the countryside in "La Strada del Bosco."

For many nights, while Martha recovered from surgery and later after her chemotherapy treatments, we were together in the house, seemingly exiled from the outside world. I created an Italian atmosphere while I cooked dinner and listened to these songs.

A few years earlier, Martha and I had traveled to Calabria, the toe of the boot, and spent a week with cousins in the village where my father's parents were born. I had already embarked on an exploration of my Italian American identity. This music carried me deeper.

About this time, while flipping through the Italian bin at a record store, I came across a CD whose cover was meant to look like a box of Ronzoni pasta. The songs were all of an era—the early 1950s through the early 1960s. Dean Martin crooned "That's Amore";

Connie Francis made everyone weep to "Mama"; Jerry Vale belted "Mala femmina"; Lou Monte sang his gimmick song "Pepino the Italian Mouse"; and for the first time I listened to two versions of "Volare," one by an Italian singer named Domenico Modugno, the other by Dean Martin. Were these songs a big part of my childhood? Not as much as, say, any number of pop songs—but I recalled them, and realized that they were as much a part of me as my last name.

I reached out to them. The rock music of the 1990s, which was coming out of Seattle, was cynical, internal, and self-absorbed. I needed voices that not only spoke of pain but could guide me out of that darkness. I needed songs that would act as a tonic to my despair.

Of course, one singer in particular could alternately make me feel as if I could conquer the world and allow me to indulge in my heavy heart: Sinatra. He was both tough and vulnerable, oozing confidence, yet also sharing his pain.

At the same time, I sought out recordings from other Italian singers; even some of the gimmicky CDs, like *Mob Hits*, got me right in the heart. Indeed, though some of the songs dripped with sap, they were still, in ways, so much more real for me than the pop music of the time.

My interest deepened, and I began searching out more songs from each of these singers. Their voices captivated me. The elegant simplicity of their singing drew me in; there was true passion in their voices. They sang about love and romance; they sang about desire and unrequited love. They told stories, but when you listened closely, you realized there was more to the stories than the words. These singers communicated a huge range of emotions with the tiniest modulation of their voices.

They helped me get myself and my wife through those scary times. When Martha got a clean bill of health, the two of us took my parents back to Calabria—a celebration.

It seemed that all these singers—or crooners, as they came to be called for their nuanced subtlety—were Italian. Of course, there were Bing Crosby and Nat "King" Cole, but I recalled my father—whose parents had emigrated from Calabria and who spoke Italian before English—displaying an Italian pride whenever a song by Sinatra, Tony Bennett, Vic Damone, or Perry Como came on the radio at home or, more likely, in an Italian restaurant.

Those songs were all from the late 1940s and the 1950s. It was during this time that Italian Americans entered mainstream American life and culture. Others have defined this period as the time between the Korean and the Vietnam wars, from the A-bomb to John F. Kennedy's assassination, or as the Eisenhower years. I define this time as the Italian decade—roughly, and generously, from 1947 to 1964; musically, from the end of the big bands to the Beatles, or, more specifically, from Frank Sinatra's last number one hit before his comeback to the heyday of the Rat Pack.

The 1940s and 1950s were decades when Italian Americans were breaking out of their working-class neighborhoods of Brooklyn, the Bronx, South Philly. For the first time, sons of Italian immigrants—like my father—tore loose from their own fathers' masonry businesses, from their grandfathers' barbershops, from their bars. In Frank Sinatra's voice you can almost hear the suppression of decades of immigrant frustration and anger.

This was the time when Italian Americans entered the mainstream of employment, and when they broke into popular culture. With television, these singers entered Americans' homes. These sociable, outgoing Italian American crooners were eager to connect with people.

First—at the very beginning of the twentieth century—there was the Neapolitan tenor Enrico Caruso, America's first recording sensation, on 78s; then, in the 1930s, Russ Columbo, born in Camden, New Jersey, pumped pride into the hearts of Italians in America.

In the early 1940s, a skinny kid with great blue eyes and a bow tie drew crowds as no one had before. He captivated the teenage girls, who screamed out to him. Frank Sinatra became the first modern American singing idol. Before Elvis Presley, before the Beatles, Sinatra developed a teenybopper cult. Young people were the fans rather than their parents.

Sinatra created a style—both onstage and off—that dozens of other performers would emulate. Vocally, he incorporated two forms of Italian singing into his music: the bel canto, or beautiful singing, style of eighteenth-century Italian opera, and the romanticism of Italian, especially Neapolitan, folk songs, which Italians of all backgrounds adopted as their own once they arrived in America. There was a smoothness and ease in his singing. Sinatra's voice was graceful—but with an edge.

The Italian American singers had a kind of charisma not seen before. They sang with a passion that nevertheless appeared casual and easy. Their seeming effortlessness reminds me of an old Italian saying—"never let them see you sweat." They embodied the Italian idea of *la sprezzatura*—making hard work appear easy. *La sprezzatura* was the concept of the fourteenth-century Italian writer Baldassare Castiglione, who in his book *Il Cortegiano*, or *The Book of the Courtier*, explained how courtiers—those who attend the court or homes of royalty—should appear to their rulers. Originally meaning to exude nonchalance, the term came to mean to remain cool.

Sinatra parted the stage curtain to a full cast of Italian American singers. Like the Jewish comedians, Italian singers found audiences among their own. The comedians, hired by Jewish promoters, performed in the "borscht belt" Catskill resorts to Jewish families; Italians were hired by Italian club owners in New York, Chicago, and other large cities, and performed to the Italian audiences who knew and loved their style. And as the list of great Jewish comedians runs long (Jackie Mason, Sid Caesar, Woody Allen, Lenny Bruce), so does the list of great Italian singers.

Through those stage curtains came generations of Italian Americans who, with song, wooed women and made men cry.

There was Perry Como as well as the New Orleanian Louis Prima, followed by Vic Damone, Frankie Laine, Dean Martin, and Tony Bennett. Their influence reached France, England, Russia, Japan—and their style even began to redefine music back in Italy, back in the Old Country.

Italian Americans must have felt a sense of pride at their success—not just a sense of belonging, but proof that they could hold their own in this country.

Now, of course, Italian Americans are established in American society. There are Italian American college presidents, Supreme Court justices, and Fortune 500 chief executives, as well as star musicians and ballplayers. So why do these singers still mean so much to me? Why am I nostalgic for a time that is not mine? Why do I yearn to recapture the experiences of my parents and grandparents?

I think it is because there really was a distinctive Italian American style—cocky and tender, tough and vulnerable, serious and playful, forward-thinking and nostalgic—and it is found nowhere so powerfully as in this music.

Although the Italian American singers and their songs may sometimes seem sentimental to our ears, their lack of cynicism is refreshing in an increasingly confusing, information-laden world. Their songs came at a time when Americans wanted, needed, to feel good—during World War II and the Korean War. America was celebrating its postwar prosperity. Italians knew how to live the good life. They knew how to celebrate when celebration was called for; they had had plenty of experience in taking the good from the bad. Even in hard times, one can find a hint of *la dolce vita*, the sweet life.

Think of Dean Martin's "That's Amore"; Frankie Laine's "S'posin'"; Perry Como's "I'm Gonna Love That Gal (Like She's Never Been Loved Before)"; Louis Prima's "Just a Gigolo"; Bobby Darin's "Mack the Knife"; Tony Bennett's "Rags to Riches"; and Frank Sinatra's "I've Got the World on a String."

To listen to American pop music is to listen to the voices of Italians as they assimilated into American culture. This is my Top 40 list of Italian American hits. Through these songs—written by other Americans—the Italians told their story. This is the story of how Italian Americans gave style to pop music.

Part One

The Old Country

1

"I Have But One Heart" ("O marenariello")

FRANK SINATRA AND VIC DAMONE

Frank Sinatra tossed his cards on the table.

"I fold," he said. He was playing poker at a friend's apartment in Manhattan. It was the summer of 1946, and WHN was broadcasting a game between the New York Giants and the Brooklyn Dodgers. That evening's hard rain had delayed the game, and music filled the gap.

The smoke from cigars and cigarettes rose from the table; whiskey-soaked ice clinked in glasses.

"Night and Day" came on the radio, the Cole Porter song from the musical *Gay Divorcee*.

"Hey, Frankie. Is that you?" asked his friend Sammy Cahn, the composer and songwriter.

"Yup," Sinatra answered, still concentrating on the game. Jimmy Van Heusen, another songwriter, nodded in agreement. Sinatra had had a hit with his version of the song, arranged by Axel Stordahl, in 1942 and again in 1944.

They continued to play, and at the song's end the radio announcer said: "And that was the voice of Vic Damone."

"Who?" Sinatra said, pushing his chair back. "What the hell did he just say?"

Sinatra got up from the table, picked up the phone, and dialed the radio station.

"This is Frank Sinatra, and I want to speak with this Vic Damone," he demanded.

The announcer tapped on the booth where Damone, backed by a small ensemble, had just finished singing. "Some guy says he's Frank Sinatra wants to talk with you."

"Yeah, like Frank Sinatra is going to call *me*," Damone said. It must be the guys back in Brooklyn, he thought, playing a prank. He picked up the line.

"This is Frank Sinatra, and I want you to stop singing my songs."

"Yeah, if you're Frank Sinatra, then I'm the pope."

Damone, laughing, hung up on the man known to everyone in the music world simply as "The Voice."

That's how Vic Damone told me the story one day nearly sixty years later.

"I was imitating him. That day, I was live on the radio. I paid an arranger to copy Sinatra's Stordahl arrangements, and I was singing it live. All of us singers then wanted to sound like him."

We were talking on the telephone. A few weeks earlier I had sent Damone a letter, along with a book I had written. In the letter I asked for an interview. I didn't expect to hear back from him: the word was that he had retired from show business after suffering a stroke a couple of years earlier, and that he hadn't spoken with writers in some time. One night I came home to a message on the answering machine: "Hello. This is Vic Damone. I was a singer—am a singer. I got your letter, and I'd be happy to talk with you."

I played the message several times, listening to the voice, at once humble and confident, over and over. The voice that generations of people had heard on the radio and in concert halls was now on my answering machine—in my home. I felt I had reached right back to the late 1940s, when the voice of Vic Damone and singers like him filled the homes of people across America with music—Italian American music.

Within four months of each other in 1947, Frank Sinatra and Vic Damone released versions of "I Have But One Heart." It was a song in English, based on an Italian folk song called "O marenariello" (The Sailor). Damone's version came out first. He was eighteen years old, and it was the first song he recorded for a major label, Mercury. Released May 30, it went up to number seven on the *Billboard* charts—just months after he had sung during the Dodgers–Giants rain delay, and before anyone outside of Brooklyn had ever heard of him—and stayed there for seven weeks. On September 20, Sinatra released his version, which stayed on the charts for just two weeks, reaching only number thirteen. Judging by Damone's numbers, his version was filling living rooms across the country, making its way into the hearts of teenage girls.

The competition certainly wasn't a catalyst for Damone's rise or Sinatra's fall. But it reflected a change in a momentous year for both singers. For one thing, Sinatra, thirty-one years old and no longer the young darling, was starting to get bad press—for being a Communist, according to conservatives then coming into power; for being linked to the Mafia; for cheating on his wife; and for lashing out, both verbally and physically, at reporters.

For another, that same year Italian Americans, long a poor and embattled minority, began entering public consciousness en masse. Nearly seven million Americans of Italian descent were living in the United States. For decades they had lived in neighborhoods of their own, enclaves within the big cities. Suddenly they were visible nationwide.

In boxing that summer, titles had been won and lost by Italian Americans within a couple of months of each other. In July, Rocky Graziano (given name: Thomas Rocco Barbella) won the world middleweight title against the Polish American Tony Zale, and a month later Willie Pep (Guglielmo Papaleo) successfully defended his world featherweight title against Jock Leslie. The middleweight Jake LaMotta (Giacobbe LaMotta) lost to Billy Fox. In September, Joey Maxim (Giuseppe Antonio Berardinelli) defeated Clarence Jones, and Roland La Starza knocked out Jim Johnson. That year, Rocco Francis Marchegiano fought his first professional bout under the name Rocky Mack. He soon changed his name to Rocky Marciano, and he would become the only undefeated heavyweight champion in history.

But it was a trio of figures who would be recognized forever among the great Americans of the twentieth century: La Guardia, DiMaggio, and Sinatra.

In 1947 those three names rolled off the tongues of Americans as never before. And Italian Americans in New York and throughout the country wore those names like badges of honor, signs that they, and their people, had made it in America.

Fiorello La Guardia—known as "the Little Flower" on account of his first name and his size (he was just over five feet tall)—had served as mayor of New York City from 1934 until 1945. He held the city's hand through both the Great Depression and World War II. He was America's first Italian American mayor of a major city.

Born in 1882 on Varick Street in Greenwich Village to an Italian father (whose family came from Apulia and Sicily) and a Jewish mother from Trieste (then part of the Austro-Hungarian Empire), La Guardia grew up Episcopalian and spent his early childhood in the Arizona Territory. In his late twenties, he worked as a translator at Ellis Island, becoming a champion of the little guy, the voice of the immigrant and the labor unions. In time, he became a congressman, representing Italian American East Harlem, and then, on the Fusion ticket, was elected mayor of New York City.

After declining to run for a fourth term as mayor, La Guardia stayed in the public eye, serving on various boards and committees, but two years after leaving office, on September 20, 1947, he died of pancreatic cancer. Nearly forty thousand mourners filed past his open casket the next day at the Cathedral of St. John the Divine in upper Manhattan.

On September 30, Joe DiMaggio, a Sicilian fisherman's son from San Francisco, played in the first televised World Series as the Yankees faced the Brooklyn Dodgers. The big story was the presence of Jackie Robinson, who had joined the Dodgers that season, breaking baseball's color line. But there were plenty of Italian Americans on both sides: Joe DiMaggio, Yogi Berra, Phil Rizzuto, and Vic Raschi playing for the Yankees; Carl Furillo, Ralph Branca, Al Gionfriddo, Cookie Lavagetto, and Vic Lombardi for the Dodgers. In game six, Gionfriddo caught a DiMaggio fly ball at the wall in Yankee Stadium, denying him a home run and forcing a game seven. The Yankees won the series, and DiMaggio earned his third American League Most Valuable Player Award.

The third member of that Italian American pantheon was Francis Albert Sinatra, who grew up just across the Hudson River in Hoboken.

On the radio in 1947, Americans tuned in to Buddy Clark's "Peg O' My Heart," the Andrews Sisters' "Near You," Louis Jordan's "Ain't Nobody Here but Us Chickens," and Dinah Shore's "Anniversary Song." Perry Como crooned "I Wonder Who's Kissing Her Now," while Frankie Laine belted out "That's My Desire," and Tony Pastor performed "Red Silk Stockings and Green Perfume." That year Bing Crosby released the version of "White Christmas" we all hear today.

Frank Sinatra also recorded a version of the song, but with less success—Crosby sounded like a father singing to his kids, Sinatra like a young man singing to his girlfriend. Every year since 1943, Sinatra had been one of the top-ten recording artists, reaching the top three in 1946. That year Sinatra had eight Top 10 hits (Bing Crosby had five). His songs were played everywhere all year long: on the radio, on jukeboxes, on home record players.

8 *The Old Country*

In the first half of 1947, Sinatra had hits with "I Believe" and "Mam'selle," which reached number one and stayed on the charts for ten weeks. Then that was it. By year's end, his career was in a decline that would last nearly seven years. Meanwhile, for Damone—and many other singers—1947 represented their big break, marking a rise in the popularity of Italian American singers. Damone represented the many Italian Americans who were just beginning to leave their close-knit urban neighborhoods.

Italian Americans were in the news—as great ballplayers, boxers, singers, and politicians—though America's attitude toward them as a group was slow to change. Italian Americans were either violent mafiosi or girl-chasing, macaroni-eating romantics. Sinatra attracted both the pride and the prejudice. In many ways he became emblematic of all Italian Americans.

Whatever anyone felt about Italians, though, Italian-inspired songs were making their way onto the lips of Americans across the country.

I heard Vic Damone's version of "I Have But One Heart" long before Frank Sinatra's, on a CD release of his first recordings on the Mercury label. And while I like both versions, Damone's is exceptionally smooth, lyrical, rich—even Sinatra lauded Damone as having "the best pipes in the business." Listening to it—late at night after a glass or two of wine—I see the waters off the coast of Naples, Sorrento, or Amalfi. The sun is setting, and the rhythm is that of a boat being gently rowed over glassy water. With each oar stroke, a phrase is sung. Damone's rich voice brings to life the voice of the sailor of that song's title, tired, but proud of his full net of fish:

Vicin' o mare, faciammo 'ammore
a core a core, pe'nce spassa . . .

The literal translation (not the lyrics of the hit) is:

By the sea we are making love,
Heart to heart we spend the time . . .

The song was written in the late nineteenth century by two Neapolitans, Salvatore Gambardella, a musician and songwriter, and Gennaro Ottaviano, a poet. For Italian Americans, "O marenariello" was as popular as "Danny Boy" is for the Irish, or "Guantanamera" for Cubans. Italian Americans had heard versions of the song performed by the great opera singers Enrico Caruso, Tito Schipa, and Carlo Buti. In the 1940s it was adapted by Johnny Farrow, with Marty Symes writing English lyrics. Unfortunately, the lyric the radio listeners of 1947 heard—"I have but one heart, this heart I bring you, I have but one heart to share with you"—was pedestrian love stuff, without a hint of Italy in it.

Within months of the release of the Sinatra and Damone recordings of "I Have But One Heart," songs both Italian-sounding and sung in Italian would be played on the radio. Perry Como sang "Chi-baba, Chi-baba (My Bambino Go to Sleep)," which was also recorded by the Charioteers and Peggy Lee; the Andrews Sisters sang "Bella Bella Marie" with the Italian American Phil Brito; Eddie Fisher sang "Anema e core"; the Gaylords sang "Tell Me You're Mine" (from the Italian "Per un bacio d'amore"); Tony Martin (who changed his name from Alvin Morris) sang "Luna rossa" and "There's No Tomorrow" (based on "O sole mio"); Vaughn Monroe sang "Vieni Su, Say You Love Me Too"; and Rosemary Clooney had hits with "Botch-A-Me," "Mambo Italiano," and the Italian-accented "Come On-A My House." And the Italian American hits continued—"Eh, cumpari" (Julius La Rosa), "Darktown Strutters' Ball (Italian-Style)" (Lou Monte), and "Angelina" and "Oh, Marie" (both Louis Prima).

In 1949, Vic Damone recorded another Italian-inspired song— "You're Breaking My Heart," which was based on "Mattinata" by Ruggiero Leoncavallo, who had written the nineteenth-century opera *Pagliacci*. Written and arranged by Pat Genaro and Sunny Skylar, the song went right up to number one.

But more than just Italian-sounding songs—or songs that evoked an Italian feeling—Italian American singers appeared in full force. They came from New York City, New Jersey, Chicago. Theirs was an urban sound. The music they sang wasn't the high lonesome of the rural South, nor was it the sound of the rugged mountains of the Old Country. It was the sound of the streets, the mixing together of songs, arrangements, and interpretations by artists from all backgrounds.

Flipping through the pages of Joel Whitburn's collection of *Billboard* hits from 1940 to 1954, I counted only five Italians making the Top 40 list before 1947: Phil Brito, Jimmy Durante, Louis Prima, Perry Como, and Frank Sinatra. Then, in 1947 alone, Sinatra, Damone, Perry Como, Buddy Greco, Frankie Laine, and Louis Prima all had Top 10 hits.

And then came the *grande bacio*—the big Italian kiss.

During the first part of the Italian decade—from 1947 to 1954, the year of Frank Sinatra's comeback—more than twenty-five Italian Americans brought music to America: Tony Bennett, Don Cornell, Jerry Vale, Al Martino, Alan Dale, Johnny Desmond, Jimmy Durante, Joni James, Julius La Rosa, Mario Lanza, Dean Martin, Lou Monte, the Gaylords, June Valli, the Four Aces, the Four Lads, Liberace, Mantovani & His Orchestra, Tony Pastor, and Ezio Pinza. And that was just the first seven years.

Eight months after Vic Damone hung up on Frank Sinatra at the radio station, the young singer himself, with his "I Have But One Heart" hit, made his first appearance at Madison Square Garden at a charity fund-raiser hosted by Ed Sullivan. He was on the same bill as his idol.

"I'm waiting backstage, and there's Frank Sinatra," Vic Damone remembered. "Someone whispered something in his ear, and I see Sinatra look at me. His eyes narrowed; he just stared at me."

Sinatra then pointed to him and with a crooked index finger motioned Vic Damone over.

"Who, me?" Damone said.

"Yeah, you."

Damone hesitantly approached Sinatra. His idol poked him in his chest with a force that pushed him back a couple of steps.

"What are you, some sort of wise guy?" Sinatra said.

"Wise guy?" Damone said nervously. "Mr. Sinatra, I don't know what you're talking about."

Frank Sinatra recounted the incident at WHN, and it occurred to Vic Damone then that it really had been Sinatra on the phone.

"Was that you?"

Sinatra laughed. He gave Damone another look and said, "Okay, kid. I'm going to introduce you tonight."

Sinatra told Sullivan that he wanted Damone to sing after Sinatra and that he would like to introduce Damone himself. Sinatra went onstage, sang a couple of songs, then spoke to the audience: "I'd like to introduce to you Vic Damone. This kid's a really great singer. He's got stardust on his shoulders."

With those words, Frank Sinatra ushered in the Italian decade, then stepped offstage.

It was as if he were referring not only to this teenager from Brooklyn who had a hit with an Italian popular song but to all the Italian American singers who would interpret pop standards for American audiences—singers who had grown up listening to their parents' songs from the Old Country but who lived entirely in the new.

2

"Vesti la giubba"

ENRICO CARUSO

America's first pop music star was an Italian opera singer.

In 1904, Enrico Caruso recorded his first aria for the Victor Talking Machine Company, "Vesti la giubba" from the Italian opera *Pagliacci*. It became his signature aria—and it would determine the course of how music was recorded and, through the purchasing power of its millions of listeners, how records were bought.

Just a year earlier, Caruso had entered the American consciousness with his first appearance at the Metropolitan Opera House. He transformed the opera experience for many Americans. At the time, the Metropolitan Opera House was known for programming German operas featuring German opera singers; it was through Caruso's heart-on-his-sleeve singing style that American opera moved away from the German-centered repertoire toward the Italian operas. Because the Met was making so much money from Caruso's performances—and Italian opera in general—the house shifted to accommodate its star's repertoire.

On East Nineteenth Street between Avenue S and Avenue T, deep in the quiet residential Gravesend section of Brooklyn, is a two-story wood-frame house. Aldo Mancusi, a trim, nicely dressed man in his eighties with a thin mustache, greets you at the door, invites you in, and immediately directs you to the second floor, as he and his wife occupy the first.

You emerge in the largest space of what is a three-room museum, the walls of which are covered with rows and rows of photographs of Caruso, as well as an impressive collection of Victrola record players and even a very early jukebox that played 78s.

On display in glass cases are several of the great opera singer's pipes; black-and-white cap-toe shoes; and a 24-karat Tiffany gold coin, of which Caruso had dozens custom-pressed to be handed out as gifts to friends.

Like those of superheroes on lunch boxes or athletes on Wheaties boxes today, Enrico Caruso's name and image appeared on countless items: Caruso tins for sewing needles; cans of Enrico Caruso Olive Oil based in Carlstadt, New Jersey (100 percent olive oil for Italians; a blend of 75 percent peanut and 25 percent olive oils "for 'merican'"); Caruso Grated Parmesan Cheese; Caruso Soup Mix; and Caruso Mushroom Sauce. There was also an assortment of macaroni (spaghetti, pastina, egg noodles), along with a booklet that included such recipes as Caruso Spaghetti with Clams. A housewife could save the coupons from each of these items in a booklet that could be redeemed for, among other items, a clothes iron.

In one case, I noticed a matchbook from a onetime New York institution called Mamma Leone's, which was a restaurant located in the bottom floor of a house on West Thirty-fourth Street. Mamma Leone cooked for Caruso out of her kitchen, until Caruso bought her a restaurant. He would bring dignitaries there, showing them the real (that is, Italian) way to eat and drink. (In 1967, Harper and Row published *Leone's Italian Cookbook*; Dwight D. Eisenhower contributed the introduction.)

Just as I was leaving, I caught sight of Caruso's death mask. He seemed to have died with a slight smile on his face.

For Mancusi, a retired designer of office and retail space whose father had emigrated from Naples and had been a great admirer of Caruso, the museum is a labor of love, a way of keeping his father's memory alive. He built upon his father's collection of records and memorabilia, gradually acquiring items from other collectors. The Caruso museum, which Mancusi opened in 1990, is the largest in the world; there are two other much smaller museums, one in Milan and one at a restaurant in Sorrento, just south of Naples. The museum in Brooklyn is a destination for scholars of Caruso and opera in general.

At the turn of the twentieth century, there were 1.5 million Italian Americans living in the United States, the population having grown from 40,000 in 1840. The years between 1880 and 1920 marked the great immigration of Italians to America. They fled from famine, drought, and earthquakes; they fled from poverty, political unrest, and social injustice. They were unskilled, and many illiterate, and what they settled for was dark, crowded tenements and long days spent at menial labor for little money—all for the sake of sending some money back to their families in Italy or starting their own businesses.

By the time Caruso came to New York, Italians were the third-largest immigrant population, following the Germans and the Irish—and they were near the bottom rung of the socioeconomic ladder. They were generally Catholic and dark-skinned; they spoke a foreign language and were considered racially inferior.

Enrico Caruso embodied the American dream held by immigrants of any nationality, and his life was not atypical for immigrants. In Caruso, Italian Americans had a goodwill ambassador, beloved by wealthy Americans as well as the poor.

Caruso was born in February 1873 into a poor family in a slum neighborhood in Naples. He was the first of seven children, and he managed to survive the cholera epidemic that swept Naples at the time.

Naples is the third-largest city in Italy, following Milan and Rome. The port city was built along the Bay of Naples; if you are standing at its northwesternmost tip, your eye follows the urban crescent that reaches Mount Vesuvius at its eastern point. Looking out to sea, you can see the islands of Procida and Ischia and, to the south, the island of Capri and the province of Salerno. The Greeks founded the city nearly three thousand years ago and named it Neapolis, or New City. From the thirteenth century until the seventeenth, it was the capital of what was called the Kingdom of Naples, which became the Kingdom of the Two Sicilies. Its size and cultural influence in Europe were second only to Paris's.

It is from Naples that we get what Americans think of as quintessential Italian foods—spaghetti with thick red sauce, pizza, linguine, and clams and mussels marinara. It is also the city that inspired a good deal of Italian popular music. It was long an artistic center of not only Italy but also Europe. Along the narrow streets of its oldest neighborhoods on weekends, musicians and singers roam, and vendors of all kinds sell their wares, with the smell of pizza and fried zeppole filling the alleyways.

It is also a place of pickpockets and crimes both petty and mortal, where the garlicky aroma of tomato sauce battles the stench of garbage and dead fish. During Caruso's time, with the exception of a few privileged neighborhoods, Naples was basically a densely populated slum of half a million people.

It was to Naples that many Italians from the continental south made the trek in order to depart for America.

By age twenty-one, Caruso had begun his professional career. He performed throughout Italy and Europe and as far away as St. Petersburg, Cairo, and Buenos Aires.

At one performance—his first engagement at the famous La Scala in Milan—he sang Donizetti's *L'Elisir d'Amore*, conducted by Arturo Toscanini. At the end of the performance, the famously harsh and critical conductor was heard to say, "By God, if this young Neapolitan continues to sing like this, he will make the whole world talk about him."

On December 30, 1901, at the age of twenty-eight, Caruso returned home to Naples to sing for the first time at one of the most prestigious opera houses in Italy, the Teatro di San Carlo, whose directors must have finally deemed him worthy to perform there.

Perhaps Caruso had gotten cocky after so much success around the world; perhaps he didn't ingratiate himself, as performers usually did in Naples, to the operagoing socialites. Whatever the reason, the audience reception was cool, with forced applause. The press butchered him the next day, saying that his performance was "not beautiful," his singing "baritonal and throaty," and his acting terrible.

Caruso said he would never perform again in his hometown: "I'll only come back to Naples to see my dear stepmother and to eat spaghetti and clams."

Like many Italians, he felt America's pull.

In a story of unrequited love and vengeance, his city of Naples had rejected him; now he would leave and prove it wrong.

To fully appreciate and understand the great Italian American pop singers, you have to go back to the Old Country.

Songs echoed from across mountaintops and within valleys, traveled across the fields, floated on waves in the sea. They came from shepherds, farmers, and fishermen. They were songs of work, of love, of sorrow, of desperation, of religion, of faith—they were the sounds of youth and old age. They came from the bosoms of mothers as they sang lullabies of hope and fear to their children.

In the fields of southern Italy, workers filled the dewy morning silence with a kind of call-and-response, like Negro spirituals sung in America. Well before the sun rose, Italian men and women would leave their compact villages to walk perhaps a couple of miles to fields where they would sow their seeds and reap their crops. One would sing a verse, the others would respond. Sometimes, on particularly fruitless days, a man might sing alone, crying out to the rest of the workers, too despondent to answer.

Out on the seas, a similar call-and-response rode the waves as fishermen hauled in their nets of tuna or swordfish in the early hours. Their singing rolled over the water to other fishing boats yards away. The waves lapped the boats on gentle Mediterranean seas, the fishermen calling to one another as they spotted the fish.

In the 1950 movie *Stromboli*, Ingrid Bergman, playing an English-woman, meets and marries an Italian man on the remote island of the movie's name off the toe of the boot. The Italian is a fisherman, and in one scene the director, Roberto Rossellini, shows actual footage of the brutal beauty of the *mattanza*, or slaughter, as fisher-men corral bluefin tuna and plunge spears into them. The white frothy water darkens with blood.

"Forti iusi fó / 'rtu uysu / 'rti iusu 'n tierra," calls one fisherman in a 1954 recording by the music ethnographer Alan Lomax. The fisherman is Calabrese, and he is fishing the waters close to the island of Stromboli. "More strongly down, landward!" he calls in dialect to his fellow fishermen, "It's going toward land!" I picture the boats getting closer, closing in on the school of tuna. I imagine an eerie calm as the boats tighten the ring and pull in the nets. A ripple of water breaks the waves, then the splash of a fin. Then an eruption of fins as dozens of fish are hauled in. The fishermen spear them and smash their heads with clubs. The singing gets louder, battling with the sound of the waves and the tuna slapping the water.

After the day has ended, there are songs of dance, such as the lively tarantella, in which *zampogne*, or bagpipes, and tambourines reach high levels of intensity, building speed. Historically, the dance of the tarantella is meant to shake and sweat out poison from the body following a tarantula bite. It's frenetic. The dancers spin around; onlookers clap and whistle and yell out. It's rhythmically mesmeriz-ing, and cathartic for its participants.

The bagpipe drones; the tambourine shakes out beats so quick dancers can barely catch their breath—as if breathing would allow the devil to enter them.

In the villages themselves, the lyrical cry of vendors selling their wares would echo within the alleys. The southern Italian immigrant vendors brought these cries to the dense cities of America—New York, Chicago, Philadelphia, Boston. You can still hear the sounds now in the hill villages of Calabria, Sicily, and Basilicata; you can hear these songs in the crowded streets of Spaccanapoli, the old section of Naples.

Italians preferred to live in clustered villages and go out to their farming rather than live remotely on the land. (Furthermore, not many Italians owned the land they farmed, but instead were sharecroppers who worked for feudal lords.) They enjoyed talking, communicating. Street vendors called out their produce, their wares; the fishmonger would sing out the day's catch. Social life for Italians was in the street, their windows always open wide to the sounds outside. One might hear the *pizzaiolo*, or pizza man, sing out:

Eh, c'aimm' a coce,
Vedi ch' e cchien' 'e alice . . .

Come on, we must cook it!
Look, it's full of anchovies . . .

The voices of *cantastorie*, or street singers, echoed through the narrow streets of hillside villages. *Cantastorie* are performers who bring music and stories to the village, perhaps even with a hint of gossip in the lyric.

Just as the Irish created hauntingly beautiful music about mythical heroes and warriors, and sang longingly about their green fields, Neapolitan composers and lyricists wrote about the bounty of the sea, the men who fished it, the women they dreamed of while they were away.

These songs took on new life in the new country. There's the dreamy "Santa Lucia," about the coast of Naples. It was written in the early nineteenth century, and it was one of the songs that was heard in many homes in Hoboken, the Bronx, South Philadelphia, and Boston's North End.

There were many other popular songs, mostly composed in the late nineteenth century, such as "A primavera," "Te voglio bene assaje," "Torna a Surriento," the playful "Funiculì, funiculà," celebrating the opening of Naples's funicular train in 1880, "Marechiaro," and, of course, "O marenariello"—the song on which "I Have But One Heart" was based.

But it is the songs of courtship in southern Italy that most move the heart. In a society where the sexes were kept separate, Italian men— unthwarted by the strict social confines—found ways to express their love, to court. And they did so beautifully through song, and with neighbors or other musicians looking on. "Come and sit by the window," a young man might sing, serenading a girl below her balcony, perhaps with a mandolin player present. "Listen to the one who sings you this serenade, it is the young man who loves you so." By singing to the girl in public, he makes his intentions known to the rest of the village.

The songs of love are plaintive. The singers bled their hearts in "Ed amuri t'arricuordi?" (Oh, Love, Do You Remember?). That song, too, is a wail. But so many songs celebrate the love of women, the beauty of the sunset over the sea, the memories of the home village, the embrace of something as omnipresent as the sun.

For southern Italian men, subsisting in a tough and often barren landscape, life revolves around the possibility of romance, of sex, and of love. And that possibility consumes them, whether it be the fear of being cuckolded or the yearning for a woman's heart.

In southern Italy, the singer truly wears his heart on his sleeve for the entire village to see. Generally, Italians there live by the twin philosophies of "never let anyone know what you are thinking" and "never let anyone know he's gotten to you."

My father always told me to put on a good face to the public, *fare una faccia contenta*. It is a point of pride for Italians to present a *bella figura*—to cut a beautiful, or graceful, figure.

But there are two states of mind where all this flies out the window—love and revenge. And often, the two go hand in hand. For in matters of love, Italians are not ashamed to show their emotions. For them, becoming swept up in those passions is proof that they are fully alive.

While traveling throughout Calabria in 2001, I wandered through aisles of vendors at an Easter *festa* outside a church in my grandparents' hometown, Gimigliano. A couple of booths there sold music cassettes. I looked through the boxes, finding familiar folk music like "Calabrisella mia" and songs by Domenico Modugno, Roberto Murolo, and Carlo Buti. Then I came across several cassettes with song titles handwritten or typed on colored paper. They looked like bootleg records. I asked the vendor what they were, and he shrugged his shoulders and said something about folk songs from prisoners. I told myself that I would return to buy one, but friends whisked me away to find a place to eat. I left Calabria regretting that I had not picked one up. I had imagined they would be the Italian version of chain-gang songs from Mississippi and Louisiana.

About a year after I returned to New York City, a magazine editor asked me to review a CD called *La Musica della Mafia: Il Canto di Malavita*—songs of the underworld. These were the prisoner songs that I remembered from Calabria, but they were nothing like what I had imagined. They were not the equivalent of songs of chain-gang prisoners, which were, say, voices singing in unison to the rhythm of the pounding of a hammer. They were the songs of revenge inspired by the dreaded 'ndrangheta, the Calabrese Mafia, written by mafiosi for their members, and often sung by local village musicians. The songs here were composed and recorded by a group of musicians led by a man named Mimmo Siclari, a Calabrese record vendor who himself had been fascinated by this music at a young age. The songs have been banned in Italy; a German record company released the CD I had been given.

These songs were heard at the village cafés and bars—songs by men about love—both of the sweet, desperate kind and of the bitter, unrequited kind. Some songs came from the tormented souls of men who'd been cuckolded. Others were by men who were betrayed by other men, *pentiti*, Mafia turncoats.

In a country that had been conquered and ruled by so many outsiders, southern Italians had come to distrust any ruling party—especially since virtually all of them were foreign, be they Bourbons or French or Normans. Southern Italians developed their own laws and codes of ethics. They petitioned their concerns through their own, self-appointed lawmakers. And thus began what has come to be known as the Mafia. Legend has it that it was first formed to protect the natives; but these groups of Robin Hood–like intermediaries became seduced by their own power.

The mafiosi sang songs of revenge—against those who had framed them, against those who had broken the code of silence that bound them. In one song, "Omertà," a member of the *'ndrangheta* sings:

> While the sawn-off shotgun sings
> The traitor screams and dies . . .

Another song, dating back to the mid-nineteenth century, juxtaposes violence and tenderness: "Tarantella guappa." A betrayed mafioso sings:

> My knife it knows its art so well
> First, traitor, I'll slash your face and watch you die . . .

He then ends his song as if returning to his lover's bed after a day's work:

My Nannaredda came to make the bed
Her skin as white as milk.

In some instances, revenge and love come together in a single
song. Throughout southern Italy, it was not uncommon for a man
who believed he'd been cuckolded to sing through the streets,
declaring a woman untrue (although she could have simply not
returned his affections). Here the man will trade the embarrassment
of unfaithfulness, being known throughout the village as a cuckold,
for the satisfaction of revenge. One *stornello a dispetto*, or derision
song, goes like this:

Because I pass through this street, you think I'm passing you . . .
I spat on you and rejected you, scoundrel,
And I'd spit on my hands if I touched you.

By singing these songs, the man is defaming the woman's virtue.
She, too, will be alone. Or worse, his insinuations will leave her no
choice but to turn to that age-old occupation—that of a *puttana*, a
whore. Whatever the outcome, the man will be able to marry someone else, but the woman's fate may be far worse.

Italian life is an opera. And opera is perhaps a kind of pressure valve
for Italians. It allows them to cry.

By the nineteenth century, Italian composers had developed what
would become known as the bel canto, or beautiful singing, style of
vocal writing. They had tired of the heavy operas of the time and
begun composing more complex vocal roles with a lighter tone. Bel
canto style is marked by smooth, legato singing and fleet and airy
delivery, especially in the higher registers.

Gioacchino Rossini was the first to incorporate bel canto style in
his operas, composed in Naples for the Teatro di San Carlo, including *Otello* and *Il Barbiere di Siviglia*.

Following him was Gaetano Donizetti, composer of *Lucia di*

Lammermoor, Anna Bolena, Don Pasquale, and *L'Elisir d'Amore.* Vincenzo Bellini worked in the bel canto style through various ariettas and operas such as *Il Pirata, La Sonnambula,* and *Norma.*

By the early twentieth century, bel canto had faded, giving way to the weightier style of Giuseppe Verdi, who composed *La Traviata, La Forza del Destino, Il Trovatore,* and *Simon Boccanegra,* as well as *Otello* and *Falstaff,* among others.

But it was Giacomo Puccini who brought to opera the voices and passions of the peasant. Although Puccini didn't write bel canto operas, the style was in his blood. He wrote twelve operas, of which *La Bohème, Tosca, Turandot, Madama Butterfly,* and *La Fanciulla del West* are staples of opera company repertoire today. Whether set in France, Italy, or Japan, the operas communicate deep lows of despair and the supreme highs of love. As one might describe many a manipulative Hollywood movie, Puccini operas are tearjerkers.

Enrico Caruso once auditioned for the role of Rodolfo in *La Bohème,* with Puccini present. When he finished singing the aria, Puccini said, almost to himself, "Who sent you? God?"

Two nineteenth-century composers set their operas in the south, namely Sicily and Calabria. And these operas evoke the southern Italian spirit of the time.

Pagliacci, written by the Naples-born Ruggiero Leoncavallo, and *Cavalleria Rusticana,* written by Pietro Mascagni, from Tuscany in central Italy, are almost always performed together—forming end pieces of traditional southern values. *Cavalleria Rusticana* (literally, Rustic Gallantry) explores the folks who inhabit the Sicilian countryside.

But it's *Pagliacci* that takes as its theme the concept of derision (*dispetto*). And it was Enrico Caruso who brought this opera to the Italians of America.

Pagliacci is set in the Calabrian countryside—somewhere perhaps in the mountain areas around Catanzaro, where my family is from. It was in those mountains that my grandfather shot a man over my grandmother in a story worthy of its own opera. My grandparents were not yet married, and at the time my grandfather was living in Connecticut, my grandmother in the small hill village of Gimigliano, Calabria. He had gotten word that a man was trying to woo her, and when he arrived in Italy, he did what was his right—he fought for his woman, whose worth was not considered much more than that of a mule. The man lost his arm, but his life was spared. Decades later, my father met the man, who acknowledged that he was in the wrong and my grandfather had done the right thing in order to save face. It was the unwritten law of the land.

Pagliacci (Clowns) is the story of a roving band of actors that travels through the countryside, putting on shows for villagers. Canio is the head of the troupe, which includes his wife, Nedda; in their performance, Canio plays the role of Pagliaccio, Nedda plays Colombina.

During a stay in the remote, rugged landscape of Calabria, Nedda falls in love with one of the villagers. A member of the acting troupe sees the two together and tells Canio. He manages to catch a glimpse of the man and implores Nedda to tell him who he is. She refuses, and they part in order to prepare for the show.

Act 1 of the two-act opera closes with Canio telling himself "Vesti la giubba"—put on your costume, the show must go on. "People pay to be here, and they want to laugh," he sings to himself. "Turn your distress and tears into jest, your pain and sobbing into a funny face." Caruso, as Canio, lets out a painful laugh.

"Laugh, Pagliaccio, at your broken love!" Make a good impression; don't let them know that they got to you.

The second act of the opera ends as Canio and Nedda are performing as Pagliaccio and Colombina in front of the entire village. Canio, driven to distraction by his wife's cheating, steps out of character and asks her who her lover is. She ignores him and continues with the play.

Canio becomes visibly enraged and sings: he is no longer Pagliaccio now but Canio. He reveals that Nedda is making him a cuckold. The crowd cheers at his passion.

Canio grabs a knife and stabs Nedda. Silvio, in the audience, rushes to her aid, but Canio stabs him as well, then turns to the audience and says, "La commedia è finita!"

The comedy is over.

This is the ultimate Italian story—the intertwining of comedy, love, and tragedy. And by 1907, Caruso's aria from this opera—"Vesti la giubba"—was the first record in history to sell a million copies.

It was also this record that, in large part, determined how the world would listen to music. At this time there were two competing formats in which to listen to recorded music—the round, flat disc used by Victor and a cylinder invented by Thomas Edison.

By choosing to record on the Victor label, Caruso effectively determined the standard recording format of the time.

3

"Core 'ngrato"

EDUARDO MIGLIACCIO AND GILDA MIGNONETTE

On the corner of Mulberry and Grand streets in Manhattan, a doorway, flanked by American and Italian flags, opens into Little Italy's past. Once inside, you're immediately confronted by a table overflowing with imported Italian ceramic plates and dishes. A handwritten sign implores you not to touch the pottery. Overstuffed cardboard boxes seem to erupt from the floor. On the walls are religious icons and kitschy bumper stickers next to cooking aprons with "Kiss Me, I'm Italian" emblazoned on them in red, white, and green.

Toward the back of the store, barely lit by a single row of fluorescent lights, are shirts hanging on the wall from various Italian soccer teams—black and white stripes for Turin's Juventus; pink and black for Palermo. In the front corner, an older man in a gray and white flannel shirt sleeps in a folding chair, clutching two canes.

The store is E. Rossi & Co., but it is more than a tourist gift shop of Italian T-shirts and espresso cups. And Luigi Rossi is not just another importer of tchotchkes. In the years before World War II, Mr. Rossi, the ninety-three-year-old man napping by the front door, was a top publisher of sheet music for Neapolitan and Neapolitan-style songs. Mr. Rossi and his store played a crucial role in the creation of what we think of as Italian American culture. From this store in America, Italian pop music, parlor songs, and opera would all come together—and from here, Italian music would be disseminated throughout the rest of the world. One song in particular would be sung by every great opera tenor in the twentieth century—"Core 'ngrato," the work of a prominent writer and newspaper publisher who used the pen name Cordiferro.

As Italian immigrants settled in North America, the songs from the Old Country became tunes of nostalgia, even anthems for them as they took up their new lives as ditchdiggers, bricklayers, miners, shirttail seamstresses. The songs were in their hearts; they were what they held of their home. The songs kept their spirits up. The immigrants knew Italy offered them nothing in the form of work or a future. So in order to have a future, many were forced to uproot their lives, leaving behind the very things with which they had the most visceral of connections—the taste of fresh tomatoes; the close proximity of family; the scent of orange blossoms; the wind whistling through fig trees; the expanse of low-lying grapevines as they cascaded down the hills; the ease and passion of the voice in their own language. The sound of music—the accordion, the mandolin—was one of the few things they could bring with them.

While a few found their way to the countryside as farmers, most Italians moved to the slums of the largest cities in the United States, the places where they had the best opportunities to find work. They lived in crowded tenements of often windowless rooms with other people from the same village. Across the street would be another tenement housing immigrants from another village—geographically, it was almost like looking across the valley to another mountaintop town. Even if the urban valley was much smaller geographically, the differences in language and food were just as apparent, with each building harboring its own regional dishes, its own customs, its own dialect.

By 1911, 340,000 Italians had settled in New York City, which had a population of 4.5 million.

Immigrant Italians experienced music in many different ways. During a game of *scopa* (a popular, fast-paced, and animated card game) or a family dinner, a member of the family could pick up an instrument—mandolin or accordion—and lead everyone in song. More prosperous Italians might have a Victrola that would be cranked by hand.

It was the live performance, however—*lo spettacolo*—to which the Italians flocked for entertainment. With enough money, one could pay for a seat at a local concert hall—but for most Italians, with very little to spare once food was on the table and rent was paid, it was enough to wander to the back of a cigar store, for instance, or to a café to hear music. Or they could simply wait until any one of a number of Italian American organizations sponsored a free show.

The Italians' approach to live entertainment was very different from that of the *americani*. It was a participatory experience. They would pile into theaters, men sitting with men smoking and perhaps drinking wine from a bottle. Women would sit with other women and their children. They would talk and gossip. A great performer would distract them from their menial lives. But once they lost interest, the conversation would continue—this time about the actors themselves. Italians would cheer the hero and hiss at the villain. They would boo any performance that failed to capture their attention; yet they would cry when their hearts were touched. The theater was an extension of their living rooms and kitchens.

They filled theaters built by the Irish and Germans who had lived in the neighborhood before them. There was the Bowery Theatre; Webster Hall on East Eleventh Street; the Spring Street Teatro Italiano; the Grand Theatre at Grand Street and Chrystie; Arlington Hall at St. Mark's between Second and Third avenues; the Giglio Theatre on Mulberry Street. At the Teatro Dei Pupi at 109 Mulberry Street, people could attend performances of the Manteo Marionettes.

But as much as Italians wanted to be entertained, they wanted to learn about this country they had adopted. Many of them had very little contact with the America beyond their own neighborhood.

Aside from the newspaper, the theater was one of the few places where they could get a glimpse of the outside world. Or, better yet, someone could cast a light on the absurd world in which they had found themselves.

Farfariello—the little butterfly—satirized the lives of Italian immigrants and their curious existence in this strange world. Through song and theater shows, Farfariello played on Italian and American stereotypes to help ease Italians through the hardships of assimilation. He helped Italian Americans make sense of the world—and their new lives.

Farfariello was the stage name of Eduardo Migliaccio, who was born in 1882 in Salerno, a mountainous area just miles down the coast from Naples. His was a kind of opera buffa, but played out on a smaller stage.

One could usually see his shows at the Caffè Concerto Pennacchio on Mulberry Street in Little Italy, in what were called *caffè concerti*, or coffee concerts. He performed in various southern dialects, posing as a bootlegger or a street cleaner; he might also be an Irish cop or a fireman. He might begin his show with the Italian folk song "A morte d'e femmene" (The Death of a Woman), then launch into *macchiette coloniali*, or colonial skits, which were scenes of Italian American life.

Migliaccio studied design at the Accademia di Belle Arti in Naples, before immigrating to Hazleton, Pennsylvania, where his father had been living. He eventually moved to New York City, where he took a job as a letter writer for a bank. There he helped Italian immigrants write to their families back home. The people Migliaccio met during this time must have greatly informed his art.

In one skit, he makes fun of Italian men hoping to look important at social events by wearing tailor-made military uniforms. In another, "Scul-Gherl," he portrays an elementary school Italian girl who barely knows her American history but can sing any popular jazz song.

His comedy sketches were filled with Italo-Americanese, as in "Ammore all'americana" (Love, American-Style), in which an Italian man asks an American girl if she loves him. The girl, trying to sound Italian, says, "Sciu gare mony? Iu bai mi pere sciuse? L'aiscrimmia?" (You got money? You buy me a pair of shoes? Ice cream?)

In one of his most popular sketches he dons a porcelain mask of his friend Enrico Caruso and imitates him reading his reviews in song—good and bad.

When Rossi & Co. first opened in 1905, it was one of several music stores that imported music from Naples, in the form of both sheet music and records. But more significantly, these stores published music written by Italian Americans and then sent it back to Naples. They created songs that became classics back home—and throughout the world, wherever Italians had emigrated.

In New York, which was the center of the American music industry, Neapolitan popular music was transcribed and recorded, then sent back to Naples. It is because of various songwriters, music publishers, and record makers in New York City that Neapolitan music traveled throughout the world wherever Italians went— Buenos Aires, Montreal, San Francisco, Paris, Melbourne—and became as ubiquitous as it is today. From port to port, along with olives, olive oil, and dried pasta, the sheet music traveled on ships carried by musicians playing for money.

The day I saw Mr. Rossi in 2004, he was wearing dark gray pants with suspenders, and he spoke in a mixture of Italian and English. His father, Ernesto, had emigrated from Naples at the turn of the twentieth century and had a partnership with an Italian music publisher back in Naples. Now, Luigi's son, Ernie (named after Ernesto), was running the counter—and taking care of his father.

Through the 1920s and 1930s—at a time when many Americans had pianos in their houses, and many Italians had mandolins and accordions—sheet music was how people learned and enjoyed their favorite songs. A bit north of Rossi & Co. on West Twenty-eighth Street was Publishers' Row—or Tin Pan Alley—which was the sheet music mecca for all kinds of popular songs.

"We had a piano player on a pushcart outside to advertise the song," Mr. Rossi told me in Italian. "And we would sell the music for ten cents each. People would come in from all over New York and Connecticut, and as far away as Chicago and San Francisco. We would sell thousands."

Luigi Rossi dug into a box—one of several he guarded at his feet—and pulled out the music for "Senza mamma e nnammurata!" (Without a Mother and Lover) by Luigi Donadio, which was a favorite with Italian audiences in 1927. He also published "Comm'è bella 'a stagione" by Gigi Pisano, which was later sung by Connie Francis.

Other music publishers got into the action as well. The similarly titled "Senza Mamma" was written by Francesco Pennino, the maternal grandfather of Francis Ford Coppola. The music was originally printed by another music publisher, Antonio Grauso, who was also a mandolin maker. Rossi bought Grauso's store and all his sheet music in the 1930s. The song was performed in *The Godfather, Part II*. During the scene, the young Vito Corleone, played by Robert De Niro, realizes the power hierarchy of his Italian neighborhood. In the middle of a theater performance, as the tenor sings "Senza Mamma," a large man in a white suit and fedora rudely gets up from his seat to leave, blocking the view of those behind him. Corleone's friend Peter Clemenza shouts out, telling him to sit down. The man turns around, and immediately Corleone's friend recognizes him as the neighborhood boss, Don Fanucci, and apologizes. The local Mob boss was disrespectful not only of the performers but of the many audience members who pay him "protection."

Luigi's face lights up, however, when he recalls yet another song he published, "'A cartulina 'e Napule," which was sung by the then-famous singer Gilda Mignonette.

Gilda Mignonette, who had changed her name from Griselda Andreatini, was born in 1890 in Naples. She was a striking woman with dark hair that cascaded in ringlets to her shoulders. In 1926, a theater director named Feliciano Acierno brought her to America to perform for the legions of immigrant fans who loved her in Italy.

Her first performance was at Werba's Theatre in downtown Brooklyn—across the street from the site of what would become the Brooklyn Paramount Theatre, in which Russ Columbo would perform five years later. During her years in New York she performed throughout Manhattan in theaters of all sizes and sang to Italians of all classes. While she sang all the Italian classics, "'A cartulina 'e Napule" (A Postcard from Naples) was her showstopper.

"She was beautiful," Luigi says. "She let me carry her valise. I used to carry it everywhere."

In 1953, as her health was waning, Mignonette decided to return to Naples. Her last performance was on March 22 at the Brooklyn Academy of Music on Lafayette Avenue. She boarded the S S *Homeland* five days later. En route, a doctor diagnosed her with cirrhosis of the liver. She had asked that a postcard of Naples be pasted on the wall opposite her bed. Ten days later—and just twenty-four hours before the ship docked in Naples—she died. Like so many immigrants from Naples who remained in the New World, that postcard was the last image she had of her homeland.

In 1911 in Manhattan, G. Ricordi & Company published "Core 'ngrato" (Ungrateful Heart), then and now a favorite of opera tenors, performed by the likes of Luciano Pavarotti, Placido Domingo, José Carreras, and, earlier, Tito Schipa. Salvatore Cardillo, a doctor from Naples who had immigrated to New York City, composed the song; the lyrics were written by Riccardo Cordiferro—or "Iron Heart"—the pen name for Alessandro Sisca, one of the most prominent and important names within New York's Italian community. "Core 'ngrato" was written for Enrico Caruso.

Sisca was born in Cosenza, Calabria, in 1875, and at the age of eleven was sent north to Naples to enter a Franciscan seminary. But as he got older, he became more interested in poetry and political issues than in religion. He began writing under the Riccardo Cordiferro alias—most likely a comment on his activist socialist politics—and in 1892, he immigrated to the United States, where along with his father, Francesco, and brother Marziale he founded *La Follia* in 1893. The offices were at 202 Grand Street, just a couple of blocks from Rossi & Co. (Decades later, Marziale's son, Michael, would take over the newspaper and help open the Enrico Caruso Museum.)

La Follia was one of the first Italian-language papers published in this country, and if it wasn't the first, it was one of the most important and far-reaching. (It was called a folly because the founders never thought it would last beyond a few editions.)

It was in this newspaper, with its socialist leanings, that Italians throughout the United States looked for news, essays on the state of Italians in America, and reviews and comments on Italian singers and performers. It was from accounts in this newspaper that Italian performers such as Gilda Mignonette, Eduardo Migliaccio, and Enrico Caruso entered the lives and homes of the millions of Italians who settled here. Sisca battled police shutdowns of his controversial newspaper. With his far-left political leanings, he often gave public speeches and drew the support of union workers and anarchists alike.

I first encountered "Core 'ngrato" on the first of the *Three Tenors* albums. José Carreras, the third part of the Pavarotti and Domingo trio, who had recently been battling cancer, sang a heartrending version. I then found a version by a once-famous Neapolitan tenor named Tito Schipa, who settled and died in Connecticut. He sings the *s*'s in the song as a *sh*—a popular pronunciation in the dialects heard throughout southern Italy.

During my visit at the Caruso Museum, Aldo Mancusi played for me one of the original 1911 pressings of the song on a 1914 Victrola. He took a needle out of a case and inserted it in the arm, then gently placed it on the record. There were pops and hisses, though far fewer than I had expected. Even when I stood behind the bell, Caruso was strong and clear. I walked around to the front of the Victrola, with Caruso's voice getting louder until it filled the room:

Catarì, Catarì, why do you say those bitter words?
Why do you speak and torment my heart, Catarì?

Ungrateful heart,
you have stolen my life.
Everything is finished
and you don't care anymore!

Perhaps Catarì was a lover, a beautiful woman who wouldn't return his love. Perhaps the lyric was written for Cordiferro's wife, who died in 1897, followed by his two daughters in 1898. And perhaps it was this longing for his wife, who he knew wouldn't ever return, that inspired the song. Because it was written for Caruso, it was most likely based on Caruso's relationship with the singer Ada Giachetti, a woman he had never married but with whom he had two sons and who had left Caruso for his chauffeur.

In any case, this song, still in the standard tenor repertoire even today, was one of the first "Italian" classics to be written in America.

4

"*O sole mio*"

ENRICO CARUSO

One bright and sunny Saturday morning, my father walked into the family room singing "O sole mio."

I was ten years old. It was a cool spring day in St. Petersburg, Florida; the windows were open, letting in the breeze—and the sun—after a night of heavy rain. I was sitting at the dining table eating toast with butter and cinnamon and drawing a comic-book battle between Superman and Spider-Man. I had heard my father sing the song many times before, but for some reason it never occurred to me to ask him about it.

"Dad, what does that mean?"

"Oh, son of mine," he said, and continued to sing. Wow, he was singing a song about me. I must have done something that pleased him. I continued my drawing. Spider-Man was winning.

Throughout the day, I wondered what exactly he had been singing. And why he was singing about me.

My mother usually cooked, but this time my father was overseeing sweet sausages cooking with peppers and onions. Just before dinner, I asked my father what the rest of the song said.

And he sang, translating the lyrics as he went. "Che bella cosa na jurnata è sole." What a beautiful thing this day and sun.

I followed so far—was I that beautiful thing?

"N'aria serena doppo na tempesta." The air is serene after the storm.

What storm? I thought to myself. He continued:

Che bella cosa è una jurnata è sole . . .
Ma n'atu sole
cchiu bello, oi ne'
O sole mio
Sta 'nfronte a te.

What a beautiful thing is a day of sun . . .
But another sun
that's brighter still
is my own sun,
which is on your face.

"So what does that have to do with me?" I asked, confused.

"With you?" my father asked. "What do you mean, with you?"

"You know, o sole mio . . . son of mine."

My father laughed. "It has nothing to do with you. It's 'sun' . . . outside . . . *sole*, not *hicchiu*." *Hicchiu* was the Calabrese dialect for *figlio*, son.

I would later learn that the music had been written by Eduardo di Capua in 1898. The lyrics were penned by the Neapolitan poet Giovanni Capurro. The song, composed just as the first massive wave of Italian immigrants arrived in America, took on even greater meaning and nostalgia for those leaving their homeland behind.

Di Capua was a lawyer who had attended the San Pietro music conservatory in Naples. He had a bad gambling addiction, and he died in 1917.

"O sole mio" came to represent Naples and, soon enough, all of southern Italy. For the hundreds of thousands of peasants who left

Italy, it would become a kind of anthem for them, a love song. It would become the song through which Italians could indulge in nostalgia for the Old Country. They would always remember their "son."

Enrico Caruso stands three-quarters turned to the photographer. His front hand rests on a decorative, ornamental cane and at the same time clutches white gloves. A cuff link on his shirt is outglittered only by his pinkie ring. His back hand rests on his hip, making for an imposing, almost Napoleonic posture. He embellishes his striped suit with a light-colored vest and with a somewhat oversized silk pocket square, emphasizing the oversized personality—and build—that fills it.

A light gray fedora frames his face—thin-lipped and healthily rounded. But it's his eyes, large and dark, that impart a sense of pride. The photograph was taken in England in 1903, just before he arrived in New York. Theodore Roosevelt was in the second year of his presidency, having stepped in for the assassinated McKinley. The appearance of Enrico Caruso coincided with the great wave of Italian immigrants in the early twentieth century. Between 1900 and 1903, nearly a million Italians passed through Ellis Island; by 1910, the number of Italians in the United States had tripled.

Caruso was preparing for his November debut (*Rigoletto*) at the Metropolitan Opera. The yellow-brick opera house, designed by J. Cleveland Cady, architect of the American Museum of Natural History, was at the center of activity in Manhattan, located on Broadway between Thirty-ninth and Fortieth streets, walking distance from Grand Central Terminal.

Following *Rigoletto*, Caruso performed Puccini's *Tosca* at the Met a few days later. The New York critics enjoyed his singing—especially the aria "Questa o quella"—but thought his acting was a bit on the vulgar side. Like the man himself, Caruso's stage persona was grand. One reviewer for *The Press* described what he called a toneless voice:

He indulged frequently in the *voix blanche*, dear to the Italians but disagreeable to the Americans. He achieved some fine climaxes, however, especially in the early part of the third act, and so worked upon the feelings of the Italian contingent in his audience that he was forced to repeat a whole passage, greatly to the detriment of the dramatic integrity of the scene. The applause continued even after his concession to popular feeling.

Caruso's voice and delivery, combined with the expressivity of Verdi's and Puccini's composing styles, changed the flavor of opera in New York City forever.

Despite the mixed reviews, Caruso was a huge popular success, and within a couple of months this man who had grown up in the slums of Naples had been accepted into the ranks of New York's opera-going elite. His warm, jovial personality endeared him to nearly everyone. He was witty and observant and possessed a self-deprecating humor. He spoke in broken English—with a few French phrases thrown in—as he told reporters stories about life in Naples and indulged them in their curiosity about the Italian food he loved so much.

Through the help of *La Follia*, the Italian immigrant audience, who wouldn't have been able to afford opera tickets at the Met, came to know him. Enrico Caruso was an expert caricaturist, and he offered drawings of himself and other prominent Italians to the paper. Sisca and Caruso formed a strong relationship. Through Sisca and *La Follia*, Caruso became an inspiration to his immigrant audience—big-city Italians who were stereotyped as poor and sloppy as well as knife-wielding thieves. They were dirty ragpickers and obedient seamstresses. Caruso, though, represented to all Italian immigrants the one who had made it. And he also showed to the outside world that southern Italians could be cultured and creative.

Caruso, however, was also subject to the same schemes that plagued many common Italians. One night in March 1910, Caruso returned to his apartment following a concert and found an envelope addressed to him in type. Upon opening it, he knew immediately what it was, for the bottom of the letter inside was smeared with a handprint in black ink.

The letter demanded fifteen thousand dollars, threatening Caruso's life if he did not pay. The Black Hand was the name extortionists who preyed on Italians used. It had its beginning in the padrone system back in southern Italy, where payment was made to local strongmen in exchange for protection from the ruling party.

The system, which had been started to protect southern Italians from foreign occupiers, quickly morphed into yet another powerful force that took advantage of them. Even the greatest-known Italian performer was not immune to the Black Hand, the precursor to the Mafia.

Caruso, however, immediately contacted the police. The note said that he would be met by two men after one of his performances; he waited, with a couple of detectives off to the side, but the letter writers never showed up. The letters stopped for a while, but continued on and off for the next several years.

In 1909, a year before Caruso received that first Black Hand letter, a high-ranking lieutenant in the New York police force had been gunned down in Sicily.

Giuseppe "Joe" Petrosino was the first Italian to reach the level of lieutenant in the New York police force, which at the time was dominated by Irish-Americans. He rose quickly in the force and gained international recognition for tracking the origins of the Mafia in America. Having grown up in an Italian neighborhood, Petrosino knew exactly how these Black Hand extortionists worked, and how and on whom they preyed. After arresting a man named Enrico Alfano in the United States, Petrosino investigated his history and discovered he was wanted in Italy as well.

The forty-nine-year-old Petrosino drew the connection between crime in Sicily and crime in New York, and thought that if he had records of all the criminals in Sicily who were being let into the country, he might be able to put a stop to the Mafia here before it became too powerful.

He soon created a case strong enough that he was allowed to travel to Palermo, Sicily, to get records from the city's courthouse. But word must have gotten out to the local mafiosi, for as Petrosino was walking out of the court with boxes of papers, two men approached him and gunned him down. No one saw anything, and the papers disappeared.

Petrosino's body was sent back to New York. Tens of thousands of Italians lined up for his funeral procession—five and a half hours long—that led from the old precinct house off Mulberry Street to Forty-second Street. He was buried across the East River in Calvary Cemetery in Queens.

There was more anti-Italian sentiment brewing, in part because of fear of anarchism. Just as mafiosi came to represent Italians in the eyes of Americans, so did anarchists, socialists, and labor protesters. Having been ruled over the centuries by foreign and corrupt governments, many Italians became wary of any government, and in America they were finally able to voice their differences without fear of reprisal—or so they thought.

Down south in Tampa, Florida, the cigar factories were the scene of growing unrest for many workers. The Latin quarter of Tampa, called Ybor City—densely populated with its ornate wrought-iron balconies associated with New Orleans—housed Spaniards, Cubans, and Italians, all of whom worked in the cigar factories, which were operated by local white Southerners. It had long been the practice that each factory employed a lector (*el lector*, as they were called by the predominantly Spanish-speaking population), a man who read to the workers as they rolled cigars—be it the local paper, a novel, poetry. But the owners feared that the lectors, who tended to be left-leaning and chose what they would read to the cigar rollers, were getting too powerful and would make the workers restless and dissatisfied.

Ironically, it was the possibility of eliminating the lectors that incited the workers to protest. In 1910, hundreds of workers rallied outside the Bustillo Brothers & Diaz cigar factory in Ybor City, during which time the bookkeeper, J. F. Easterling, was shot but not killed.

The police arrested two men, Castenge Ficarrotta and Angelo Albano, both of whom were known to be anarchists, and brought them to jail to await trial. The police chief and deputy just so happened to leave the jail while a mob of about seventy-five men broke in, took Ficarrotta and Albano to a nearby field, and strung them up on a live oak tree.

The two had been handcuffed together and hung from the same limb. There's a photograph of their bodies from the time; Ficarrotta still has his fedora on, and his teeth tightly clench his pipe. Locals stand gathered below the bodies, talking and smoking as if it were a party.

The police officers in charge maintained that the lynch mob was a group of Italians and Cubans; the Italians and Cubans of Ybor City denied it. There was never any trial, and the local papers thanked the vigilantes for coming to the rescue. Even *The New York Times* sided with the mob.

A few years later, Caruso performed at the Italian Club in Ybor City.

"New Yorkers are no longer opera mad," wrote W. J. Henderson in *The New York Sun* after hearing Caruso's performance in *Carmen* one year. "But Caruso mad!" Throughout the years, Caruso grew to become a superstar. In 1914, he performed Puccini's *Tosca* at the Met. He and the soprano Geraldine Farrar took more than forty curtain calls before the audience finally let them go. Reporters followed him everywhere and described everything he wore; "sporting a creamy white suit, with a double-breasted coat, fastened with pearl buttons, a pearl-gray fedora, white shoes slashed with tan, a green cane and a cigarette holder of pure white," noted one Atlanta reporter. Caruso brought style to the opera, even if the old guard considered it ostentatious.

But Caruso was both a practitioner of the high art of opera and a populist hero. Following the sinking of the *Titanic*, he further endeared himself to the American public by singing a concert to benefit the families of the victims; after a concert in Atlanta, he posed for a photograph with Ty Cobb.

He was a champion of the unfortunate, and on tour in the South he gave a special performance for Helen Keller at his hotel. She placed her fingers on his lips as he sang the opening aria from the third act of *Samson and Delilah*.

As World War I broke out in Europe, Caruso drove hard to get Americans to buy Liberty Bonds. But as America fell in love with him, Italy criticized him for betraying his country by surrendering to the temptation of the American dollar. And when the United States entered the war, Caruso recorded one of his few songs sung in English—the patriotic anthem "Over There." He sings first in English, rolling every *r*; then repeats the song in Italian.

In 1917 thousands of Italian Americans signed up for the war. My grandfather, having emigrated five years before, realized this was a way to get U.S. citizenship. He enlisted in June and was shipped out in July of the year "Over There" was released. My father told me that Caruso was the one singer his father always listened to. I can imagine the Italian American recruits' sense of pride in listening to this Italian sing in the same accented English in which they would have spoken.

In 1916, Caruso recorded what is perhaps his best-known popular song, "O sole mio." It became one of his biggest records, selling well over a million copies.

On April 15, 1920, Nicola Sacco, a shoemaker, and Bartolomeo Vanzetti, a fishmonger, were arrested for the murder of a paymaster for a shoe company in Massachusetts. Witnesses said that the murderers were Italian and identified the two men. They were known anarchists, but neither had a criminal record, nor was there evidence of either having the money that they supposedly robbed of the pay-master. Many people at the time believed that the prosecutors and jurors had been influenced by anti-Italian sentiment. Nevertheless, while through Caruso Americans saw Italians as great artists, through Sacco and Vanzetti they also saw them as murderous criminals.

In December of that year, Enrico Caruso became ill and left the United States to return to his home in Naples, the Hotel Vesuvio. He was diagnosed with pleurisy, which later turned to pneumonia.

Overlooking the Bay of Naples and the coast of Sorrento, Caruso died at the age of forty-eight.

Enrico Caruso was, in a way, a typical Italian immigrant. He came here seeking opportunity; he encountered prejudice; he mar-ried an American woman; he never meant to stay, always dreaming of his native country. Like many Italians, he pledged to return to Italy to die. But unlike most of them, he did.

In 1921, the year Caruso died, Sacco and Vanzetti were sen-tenced to death. That year the United States enacted immigration laws to limit the number of incoming Italians to 42,057 per year. In 1924, the second Immigration Act lowered the annual quota to 3,845.

5

"Tip-Toe Through the Tulips"

NICK LUCAS

They called him "the Crooning Troubadour." With his solo guitar, his sweetly high voice, and his long, gentle face and dark eyebrows, Nick Lucas sang as if he were serenading a girl from beneath a balcony window.

In the years after Caruso's death—throughout the 1920s—Nick Lucas recorded dozens of hit songs and sold millions of copies of records and sheet music, making him one of the top-selling recording artists of the decade. He belonged to the first generation of what people would call "intimate" singers, which included Gene Austin, "Whispering" Jack Smith, Johnny Marvin, and Morton Downey.

Dominic Nicholas Anthony Lucanese was born in 1897 in Belleville, New Jersey. His father, who had emigrated from Avellino, a town northeast of Naples, was a gardener. Dominic first learned to play the mandolin and banjo before the guitar. And he and his older brother, Frank, would sing as an act together.

"Frank would drag me along, and we'd play Italian christenings and weddings," he recalled. "We even played on street corners and in saloons, and I'd pass the hat around. I was getting a lot of experience because Italian people, when they get to feeling good, like to dance all night long, especially the tarantella."

Wherever the Lucas brothers performed, they would play for hours: "My wrists got very tired, but I was getting great practical experience that paid off years later."

Frank, seven years older than Nick, eventually left Belleville to perform vaudeville. Nick graduated from grammar school in 1912 and took a job at a leather tannery, where he played guitar and mandolin for his fellow workers, who convinced him to shorten his name; by 1915, the seventeen-year-old Lucas was playing guitar at bars and nightclubs throughout Newark. For the next decade he played solo as well as with various bands, including the Ted Fio Rito Orchestra and the Russo–Fio Rito Orchestra, which took him to Chicago and to the Orpheum Theatre in Los Angeles. By the late 1920s, he had a contract with Brunswick Records.

Lucas had a list of hits, including "Bye Bye Blackbird," which was first recorded by Gene Austin in 1926, "Looking at the World Through Rose-Colored Glasses," and "It Must Be Love," which became the official song of the 1928 Republican National Convention, which nominated Herbert Hoover for president. His earliest recordings were on Thomas Edison's wax cylinders—made about the same time Caruso recorded "O sole mio" for Victor.

In a way, Lucas was a link from Caruso and opera to popular music. Like Caruso, he was a true tenor. And at the time, it was the tenor voice that translated best to records.

Around 1925, the course of live singing changed with the invention of the electric microphone. Rather than sing through a megaphone, as Al Jolson had done, singers used microphones to amplify their voices and float them over the instruments. Singers could treat the microphone itself as an instrument; the microphone picked up gentle inflections that hadn't been possible to project before. Immediately outdated was the minstrel "coon shouting" style of Jolson; even Rudy Vallée, who had originally sung through a megaphone, would have been left behind had he not been able to change his style. The microphone allowed a gentler, softer voice to be heard. It allowed for subtlety. Singing became more intimate. Born in Vermont to parents of French-Canadian extraction, Vallée was a member of the Whiffenpoofs of Yale and wrote many songs for them, including the eponymous "Whiffenpoof Song." His was a cool, crisp voice, if a bit nasal. While Austin, Lucas, Marvin, and the others before him had distinct, high tenor voices, Vallée's was one of the first baritones in American pop. In 1929 he sang and acted in a movie called *The Vagabond Lover*; it was the title song for this movie for which Vallée would become best known.

That same year, Nick Lucas starred in the film *Gold Diggers of Broadway*, about showgirls hoping to fall in love and get rich at the same time. *Gold Diggers* was the second talkie and was filmed in Technicolor; from that movie came Lucas's trademark song, "Tip-Toe Through the Tulips." In a voice that verges on falsetto, Lucas sang from the back of his throat with covered vowels, which was typical of the style at the time.

That song sold three million copies in its original pressing. In fact, Lucas sold over eighty million records in the 1920s and 1930s. Forty years later, Tiny Tim would record, in nearly the same high-pitched voice, the version people know today.

But it was through yet another talent that Lucas further made his name—his guitar playing. Nick Lucas was the granddaddy of the jazz guitar. In fact, in 1928 Gibson Guitars designed a guitar to Nick Lucas's specifications: one of the first flattop guitars Gibson offered, it had an extra-deep body for a bassier sound that resonated between a mahogany back and sides with a sunburst finish; on the inside was a round label with the image of Lucas. The guitar sold for the large sum of $125. In the mid-1960s, the Nick Lucas model was the guitar of choice for Bob Dylan—and can be heard on *Another Side of Bob Dylan* and *Bringing It All Back Home*.

"I remember when I first met Nick Lucas," said Tommy DeVito. "All I could focus on was his guitar, which to me must have cost a million bucks."

Tommy DeVito, a founding member of the Four Seasons, featuring Frankie Valli, grew up in Belleville, just around the corner from Nick Lucas. In fact, DeVito's half sister married one of Lucas's younger brothers.

"Nick Lucas was my idol. He was the one who inspired me to play guitar," said DeVito, who was about eight years old in the late 1940s when he first met Lucas, then in his early forties, who had come to Belleville to visit his family.

DeVito drove me through the Italian neighborhood of Belleville, called Spring Lake. "The town was built on a lake, so any day I went down to the basement to put coal into the boiler, there would be an inch of water."

Belleville is at the northern edge of Newark, which once had one of the largest Italian populations in the country. And today, northern Newark and the neighboring Belleville, Nutley, and Bloomfield still harbor a large Italian American population. Many of the houses in the Spring Lake neighborhood are still owned by the same families DeVito knew.

We pulled in front of Lucas's house. "You can see there at the end of the driveway a water pump. His was the only house with a well, and they would always let us get fresh water from his house." It seemed as if the Lucas family trusted groundwater for drinking or cooking more than the municipal water system.

A few streets away was where the actor Joe Pesci grew up. And on the corner was a bar named Stefanelli's, where the neighborhood Mob boss would spend his time.

"He was the meanest man you could meet," DeVito said. "He would laugh with you one minute, kill you the next."

DeVito told me the story of the time when a nineteen-year-old Pesci was hanging out at the bar with the Mob boss, nicknamed Cabert. This was in the early 1960s. On hot days, Cabert would turn on the fire hydrants for the kids to play in. One day, one of the local cops, who was wearing a riot helmet that seemed to diminish his small body, turned off the water and walked into the bar to try to enforce the law.

"Oh, no, Joey," said Cabert, pointing to the cop's head. "It looks like the Martians are invading." The cop and Cabert exchanged words: "Let the kids have fun."

When the cop walked out, Joe Pesci turned to Cabert and said, "You are funny."

"Funny?" Cabert said. "Who are you calling funny? I'm funny, like what, a clown?"

And thus was born Pesci's character—named, most likely not by coincidence, Tommy DeVito—in Martin Scorsese's *Goodfellas*.

Continuing our drive through the neighborhood, DeVito pointed out the house he had grown up in—a two-story brick and wood-frame house across the street from what had been Edison's zinc and lead plant, now a grocery store. On each corner might be a bar, restaurant, pool hall, or tailor—and in any given place, it seemed, numbers were secretly run.

The local church was St. Anthony of Padua, and down the street was a macaroni factory. On the corner was a fishmonger, where DeVito shelled clams for spare change; down the block was the butcher where DeVito's mother would send him to buy the cheaper ends of salami and pepperoni.

One day DeVito picked up the guitar owned by his older brother, a sixty-dollar Gibson. His brother came home to find DeVito playing the guitar flat on the floor.

"It was too big for me to play normally," DeVito said. His brother gave him a good beating. DeVito remembers his threat: "If I ever catch you playing this guitar like that again, I'll kick the crap out of you. And if I ever catch you *not* playing this guitar, I'll kick the crap out of you, too." Apparently, his brother recognized DeVito's natural musical talent, and this was his way of encouraging his younger brother.

DeVito shared an instrument with him until his father saved up enough to buy him his own.

DeVito admitted to fighting almost every day of his life, and committing a few crimes. He spent time in and out of boys' homes and juvenile delinquent centers. He would listen to, of all things, country music, a sound so distant, so foreign, that he could understand the loneliness in the voice of the singer.

"And it was there that I learned to play guitar—I had all the time to practice," DeVito said. "And it was Nicky Lucas who inspired me. His guitar playing was sophisticated."

Early in his career—right around 1929—Bing Crosby hired as his accompanist an Italian American guitarist and arranger named Eddie Lang, a man who had learned from Nick Lucas. Crosby was an early fan of Nick Lucas, and later told a group of radio DJs, "If you disk jockeys had been on hand when Nick Lucas hit his stride he'd be the biggest name in show business."

I recently watched a video of *Gold Diggers of Broadway*. The final scene of the film is set on the stage of a Broadway musical. The curtains rise. True to how I had pictured Lucas singing "Tip-Toe Through the Tulips," he stands below a balcony and in front of bushes of tulips. A woman in a fancy ruffled nightgown and bonnet sits at the window.

Lucas faces the audience, dressed in white pants, a dark sport coat, and a tie. His white pocket square seems to match his shoes, one of which is stepping on a chair as he strums the dark-wood guitar named after him. He begins singing, "Shades of night are creeping, willow trees are weeping," as the girl looks lovingly upon him. After a few verses of the song the stage darkens, and moments later the lights go on, and the stage has changed from quaint garden to, in Art Deco style, people dressed as tulips with the lead female, who had been sitting by the window, now tap-dancing in front of the human tulips. Another darkening of the stage, only to return to the original setting. A full moon lights the backdrop.

"And if I kiss you . . . , will you pardon me?" Lucas sings in a gentle, lilting high tenor, and invites her to come tiptoe through the tulips with him.

6

"You Call It Madness (but I Call It Love)"

RUSS COLUMBO

On Thanksgiving evening 1931, several hundred women, with their husbands, boyfriends, or girlfriends in tow, set out for the Brooklyn Paramount Theatre. They came from south Brooklyn; they came from Manhattan and New Jersey. For three months now they had heard his voice on the radio in ten- and fifteen-minute slots, the typical radio format at the time. His voice called out to them; it promised romance. They had seen his romantic visage on billboards and in the pages of newspapers—his warm eyes gazing out at a three-quarters angle, the right side of his mouth curving upward into a subtle smile. Tonight they would see him in person—"the Romeo of Song," Russ Columbo.

The Brooklyn Paramount had opened three years earlier, in Thanksgiving week 1928, with the slogan "Bringing Broadway to Brooklyn" and billing itself as "the first theater in the world to be built expressly for the showing of sound pictures." Unlike the Loew's theaters—built in major cities at the same time and housing only a theater—the Paramount was constructed as a combination theater and office building. In fact, offices of the Brooklyn-Manhattan Transit Corporation, or BMT subway, occupied eight of the eleven floors adjacent to the theater. Designed by Rapp & Rapp, the forty-five-hundred-seat rococo-inspired theater was indeed Brooklyn's answer to Forty-second Street in Manhattan.

Within a triangular block from the Paramount Theatre—an area of only 28,400 square feet—were the Brooklyn Academy of Music, the Orpheum, the New Paramount, the Strand, the New Fox, Werba's, Keith-Albee, the Majestic, Keeney's, the Casino, and the Loew's Metropolitan. Before and after shows, theatergoers would shop along Fulton Street and dine at Gage & Tollner, or head over to Joe's Restaurant on Nevins Street for drinks. Just across from the Brooklyn Paramount was a restaurant and after-theater nightclub called Enduro's, which, a few years later, would be renamed Junior's and become known for its "most fabulous" cheesecake.

For a ticket price of fifty-five cents that Thanksgiving evening, Columbo fans entered the glorious red-and-gray-marble lobby. Cocktail tables were set against mirrored walls; Art Deco chandeliers hung above. In the Florentine lounge on the lower level, patrons sat at one of two bars or in marble alcoves intimate enough for two young lovers. Goldfish swam in lit fountains. Depending on which night you went, you could also visit booths of vendors offering tasting samples of new brands of products such as "Minute Jelly," "Tao Tea," or even "Lucky Strike," "Virginia Sweet," or "Worcester Salt." A winding marble staircase covered with a rich red carpet and lined with wrought-iron railings led to the mezzanine and balcony levels, where ladies could duck into powder rooms and men into smoking lounges. For those with seats in the balconies, green and gold elevators awaited.

Gilded moldings framed the box-seat sections. The gold ornamentation continued down the walls on both sides of the proscenium to a statue on each side of women supporting a fountain. The concertgoers settled into plush burgundy velvet seats.

The stage curtain—sixty feet of velvet embroidered with satin pheasants—opened dramatically. To warm up the crowd, a movie—*Rich Man's Folly*—was shown. When it ended, the curtains closed to darkness in the hall. There was a shuffle of musicians onstage. Then silence.

"I can't forget the night I met you, that's all I'm dreaming of," sang a voice, smooth and light.

In a flash, light flooded the entire stage. Russ Columbo stood in front of the curtain in a black tuxedo with a carnation as a boutonniere; his hand lightly touched the microphone. Cheers erupted; women screamed; the theater thundered. The curtains opened behind him as the band continued the song with which Columbo opened and closed his Maxwell House–sponsored radio program—"You Call It Madness (but I Call It Love)."

But the cheers and screams drowned him out for the first two verses. It wasn't until the chorus that the audience had settled down enough to actually hear the voice coming from that romantic face, hair slicked back, with the deep brown Italian eyes.

Russ Columbo was an upstart, a twenty-three-year-old who could dethrone the already-established Rudy Vallée and compete with the twenty-eight-year-old Bing Crosby. In fact, for the next three years these crooners—Vallée, Crosby, and Columbo—would engage in a "Battle of the Baritones," highly publicized on the radio, in newspapers, and in entertainment magazines.

Ruggiero Eugenio di Rodolfo Colombo was born on January 14, 1908, in Camden, New Jersey. It was in this city of nearly a hundred thousand people, located across the Delaware River from Philadelphia, that the Victor Talking Machine Company (later RCA Victor) was headquartered—and where Enrico Caruso had been recording his arias.

When he was a small boy, Colombo's family moved to Calistoga, California. His parents, Nicola and Julia, had emigrated from Naples. His father, a stonemason by trade, had, like many Italians, grown up with music. He played the violin and guitar, and he made sure his eight kids grew up with music as well (four other children had died in infancy). Russ would later change the spelling of his last name to Columbo.

At the same time, Rudolph Valentino, who had emigrated from Apulia, was capturing the attention of women around the country. It was the silent-film era, and the "swarthy" actor played a veiled sheik, a masked gunman, anything but the strong, manly white romantic leads played by actors such as Douglas Fairbanks. Russ Columbo was also making his way in the film business, but behind the scenes. During the filming, movie studios hired musicians to perform for the actors on the set, to help create the mood of a scene. In 1925, the seventeen-year-old Columbo was hired by Paramount studios as a violinist.

In time, Columbo would become known as "the Vocal Valentino," for, like Valentino, he possessed mysterious dark looks that made women swoon and men jealous.

Columbo's violin playing caught the ears of the big-band leader Gus Arnheim, who was providing music for a film short in 1928. Arnheim also was appearing in L.A. and leading his Cocoanut Grove Orchestra in a performance on CBS radio. When one of his violinists dropped out in 1929, Arnheim picked up Columbo. Just a few months later, Arnheim brought on Bing Crosby—backed by Columbo on violin. They performed at the Grove, Crosby singing while Columbo played violin as part of the orchestra. Within two months, Columbo, who had aspirations to sing, became frustrated and quit the Cocoanut Grove Orchestra. He struck out on his own, performing on KMTR radio and in clubs such as the Pyramid Café on Hollywood Boulevard. It was while performing here, in 1931, that he caught the ear of the music producer and agent Con Conrad, who soon decided that Columbo could have a big career in New York City.

Radio stations encouraged performers to have a signature tune listeners could associate with them. In Russ's case, Conrad selected a song he had written years before: "You Call It Madness (but I Call It Love)," which Columbo helped to rewrite and record in September 1931. A month later, Columbo would have a hand in writing his next big song, "Prisoner of Love." Both songs hint at passionate love: he's caught up in the madness in one song, while he can't escape it in the other.

It's hard to imagine Crosby singing these lyrics convincingly— had he even chosen to sing them. Crosby's voice is smooth, though crisp and punchy—very appropriate for someone who was taught percussion at a young age. Columbo, the violinist, has a lighter touch. His voice glides like a bow over the strings. He's not an alpha-male singer but a romantic, lost and perhaps confused in love. He doesn't deliver the lyric with force; instead, it's almost as if he's conversing with a woman and waiting for her reaction.

Radio stations had begun emerging in 1920, beginning with KDKA in Pittsburgh, WWJ in Detroit, and, in 1921, WJZ out of Newark, New Jersey. Within a couple years, there were networks across the nation, such as CBS, NBC, and MBS, as well as several local stations in New York City, such as WOR, WNEW, and WHN. The major radio stations were competing for singers—and, ultimately, advertisers. Each performer was given a fifteen-minute time slot. The National Broadcasting Company had had great success with Rudy Vallée, and they were intrigued by this new voice from the West Coast. They slotted Columbo for the late hour of midnight. Just days later, Crosby signed with CBS.

George Burns and Gracie Allen opened for Columbo at the Paramount in 1931. Columbo worked with and influenced musicians such as Benny Goodman, who acted as his first bandleader, and the drummer Gene Krupa, an early member of his band. As a good dance band, the Russ Columbo Orchestra played at the more intimate clubs and restaurants that served alcohol and had space for dancing. He gigged at the Woodmansten Inn, in the Pelham Parkway section of the Bronx, where Guy Lombardo joined him on violin and newcomers like Ethel Merman opened for him.

By December 1931, the "Battle of the Baritones" became so popular that at one point the songwriters Al Dubin and Joe Burke came out with a song called "Crosby, Columbo, and Vallée."

There are three photographs of these crooners—the "three baritones"—taken in 1931. Vallée exudes a privileged confidence, with
his head of light brown wavy hair; the curls, waxed into perfect
waves, give the impression of a sophisticated college boy. By this
time, he had a huge following. Crosby is coolly confident, and there's
a fighter's look in his eyes—he's someone who wants to rise to the
next level. Columbo, meanwhile, looks like a man struck by Cupid's
arrow. Delicate narrow eyebrows accentuate his dark, sad eyes. He
wears his hair slicked back and smiles warmly for the camera. He
looks eager to please, almost needy of attention. He seems unaware
of his abilities.

Of the three, Columbo was strongest in the Italian communities.
At a time when most Italian Americans were doing manual labor,
and when many elitist Americans considered them dirty, uncouth,
and violent, Columbo had made it in white America, successfully
appealing to the fans of Vallée and Crosby.

Italian radio programs on any number of stations—over a dozen
in New York and New England alone—played Russ Columbo songs
to their Italian listeners. On one night in October 1931, NBC radio
turned the airwaves over to Salvatore Pino, the editor of *Il Progresso*,
one of the largest Italian-language newspapers, which was published
in New York. It was prime-time radio, and Pino spoke to the listeners in Italian.

At this time, Italy was ruled by the Fascist government of Benito
Mussolini, who was promising to bring the country back to its great
Roman founding.

Italians in America were divided in their feelings about the
regime. Many felt this was just another ruling body that would ne-
glect their families and the south in general. Others—perhaps those
nostalgic about their homeland and tired of being trodden on in the
United States—believed in a renewed, more powerful country, and
so sided with the regime. *Il Progresso* was such an influential newspaper that when Mussolini asked Italians living in America for support

in strengthening Italy's economy, thousands of Italian Americans sent their gold wedding bands. In return, they would be given steel armbands with the words "Gold for the Fatherland" stamped on them. Mussolini was popular not only with Italian Americans but with Americans in general.

As Cole Porter wrote in the original version of his song: "You're the top . . . You're Mussolini."

My grandfather Filippo Rotella was in his thirties at this time and worked as a bootlegger running liquor from Canada to Buffalo, New York. Just after Prohibition ended, he moved to Danbury, Connecticut, where he dug graves, excavated foundations for buildings, then worked as a milliner for the Stetson hat company. At home, my grandfather, who fought on the American side in World War I, took solace in a glass of wine, food, some whiskey, and, I imagine, the music that came from Italian radio stations.

I have an image of my grandfather at this time, formed in part by a poem of Lawrence Ferlinghetti's written about his father:

And my father drifts by in his fedora
   his eyes on the sidewalk
     a single Italian lira
       and an Indian-head penny
        in his pocket

I imagine my grandfather had a song in his head. He would proudly list Russ Columbo—a successful son of Italy, the first American-born—as one of his two favorite singers. The other, of course, was Enrico Caruso.

In March 1933, President Roosevelt rolled back Prohibition. Columbo decided to go west, to go home. He saw the success Bing Crosby was having with films, and realized Hollywood was the next proving ground.

The next month, he began filming *Broadway Thru a Keyhole*,

which was written by the New York gossip columnist Walter Winchell and loosely based on the life of Al Jolson. Columbo plays a singer (Jolson) who falls in love with a dancer who is the girlfriend (Ruby Keeler) of a New York Mob boss (Larry Fay).

I found a reel-to-reel print of the movie at the New York Public Library, and I viewed it in a basement room there. Columbo, presented in soft focus, was definitely cast in the role of the Latin lover. But unlike Rudolph Valentino, whose characters seemed mysterious, even threatening, Columbo appears slightly awkward and, as in his singing, hesitant. There is nothing dangerous about him; he is simply a young man in love.

While Bing Crosby would, for the most part, play role-model figures in his films—college professor, priest, husband—Russ Columbo played the lover or the interloper, roles that Valentino had taken.

Broadway Thru a Keyhole was released in November 1933 to critical raves. It became one of the highest-grossing films of its time. Before the movie was released, Russ Columbo became the subject of Hollywood gossip pages with his several love interests—Greta Garbo and Hannah Williams, the future wife of the boxer Jack Dempsey. But that year, he fell in love with the actress Carole Lombard. Russ and Carole were seen out everywhere. Both of their careers were flying high. Russ proposed to Carole, who, while not refusing him, did not immediately accept, wanting him to focus on his career.

On September 2, 1934, Columbo stopped off at the house of a friend, the Hollywood portrait photographer Lansing Brown. The two lit cigarettes and talked. On his desk, Lansing had two nineteenth-century dueling pistols that he played with absentmindedly—pulling back on the hammer and letting it go. Lansing picked up a match and struck it on the gun, and the gun went off. He looked up to see Columbo slumped in his chair, clutching his face. Columbo was rushed to the hospital, where doctors tried to remove the bullet, which had lodged in his brain. They could not, and he died that evening.

Thousands of mourners attended his funeral in Los Angeles. Zeppo Marx and Bing Crosby were two of his pallbearers. His last movie, *Wake Up and Dream*, was released a week after his death.

Columbo's siblings kept newspapers away from their mother, who had been going blind. They hid his death from her for years, writing letters "signed" by him from Europe and New York. It seems unbelievable that this Italian mother would not have known her son was dead, not have been able to somehow sense it. Such is the power of denial, one might think.

But I'm reminded of a scene in an Italian movie from a few years back called *Cinema Paradiso*, in which a boy is urged by the village film projectionist, a kind of surrogate father, to follow his dreams of being a filmmaker and leave the island of Sicily and never come back. "I don't want to hear you talk anymore; I want to hear talk about you."

7

"Sing, Sing, Sing"

LOUIS PRIMA

Every part of him is moving. His head bops, face contorting; his hands make a spastic conductor's motion; his back arches, he doubles over; all the while his feet are tapping the ground. He lifts his shoulders and raises the trumpet to his lips and wails. His legs pulsate in his baggy trousers, which ripple with each move. He blows quick blasts of his horn. His hips thrust and grind.

Meanwhile, the drummer pounds out a rhythm, his white shoes clenched to the bass drum pedal. He's hunched over the drum kit, beating the cymbals. His pomaded hair loosens with the frenzy and dangles over his brow. The rhythm of the drums bangs out a gyrating beat.

In September 1934—the month Russ Columbo was shot in Los Angeles—midtown Manhattan thundered with young men and women in nightclubs thumping their feet and swaying to a new sound: the "hot" Italian jazz of Louis Prima.

The music came from New Orleans, following the path cut by Louis Armstrong. Prima's roots were placed firmly in the "hot" jazz tradition, where speed and improvisation ruled, and he burned a trail through to Fifty-second Street. The single block of brownstones and town houses between Fifth and Sixth avenues was nicknamed Swing Street, for its row of jazz clubs.

Sing, sing, sing
Everybody's got to sing . . .

Prima played a high-spirited jazz—blowing his trumpet, calling and responding with the band members, and scatting the quickest, funniest nonsense you ever heard. Even today, when you listen to Prima's records, you forget your worries, you smile, and your feet begin to tap the floor.

It's heart-pounding jazz—Italian-style. And Prima is the consummate entertainer. He was prescient, and aware of the changing times, and he adapted his music constantly. He may not have been a traditional jazz master—but he made jazz popular.

Benny Goodman, with Gene Krupa playing a drum solo, made "Sing, Sing, Sing" famous. But it was Louis Prima who wrote the song.

When Louis Leo Prima was born on December 7, 1910, the population of the French Quarter of New Orleans was nearly 80 percent Italian. New Orleans, which had a customs facility like Ellis Island, had been attracting Italians since just after the Civil War. Most of them came from Sicily—Palermo, Ustica, and Cefalù. Unlike Boston, New York, and Philadelphia, New Orleans offered these new immigrants a way of life akin to the life they had left behind. They were not stuffed in tenements, but lived in single- and two-family houses (though crowded nevertheless) in a part of the Quarter that became known as Little Palermo. As in Sicily, there was a cultural mix—a melding of French, black, and Cajun food. Italians would develop the muffuletta sandwich (salami, mortadella, provolone, mozzarella, and an olive tapenade on a focaccia-like round bread), and their tomato sauces and spices were incorporated into the native gumbo. A Sicilian-born man named Vincent Taormina began canning beans, bread crumbs, and soups, eventually naming his company Progresso.

New Orleans was a port city made up of several different cultures—French, African, and southern. New Orleans was at just about the same longitude as southern Italy, and Italians, used to the warm air of southern Italy, only had to adjust to the humidity. A port town farther south, in Tampa, Florida, drew Sicilians who wound up making cigars.

The Italian immigrants found themselves in a city of pageantry and religious parades similar to those back in Italy. Italians worked the loading docks, opened grocery stores, and played instruments in marching bands whenever music was needed. They played especially during Mardi Gras, leading floats down Canal Street. Back in Italy, these same kinds of marching bands had played for their town's saints' days—the festivals of the Virgin or Saint Joseph. But in New Orleans, Italian marching band players—drummers, trumpeters, trombonists, and clarinetists—soaked up the rhythms of Africa. The Italians and blacks worked in the fields together, and in the Storyville section of New Orleans. But Louis Prima once mentioned that "the white and colored musicians listened to one another and played sessions." Blacks and whites would perform at New Orleans's honky-tonks, many of which were owned by Italians: Matranga's, Segretta's, Tonti's Social Club, and Lala's Big 25. They gambled, visited bars and bordellos, and played music together.

And like the blacks of New Orleans, the Italians faced discrimination. In 1891, America witnessed the largest mass lynchings in its history.

On October 15, 1890, the New Orleans police chief, David Hennessy, was gunned down by masked men. "The dagos did it" were supposedly the chief's dying words. Fingers were pointing everywhere—political rivals, politicians, people to whom he owed favors—but ultimately landed on the Italian community. Rumors of a loose network of crime—the Black Hand—had made their way into the newspapers. As the newest immigrants, Italians were looked down upon as shady criminals.

About 250 of New Orleans's 30,000 Sicilians were rounded up, and 19 of them were indicted. The court found three of the businessmen not guilty and declared a mistrial for the others. However, the Sicilians were not free to leave. They were held in prison "for their own security" against the hands of angry New Orleanians.

That night, the prison guards disappeared from their posts en masse, just as they did later in Tampa. Keys found their way into outsiders' hands, and a mob of eight thousand people flooded the prison, shooting and clubbing eleven Sicilians. When the morning sun rose over the river, there along Canal Street—down which the Mardi Gras parade passed every year—three of them were hanged on the ornate, wrought-iron lampposts.

Nevertheless, newspapers across the country chose to side with the lynch mob, even *The New York Times*, which ran the headlines:

A Gang of Vengeful Sicilians Supposed to Have Done the Work

Chief Hennessy Avenged

Eleven of His Italian Assassins Lynched by a Mob

Ten years later, in 1901, Louis Armstrong was born, and by the age of sixteen he was playing the trumpet at Henry Matranga's saloon in New Orleans—"one of the toughest honky-tonks in black Storyville." The Matranga family, originally from Monreale, Sicily, had survived the lynchings, and they now owned one of the most popular bars for Dixieland music. Growing up, Armstrong had worked for the Matrangas as a delivery boy.

An Italian ragpicker and junk collector named Lorenzo had introduced Armstrong to the Italian bars of the uptown neighborhood. Lorenzo was also a trumpet player.

"The things he said about music held me spellbound, and he blew that old, beat-up horn with such warmth," Armstrong once said of him.

Armstrong listened to Italian bands playing music in the night-clubs. He heard opera arias as he walked the streets—women and men singing from balconies, from porches.

Later, when Armstrong went to Chicago and played at the Vendome Theater, he was quoted as saying: "I got a solo on stage, and my big thing was *Cavalleria Rusticana.*" In his study of Louis Armstrong, Joshua Berrett notes that one can hear quotations from the opera in Armstrong's 1930s recordings of the Dixieland standards "Tiger Rag" and "New Tiger Rag."

In turn, the clarinet in those Creole-sounding songs must have been familiar to the Italians—the Creoles and the Italians being two saint-worshipping, pagan-informed Catholic cultures.

Southern Italians held on to their ritual of marching bands leading a funeral procession—music and death intermingled. Like the Creoles and African Americans, Sicilian musicians at times led the bereaved to the cemetery site, playing the sweet, dolorous music of the clarinet, the percussion keeping a steady beat. They marched along the narrow streets of wood and brick houses, followed by mourners dressed in black.

On more festive occasions, the same Sicilians gathered on the balconies decorated with banners and intricate, colorful handmade rugs and shawls used throughout southern Italy. They cheered and sang along with the procession, tossing down confetti as the band passed by.

One of the earliest jazz bands to be recorded was the Original Dixieland Jass Band. The members were a mix of Italian and Anglo New Orleanians, led by the cornet player Dominic James "Nick" LaRocca.

They weren't the first jazz band by a long shot, but they were the first to be recorded. Just weeks after the United States entered World War I in 1917, the Original Dixieland Jass Band made their first record: "Livery Stable Blues" on one side, "Dixie Jass Band One Step" on the other (later that year, the band would change the spelling to "Jazz"). It would go on to sell over a million copies—outselling Caruso that year. LaRocca is credited with having written one of the biggest jazz standards of the time, "Tiger Rag."

Louis Prima's older brother, Leon, played the cornet, and Louis cottoned to that brassy sound.

Their father had a soda pop route on a horse-drawn wagon, and often Louis would accompany him, getting to know local bar owners and everyone in Little Palermo. But at night he would sneak out to the bars in the French Quarter to hear other musicians, in particular Louis Armstrong—studying the beautiful phrasing, the timing, the blowing behind the beat. In his early teens, he put together a band with a twelve-year-old clarinetist named Irving Fazola; Prima added the even younger Johnny Viviano on drums and Jacobo Sciandra on clarinet to form Prima's Kid Band.

In 1934, the Canadian big-band leader Guy Lombardo was visiting New Orleans during Mardi Gras, walking the streets listening to the sounds typical of the area.

Lombardo—Gaetano Alberto Lombardo, born in 1902 in Ontario—would become known as "Mr. New Year's Eve." Since 1929, he had been performing at New York City's Roosevelt Hotel, and later at the Waldorf, every New Year's Eve, and his name had become synonymous with the Scottish song "Auld Lang Syne." He had performed with Russ Columbo's band at the Woodmansten Inn back in 1931.

As he passed a saloon called the Shim Sham, he heard the most incredible trumpet playing. It wailed—"more piercing than any I had experienced," Lombardo recalled in his autobiography. He entered a bar, which was mostly empty, and saw a young musician jumping around on the stage, sweating away as if the place were packed. "On the bandstand was an olive-skinned trumpet player, hardly more than a boy."

Lombardo was astounded. He approached Prima and insisted that he come to New York. It seems odd that the man who played "the sweetest music this side of heaven" would support "hot" jazz shows, but there it was.

It took Prima over six months to land a job in New York City. On one occasion, a club owner was ready to hire him on Lombardo's recommendation alone. But when the owner saw Louis Prima perform, he bristled and reneged. It turned out that he mistook Prima, with his dark complexion, tight curly hair, broad nose, and raspy voice, for a half-breed Creole. The problem was that this "mulatto" was being backed by a white band. And in those days, blacks and whites could not appear onstage together.

On Prima's behalf, Lombardo contacted the owner of the Famous Door, a club on Fifty-second Street.

Story has it that by eleven o'clock on Prima's opening night in November, hardly anyone had shown up. But Louis Prima and His New Orleans Gang were nevertheless jamming to the empty room—playing as if it were packed. Prima had been used to playing honky-tonks, full of only drunks and prostitutes.

But suddenly, after midnight, the place was mobbed with musicians getting off their own gigs. The Famous Door would become the place where musicians went to listen to music, relax, and party like the people they had been entertaining all night long.

I saw a grainy film of one of Prima's shows, recorded at a club sometime in the 1930s.

Prima, dressed in a white suit and bow tie, engaged with his clarinetist, Pee Wee Russell, in the New Orleans call-and-response form. Prima would call a tune on his cornet, and Russell would respond on his clarinet. Prima would later play this scenario out with the saxophonist Sam Butera, which would develop into a kind of scatting—Armstrong-style.

With Russell, Prima had his straight man. The instruments seemed to have conversations—on "Chinatown, My Chinatown," a mock argument plays out as the song evolves into "Yankee Doodle."

Prima's trumpet plays "Yankee Doodle went to town."

Russell responds, on his clarinet, "Riding on a pony," though the last note trails, as if Russell's lost interest or can't remember the last word.

"Pony," Prima plays, with an exclamation point.

"Oh, yeah?" Russell seems to play.

"Yeah!" Prima responds.

"Screw you."

"No, you!"

Within six months of his first success on Swing Street, Prima and his band were a national hit. They had conquered New York—performing "The Lady in Red," "Chinatown" (in a very similar version to Louis Armstrong's), and the New Orleans–inspired "Let's Have a Jubilee."

Because of his ambiguous skin color and head of tight curls, Prima was one of the only white jazz musicians able to play on black stages. He had a nice run of shows at the Apollo Theater in Harlem in 1939. During the run, a young black tap dancer from Harlem made his first appearance at the Apollo. He performed with his father and a man he called his uncle in the Will Mastin Trio. His name was Sammy Davis Jr., and he was fourteen years old.

But Prima's main following was still downtown, where he would introduce Italian lyrics and songs into his jazz.

8

"All or Nothing At All"

FRANK SINATRA

"I'm going to make it," Frank Sinatra told the bandleader Harry James. "But I'm going to make it with my Italian name."

A WNEW radio program called *Dance Parade*, which was heard throughout New York and New Jersey, was broadcast from the Rustic Cabin in Englewood Cliffs, New Jersey. One night in the spring of 1939, while staying in a hotel in New York City, the wife of the bandleader Harry James heard Sinatra on the radio and suggested her husband check him out; the next night James drove out to New Jersey to hear him sing in person.

As it happened, Sinatra wasn't slated to perform that night—but after a last-minute cancellation, he filled in for the originally scheduled singer.

The first song was Cole Porter's "Begin the Beguine."

"I felt the hairs on the back of my neck rising," said James. "I knew he was destined to become a great singer." Shortly thereafter, James hired Sinatra.

James was thinking about how to promote his band and this new singer. He wanted a name that was catchy, something that wasn't too ethnic.

"I've got an idea," he told Sinatra. "What about if we change your name to Frankie Satin?"

Sinatra paused for just a second, but his proud Italian back was up. "You want the voice, you take the name."

The Rustic Cabin was a sprawling stone and wood restaurant—a building that lived up to its name—that advertised steaks and chops. It was set in a wooded area of Englewood Cliffs off Route 9W, which wound its way up the Palisades, alongside the Hudson River. Although it was located just a mile across the river from Manhattan, the setting lent a feeling of seclusion to the club. Now it's a gas station on a heavily trafficked road.

Sinatra had taken a job there as a singing waiter. He sang from table to table, really learning how to engage patrons who had other things on their minds—namely, eating and drinking. So it was in the "saloons" that Sinatra learned to sing to a crowd.

That same year, Joe DiMaggio was in his fourth season with the New York Yankees. *Life* magazine put him on its cover. But his success didn't dispel the stereotypes. Inside, alongside a spread of photographs, the Yankee Clipper was shown with a bright, all-American toothy smile, while the text marveled, "Although he learned Italian first, Joe, now 24, speaks English without an accent and is otherwise adapted to most U.S. mores. Instead of olive oil or smelly bear grease he keeps his hair slick with water. He never reeks of garlic and prefers chicken chow mein to spaghetti."

Sinatra did not come from a typical large Italian family. He was an only child, born to Dolly and Marty Sinatra in Hoboken, New Jersey, on December 12, 1915. Even Sinatra's parents' background wasn't typical. Marty, Anthony Martin, was born in Agrigento, Sicily; shortly after his birth, his family immigrated to America. He was a blue-eyed, ruddy-complexioned boxer who changed his name to O'Brien in a time when people didn't take Italians seriously as fighters. Later, he held various positions before getting a job, thanks to his wife, with the Hoboken Fire Department.

Natalie Catherine "Dolly" Garavente was a strong-willed, political-minded person who was born in the northwestern port city of Genoa, famous for its basil pesto and focaccia bread, and the ancestral home of Christopher Columbus and the composer Niccolò Paganini. Marty's family saw her as a snobby Northerner, while her family looked down on Marty's people as poor Southerners.

Dolly's blond hair, blue eyes, and Irish-sounding first name enabled her to travel effectively between the Irish and the Italian communities. Accepted by the Irish and by Irish politicians, she could be counted on to get out hundreds of Italian votes for whoever was mayor—usually an Irishman.

The Sinatras lived modestly, but they owned their own house— and over the years they did well enough to keep trading up. Dolly made sure her son always looked nice, often in expensive trousers. He had so many pairs of pants that kids called him "Slacksey O'Brien."

"Someday, that's gonna be me up there," Frank Sinatra whispered as he leaned over to his new girlfriend, Nancy Barbato.

The year was 1935, and Frank and Nancy were at the Loew's Theatre in Jersey City to hear Bing Crosby. The nineteen-year-old Sinatra knew that he wasn't going to be just like Crosby. No, he was going to be better.

Sinatra's dark brown hair was neatly trimmed above his ears and combed back. A rebellious curl dangled on his forehead. He made no effort to hide the scars on the side of his neck and face—scars left by the forceps used to deliver him. His wry smile belied an eagerness to be where Crosby now stood.

Loew's Theatre is in Jersey City's Journal Square—across the street from the Stanley Theatre, and just a block down from the Majestic. Jersey City was pulsating with energy in 1935. The Canton Restaurant—with its ornate coves of tables surrounding a large dance floor and a big-band stage—had just opened. It served Chinese food and cocktails in large glasses shaped like volcanoes or Buddhas to couples and groups of friends ready for a night on the town.

In the Loew's Theatre (pronounced "LOW-eeze" by the locals), Sinatra and Barbato were two of thirty-one hundred people. To date, Sinatra had sung with his high school glee club, for parties at his mother's Democratic meetings, for weddings.

Sometime during the Depression, Dolly had opened a restaurant in Hoboken. She named it Marty O'Brien's and ran it with Marty as a speakeasy. She would allow the teenage Frank to sing at the bar for tips—his very first saloon.

Bing Crosby exuded an effortlessness that appealed to Sinatra. Sinatra must have seen Crosby in many of the faces of his neighborhood. Crosby was the bus driver, the chief of police, the chief of the fire department. Crosby was the mayor of Hoboken, for whom Sinatra's mother collected Italian votes.

While Sinatra was absorbing Crosby, he was also taking in the songs of the late Russ Columbo from 1931: "You Call It Madness" and "Prisoner of Love." Columbo didn't have Crosby's confidence, but he did know how to woo his female listeners. Columbo seemed a bit young, a bit naive, a bit nervous. And the girls had been drawn by his vulnerability, just as they would be by that quality in a young Sinatra.

Sinatra later gravitated toward soulful music, heartfelt and introspective. He turned to the blues, and it was there that he found his other influence: Billie Holiday. Through her he learned his trademark timing, a way of singing behind the beat. In the socioeconomic hierarchy, Italian immigrants came in just above blacks and just below the Irish—working side by side with both—so it's hardly a surprise that Sinatra learned from and successfully incorporated the influences of both cultures. Irish was what his head said; black was where his heart was.

But to that Sinatra would add his own brand of Italian style—not anything that he learned at home, but from the songs he heard at the local *salumeria, latticini*, the olive store, the cheese store. The songs he learned at Italian weddings and first Communions. The Caruso arias he heard on the Victrola in Nancy Barbato's family's living room. The style he used, he later explained, was that of bel canto—gracefully singing with the open vowels of the Italian language. He would incorporate the feelings he felt in the popular Italian love songs he heard.

In Crosby, Sinatra could hear the clarity and softness that only a microphone could pick up. Columbo had been even more delicate. The women in particular swooned for Columbo—in fact, a large percentage of his fans had been women, whereas Crosby had a mixed following. Sinatra, like Columbo, and like Valentino, was soon to inspire the love of women and the ire of men.

I can imagine Sinatra's attraction to Crosby's singing. At the time, Crosby was a better singer than Columbo had been, more versatile; he had more experience than Columbo, whose life and career had been cut short. But what's more, he was not Italian. I could imagine that Sinatra, with his parents as role models, wanted to get to the next socioeconomic level. If he followed Columbo, he risked being just another Italian singer, another dark, mysterious Latin lover. Instead, he chose to emulate Crosby while still—and perhaps unconsciously—continuing the tradition of Columbo.

Nancy and Frank were married on February 4, 1939, in Our Lady of Sorrows church in Jersey City. It's a small, inconspicuous church, tucked away within streets of wood-frame, late-Victorian houses. There's a cloistered feel about the stuccoed church and the neighborhood—like that in an Italian village.

The soundtrack to their courtship would have been the music of Count Basie, Benny Goodman, Duke Ellington, Glenn Miller, Artie Shaw, and Harry James. The bandleaders themselves were the headliners, playing sax, trombone, piano—but the band's showpiece was often a vocalist. It was Frank's generation of singers that got its start fronting the big bands.

It was also at this time that Sinatra, very aware of his Jersey accent, began taking speech and diction lessons.

"You can't sing what you don't understand," John Quinlan, his diction coach, told him. It was probably one of the best things his instructor said. With Frank Sinatra, you always feel as if he is telling you a story, not just performing a song. And this lesson stuck with him—by understanding the lyrics, by making them his own, he was able to communicate them to the world.

A month after their meeting at the Rustic Cabin, Sinatra and Harry James recorded for Columbia Records; their only memorable song out of ten they would do together would be the appropriately titled—for Frank Sinatra—"All or Nothing At All," recorded in late August. Clarinets exchange phrases with muted horns. Sinatra's voice is crisp, clear, and forceful.

"All or nothing at all," he croons, floating the phrase over the band. "Half a love never appealed to me." He lingers on notes just a bit longer than other singers do. It's the duality of Sinatra, insistent and confident, though asking for acceptance. He's young—he's got a youthful cockiness coupled with insecurity. He's got a young man's naive hopes, which, with just his inflections, he confesses to the audience. He holds that note; he's in control. But then he bends it a bit, questioning. He's Crosby cool, yet Columbo vulnerable. He opens the vowels, as Caruso does in "O sole mio." He finishes the song in a smooth, operatic flourish, "all, or nothing at all." And hearing that ending, you knew he wasn't going to settle for anything less.

In December of that year, Sinatra left James's band for one led by the trombonist Tommy Dorsey.

The three years he spent with Dorsey's band were a kind of boot camp for Sinatra. Dorsey was a famously exacting taskmaster, and he showed the singer how to work with musicians and how to select repertoire. But most important, the twenty-five-year-old skinny Sicilian with the piercing blue eyes perfected his phrasing, the art of holding and bending notes.

"The thing that influenced me most was the way Tommy played his trombone," Sinatra would later say. "He would take a musical phrase and play it all the way through, seemingly without breathing, for eight, ten, maybe sixteen bars."

Sinatra shared the Dorsey stage with Connie Haines, Jo Stafford, and the Pied Pipers.

"He came on and sang 'Stardust' and it was quite an experience. You knew after eight bars that you were hearing something just absolutely new and unique," Stafford said.

It was with Dorsey that Sinatra first connected with the song-writer Jimmy Van Heusen and the arranger with whom he would later work, Axel Stordahl.

His first number one record with Dorsey was "I'll Never Smile Again." Sinatra, harmonizing with the Pied Pipers, sang along with the vibes. He tells the story, narrating it in a warm, powerful voice.

His smooth style beautifully complemented the big-band swing sound. His voice was an instrument, like any other in the band. He was what big bands needed. His romantic renderings—sweet and rich—fit beautifully with the lush sounds of Dorsey's brass. Dorsey and Sinatra would sell millions of records, including "Fools Rush In," "Polka Dots and Moonbeams," "Stardust," and "Oh! Look at Me Now."

Five days before Sinatra's twenty-sixth birthday, the Japanese attacked Pearl Harbor, and America entered World War II. Six months later the studio musicians would strike, bringing the recording industry to a standstill. It was the beginning of the end of the big bands, an era that had lasted ten years.

The popularity of the singer—the voice—eclipsed that of the bandleader.

9

"Night and Day"

FRANK SINATRA

It was December 30, 1942, and Benny Goodman, "the King of Swing," had invited Frank Sinatra to share a bill at the Paramount Theatre on Forty-third Street and Broadway in Manhattan. Apparently, Benny Goodman didn't know much about Frank Sinatra— other than that he had fronted Dorsey's band. Goodman himself hated to be upstaged by singers.

Peggy Lee was Goodman's featured singer, and when she finished her number, the band left the stage. The announcer introduced Frank Sinatra to a deafening cry.

"What the hell was that?" Benny Goodman said backstage.

The theater erupted in screams and cheers for "Frankie."

Teenage girls gyrated beneath their pleated knee-length skirts and squirmed within sweaters that covered pert white shirts. They tapped to the music and leaped off their feet in their black loafers or saddle shoes and white bobby socks.

Frank Sinatra took the stage in a dark suit, with a bow tie and a pocket square. He pressed his lips close to the microphone, and with a gentle touch he cradled the device in one hand, almost as if it were the back of a girl's head. He swayed ever so slightly, while his free hand gestured toward the lights or held on to the stand.

"Night and day," Sinatra sang, crooning his first solo hit. "You are the one. Only you 'neath the moon or under the sun." He sang as if it were just him and any one of the girls sitting on a couch, knowing that the bedroom was upstairs.

He wasn't your typical heartthrob. He was the guy next door. "He weighed 120 pounds soaking wet," Benny Goodman would later say of Sinatra. "Twenty of which was hair."

"I was the boy at every corner drugstore, the boy who'd gone off, drafted to the war," Sinatra would later explain.

The suits draped his thin frame. The floppy bow ties—sewn by his wife, Nancy, to cover up his Adam's apple—framed his gawky face. The cheekbones, the scars on his face, were all eclipsed by the radiant blue eyes. He was the young man girls wanted to take care of.

This was a new generation of girls from working-class and immigrant families—Italian, Irish, Jewish, German, Polish. They were the wartime audience who wanted their part of the American dream. These teenage girls were the "swooners"; they were the bobbysoxers. That evening, Sinatra's publicist, George Evans, paid a few girls to start screaming, which they did—and it quickly spread to all the girls in the theater. In ways, this was a release for girls at a time when such reactions were not culturally accepted.

That night, Benny Goodman—and everyone else—witnessed the "Sinatra Swoon" for the first time.

Men were leaving for war, and their girlfriends were staying behind, dreaming of reuniting at a better time. Sinatra was the man who was singing to the young women. He was a distant lover, he was a close boyfriend, he could be their husband.

He was the voice of the soldiers, who whispered through letters "just as though you were here." And he warned these girls to "be careful, it's my heart."

Sinatra was one immigrant son interpreting the lyrics of song-writers who were themselves immigrants or the sons of immigrants:

Jerome Kern, Arthur Schwartz, Irving Berlin, George Gershwin, Richard Rodgers, Lorenz Hart, and Oscar Hammerstein. (Of course, he didn't overlook the songs of Cole Porter and Johnny Mercer— old-stock, blue-blooded Americans.)

Sinatra, as he interpreted the songs, is the sound of the city. And he was a city man singing to city girls.

Sinatra's initial two-week run at the Paramount with Benny Goodman was immediately extended to eight weeks. Sinatra later boasted that he performed eleven shows a day at the thirty-six-hundred-seat hall (though, by many accounts, as many as five thousand fans attended that first performance). Each show lasted forty minutes, well worth the forty-to-eighty-five-cent price of admission. Girls lined up for each show; the promoter's challenge was to get them to leave afterward, but many insisted on staying for the next show.

A reporter from *Time* magazine remarked, "Not since Rudolph Valentino has American womanhood made such unabashed public love to an entertainer."

Of course, Sinatra had his detractors.

"Mr. Sinatra's baritone had little volume and little carrying power beyond what the amplifier gave it, and it was utterly inadequate in 'Old Man River,' but the singing was definitely unique in style, and the singer's pleasant and friendly and somewhat dreamy personality matched," said a review in *The New York Times*.

Even his limitations didn't hold him back. He came to be known as "the Voice," and by 1943 his popularity rivaled that of Dorsey's.

Sinatra was now performing at larger venues and occasionally had to break engagements, one of which was at the Riobamba on East Fifty-seventh Street in Manhattan. But his management made the calls to other managers to find a substitute—and that they did, a twenty-six-year-old tall, dark, and handsome Italian guy from Steubenville, Ohio, named Dean Martin.

American men were being called up for duty, and Frank Sinatra was no exception. Sinatra was examined by the Army in Jersey City, and on December 9 he was declared 4-F, unfit because of a ruptured eardrum, caused during his difficult delivery. The men and boys who had gone to or returned from the war came to resent him. They became jealous that through his music he was making love to their girls. Outside the Paramount Theatre, GIs and other young men threw tomatoes at the posters for his show.

By early 1944, the crooner Dick Haymes, Crosby, and the newcomer Perry Como were battling it out with Sinatra for *Billboard* hits. Nat "King" Cole released "Straighten Up and Fly Right," and Sinatra sang Jerome Kern and Oscar Hammerstein's "Ol' Man River," though he refused to sing the lyric "Niggers all work on the Mississippi," changing it to "Here we all work on the Mississippi."

Shortly before the Allies liberated Rome in the spring of 1944, Sinatra moved Nancy and his two children to California, where he began work on the movie *Anchors Aweigh* with Gene Kelly, which would be released the next year.

That year, Sinatra made a short, socially conscious film called *The House I Live In*. It spoke out against religious and racial intolerance.

"I grew up being called a guinea and a wop," he said. "And words like 'nigger' and 'kike' are hurtful and shouldn't be used."

"Prejudice is nothing new to me," Sinatra said, as his daughter Tina remembered in a book published many years later. "In Hoboken, when I was a kid, I lived in a tough neighborhood. When somebody called me a 'dirty little guinea,' there was only one thing to do—break his head. When I got older, I realized you shouldn't do it that way. I realized you've got to do it through education—maybe with a few exceptions."

The screenplay of *The House I Live In* was written by Albert Maltz, a Jew and a Communist who would soon become known as part of the Hollywood Ten: artists who were blacklisted because of their political convictions. In the film, Frank Sinatra takes a break from a recording session and steps outside to smoke a cigarette. There he finds a group of kids chasing a small boy, calling him a kike.

"Hey, what's this all about?" Sinatra says, breaking up the fight.

"None of your business!" one smart-ass kid says.

"What?" Sinatra says with a Jersey-tough attitude. "You're afraid to tell me?"

The kid tells Sinatra that they don't like the kid's religion, to which Sinatra replies, "You must be one of those Nazi werewolves I've been hearing about."

The tough kid tells Sinatra that his father fought and was wounded in the war; the Jewish kid says that his parents donate blood for the war cause.

"I betcha his pop's blood helped save your dad's life," Sinatra says. "My dad came from Italy, but I'm American, but should I hate your father because he came from Ireland, France, or Russia?" That sentiment aside, the script nevertheless refers to "Japs," our wartime enemy.

On October 11, 1944, Sinatra returned to Times Square to perform at the Paramount, where ten thousand fans awaited him, most of them teenagers. The fans inside refused to leave for the following show. Kids outside waited for hours; they became hostile and started chanting, and some of them began stampeding into the theater. It took the police until the evening to calm everyone down. The New York newspapers called it the Columbus Day Riot, noting that the disturbance occurred on a national holiday honoring an Italian.

10

"Angelina"

LOUIS PRIMA

"I'm not worried about those Italians," President Roosevelt said when asked about them in 1942, with the United States freshly entered into the war against Hitler's Germany and Mussolini's Italy. "They are just a bunch of opera singers."

Roosevelt had nevertheless asked the head of the FBI, J. Edgar Hoover, to investigate the threat posed to the United States by Italians living in America. America was at war, and Italy, Germany, and Japan were our enemies. By now, the story of the Japanese citizens held in internment camps in the West is well-known—but there also existed camps for Italians, albeit to a much lesser degree. Little is said about them even today, and those who do remember refuse to talk about them.

Just as it's considered bad form for Italians to be too obvious about their ambitions, they don't like to admit their hardships—because who really cares, anyway? And, of course, if it's not acknowledged, it's not real. One doesn't present a *bella figura* by acting as if the world's against you, even if it is—and in that case, don't let them know they got to you. You are stronger than that. We *are* American, Italian Americans would tell themselves.

By June 1942, Hoover's FBI had arrested 1,521 Italian aliens (noncitizens) as a threat to national security. The United States required that 600,000 Italian "resident aliens" carry identification cards, and began arresting those who broke curfew, or didn't have papers on them, or just plain looked suspicious.

Nearly 250 Italians were held for up to two years in Fort Missoula, near Missoula, Montana—not to mention another couple hundred held in California, and at Ellis Island. Never mind that nearly 500,000 Italian Americans served in World War II—the largest minority to fight for the United States in the war.

The number interned doubles when Canada is taken into account, for Italians were rounded up in Montreal, Toronto, everywhere, and sent by train to cold, remote places in the Canadian tundra.

During this time, many Italian American fishermen were forbidden to board boats. In fact, as "the Yankee clipper," Joe DiMaggio, was about to start two years of service in the U.S. Army Air Force, his father, a fisherman in San Francisco, was banned from going within twenty yards of the docks.

At the same time, Swing Street was living up to its name, and Louis Prima was putting his Italian sound to jazz, first in music, then in lyrics. He sang about what he knew: he sang about his upbringing. Prima, who craved the public eye, did whatever he could to stay there. But one great sensibility that would inform all of his music was his self-deprecating humor. Whether people laughed with him or laughed at him, he knew they were enjoying themselves. And by laughing at yourself, you lessen the blow when others laugh. You have control; therefore, you are not a victim.

In the early 1940s, Prima wrote one of the songs for which he would be most remembered, inspired by his mother, Angelina. "Angelina" is about an Italian waitress the singer meets in a pizzeria. He starts off with a typical Italian meal:

I eat antipasta twice
Just because she is so nice, Angelina . . .

With this song, which hit the Top 10, Louis Prima introduced the southern Italian tarantella—fast-tempo music for dancing, usually in 6/8 time—to America.

From that gentle 6/8 (in the popular version we now know), he goes to a rollicking 4/4, segueing into the traditional Italian "Menzu 'u mare" which starts, "C'è la luna 'n menzu 'u mare, mamma mia m'a a maritari." The song, when sung by Italian men, often has more sexually suggestive lyrics. And Prima didn't shy from sharing the double entendres with his audience. His own little joke.

The story is about a fireman, with his long hose, who "comes and goes, goes and comes . . ." You get the idea.

Prima worked these double entendres into his songs. Most Italians knew the songs, and for the Americans it wasn't difficult to figure out what they were about.

Prima sang "Please No Squeeza da Banana," about an Italian fruit vendor who has to watch as a police officer fondles all of his fruit every day, only to take off without paying.

He sang a song called "Baciagaloop (Makes Love on the Stoop)." Because Italian families were typically large, young lovers wooed each other anywhere else but in the apartment—on a park bench, in a car, on the stoop. Later, another Italian American comic singer, Lou Monte, would come up with a song about Baciagaloop, whom he would call Paul Revere's Horse.

A song called "Felicia No Capicia" was even more successful for Prima. The public had come to understand Prima's wry humor, and it also came to the attention of New York City officials. *Life* magazine interviewed Mayor Fiorello La Guardia at the time and asked him if *capicia* meant anything nasty. La Guardia, perhaps evading the question, responded that *capicia* was dialect of *capisce*, which means to understand—therefore, the only thing Felicia doesn't do is understand.

While the FBI was rounding up "threats" to the United States and putting them in internment camps, their relatives were fighting on the other side of the ocean. But the Italians here still considered themselves Americans. And they played an important role, both at home and on the front.

The men in the ports heard the news; they knew the inside scoop. The same Italians working for the Mob kept an eye on the waters for German subs. The U.S. government reasoned that it was the Italians here who knew Italians there best, and so they looked to the Mob to help with the invasion of Sicily. They released from prison Lucky Luciano, credited with being the father of organized crime in the United States, who, in turn, enlisted the help of his associates both here and in Italy.

Legend has it that Luciano put word out to his compatriots in Sicily that the Americans were landing, and not to engage them. When the Allies landed, it was the Germans they fought, not the Italians, who were eager to change sides.

In 1942, Louis Prima performed at the Howard Theatre, a traditionally black performance hall in Washington, D.C. In attendance was First Lady Eleanor Roosevelt, who was vocal in her support of civil rights for Negroes. She was so taken by Prima that she introduced herself after the show and invited him to President Roosevelt's birthday party at the White House a few days later.

Prima had no idea how he should introduce himself to the president. When the time came to meet him, he decided the best way was to be himself. In his hepcat speak, Prima said, "Hello, Daddy!"

On Columbus Day that year, President Roosevelt announced that Italian Americans should no longer be considered enemy aliens.

11

"I'm Gonna Love That Gal (Like She's Never Been Loved Before)"

PERRY COMO

Pierino Como was the seventh son of a seventh son, born in 1912 in Canonsburg, Pennsylvania, a town south of Pittsburgh known for its uranium-refining factories. His parents, Pietro Como and Lucia Travaglini, had emigrated from Palena, a mountain village in the Abruzzi e Molise—located west of Rome, but considered part of the *meridione*. After 1963, the two regions separated, and Italian immigrants identified themselves as having come from either Abruzzi or Molise.

Como was one of thirteen children growing up. His father worked as a mill hand in the working-class town, and as in any large Italian family the children found themselves working after school. At age eleven, Perry Como got a job at the local barbershop, lathering beards, cleaning clippers, sweeping the floor. It was here, in the familiar environment of the barbershop, that Perry Como discovered what he wanted to do. He saw the comfort a barber gave. It seemed like a steady business—there was always someone waiting to get a haircut. It didn't seem too taxing, not like working in a mine.

At age fourteen, he had saved enough to put a down payment on his own barbershop, which was located next to a Greek coffee shop. While he was in class during high school, he hired two men to work the day shift. Como would take over when school got out; when the demands of school became too much, he hired someone to cover the late-afternoon shift.

Barbershops were the refuge of men. Here they could talk openly. The smell of tobacco smoke mingled with the scents of pomades and tonics. This was where they could feel civilized; for some of them a crisp haircut was the only way they would take care of themselves—or let themselves be taken care of, however grudgingly. They were men, after all, hardworking, callus-palmed. Here they could feel the weight of their hair, however slight, be taken off, and with that the weight of the day. Men could listen to others in ways that they wouldn't listen to their wives. In Italy, barbers not only shaved your face and cut your hair, they also acted as dentists or doctors, called on to perform bloodletting or other minor surgeries. (While staying in Calabria with his mother, my father developed a boil on his arm. He was directed to the corner shop, where he waited for the barber to finish a game of *scopa* before lancing it.)

Como kept a guitar in his barbershop. He played and sang in various barbershop quartets. In the evenings, he went to parties and dance halls. His friends realized that he had a decent voice, and he was soon asked to sing at those parties. A neighborhood friend, Jimmy Palmer (who would become a big-band leader in the early 1940s), encouraged him to perform.

For many Italians, though, singing was looked on as a job—true, one that brought in a better-than-decent paycheck and afforded one some form of popularity—but still a job, like running a coffee shop, cutting hair, or laying brick. Except you kept your hands clean.

In 1933, at age twenty-one, Como, looking for a vacation spot, found his way to Cleveland, Ohio, where a friend just so happened to introduce him to a musician friend who lived there, Freddie Carlone, who, upon hearing Perry's smooth baritone voice, asked him to join his band.

Como returned to Canonsburg and gave it serious thought. With some encouragement from his father, he decided to try it out. ("If you decide you don't like singing," his father said, "you can always come back to Canonsburg.") Just before leaving, Como asked his sweetheart to marry him. On July 31, 1933, he wed that girl, Roselle Belline, whose family had emigrated from France and lived a couple towns away from Como. The two had met at a wiener roast festival in Canonsburg. The father of his friend Jimmy Palmer took over the barbershop.

He performed with the Freddie Carlone Orchestra mostly throughout the Midwest, where his "voice, his easy manner, and his handsome appearance, won him many fans," observed one reporter.

When, in 1936, he received an offer from a bigger bandleader, Ted Weems, Carlone understood and let him go. Ted Weems traveled much farther than Carlone's band had, performing on both coasts. "When I look back on it now," Perry said in an interview, "I realize that joining Weems was like joining the Foreign Legion. Those one-nighters—ugh!"

In 1942, Ted Weems joined the Merchant Marine and broke up the band. Como knew he didn't want to join another band. It was too much traveling, too much work—even while making a comfortable $175 per week. Assuming he would never get a break without a band backing him, he decided to return to the barbershop in Canonsburg.

He and Roselle, on the way back from Weems's last gig, stopped off in New York. Como met up with a friend who convinced him to hang around just a bit longer. And as it happened, luck was on his side—he was offered a contract to perform at the Copacabana. He was tired of being on the road, and the only thing that convinced him to stay rather than move back to Canonsburg was that he wouldn't have to travel.

The low-key former barber settled not in Manhattan but in Sunnyside, Queens, just across the East River via the Queensboro Bridge. He chose as his home an apartment, most likely the Phipps Garden Apartments building, in Sunnyside Gardens, one of America's first planned communities, with two-story brick row houses enclosing blocks of private and communal gardens—an oasis within the chaos of New York City.

That year he was approached by a producer from RCA Victor.

In 1943, RCA released Como's first record, "Goodbye, Sue." Because it was recorded during a strike by the American Federation of Musicians, he was accompanied solely by vocals, not instruments. The next year he came out with "Long Ago and Far Away," which was the song for the movie *Cover Girl*, starring Rita Hayworth. But 1945 was Como's year. Como started with "I'm Confessin' (That I Love You)," which had been a hit for the Guy Lombardo Orchestra back in 1930, and continued with "If I Loved You" and "I'm Gonna Love That Gal (Like She's Never Been Loved Before)," which reached numbers three and four, respectively, on the charts. Then "Till the End of Time" reached number one and stayed on the charts for seventeen weeks.

"Black-haired and black-eyed" is how one journalist described Como, while another, noting his Italian looks, painted him as "an admittedly lazy young guy, with dark hair and sleepy brown eyes in a Rudolph Valentino face."

Yet another article at the time said that Como, who was listed in various polls as one of the top-ten best-dressed men, with the appearance of a "husky college freshman."

Perry Como was viewed at once as dark, Italian, and all-American. Perry Como was the Italian who became white.

While Sinatra romanced women, and while Crosby was the ubiquitous father, Como had sex appeal, albeit of the boy-next-door variety. He was open and friendly, and without the arrogance that both Sinatra and Crosby possessed.

Como finished the year with "Dig You Later (A-Hubba-Hubba-Hubba)." He must have realized the success Crosby had in 1944 with his Irish lullaby "Too-Ra-Loo-Ra-Loo-Ral," and RCA released a version of an Italian lullaby Como knew from childhood.

This was "Chi-baba, Chi-baba (My Bambino Go to Sleep)," which stayed high on the charts for 13 weeks in 1947.

By 1945, Como had become the first pop singer to have two songs sell over two million copies at the same time. Como would earn the moniker "King of the Jukes," for he had seventy-three *Billboard* hits from 1945 to 1954. This was a tremendous feat, considering Crosby had seventy, and Sinatra had only fifty-eight. *Billboard* would later rank Como as the third most successful recording artist from 1940 to 1954, below only Crosby and Glenn Miller and above the Andrews Sisters and Sinatra.

The war had ended, American troops were coming home, and Perry Como sang "I'm Gonna Love That Gal (Like She's Never Been Loved Before)." A swoosh of bright brass opens the song, which swings as if it were the Roaring Twenties. A New Orleans jazz clarinet carries the melody. "I'm gonna show that gal she's the baby that I adore," Como declares. When she's in his arms again, they'll forget all those years apart. He insists they're going to begin anew.

As always, Como's vocals seem effortless. He sings the song as if telling a story to friends gathered in a barbershop.

12

"Prisoner of Love"

PERRY COMO

The next year, 1946, Perry Como had his second number one hit with "Prisoner of Love," which Russ Columbo had sung fifteen years earlier. The song made clear that while Crosby was Como's obvious influence in matter of style and persona, Como was a vocal heir of Columbo.

"Prisoner of Love" was Russ Columbo's big song—his theme song—and it proved to do just as well for Como, staying on the charts for twenty-one weeks.

> Alone from night to night you'll find me,
> Too weak to break the chains that bind me . . .

Columbo sings the song like a young man hopelessly in love. He delivers the lyric dreamily, then during an interlude hums happily, as if he's enjoying his amorous incarceration.

Como sings the song in the same key over lush strings. His voice is more covered, as if it had a governor on it. Yet it is resolute, as if he is stoically resigned to being captive to love—a love it is too late for him to escape.

It's almost as if Como is Columbo, grown up. Columbo was only twenty-four when he recorded the song; Como was thirty-four. His voice, mellow as always, doesn't have the desperation that Columbo's did; instead, Como accepts his fate, crooning, "I'm just a prisoner of love."

Just as Columbo had made his way into the homes of listeners of all kinds through radio, so Perry Como, two decades later, made himself present in American living rooms through the relatively new medium of television.

On Christmas Eve 1948, Como hosted his first TV show, NBC's *Chesterfield Supper Club*, named for its cigarette sponsor. This began a tradition of Perry Como Christmas specials.

Watching one of his shows from 1951 on the Museum of Broadcast Communications website, I was struck by how warm he his. His sponsor, Chesterfield, couldn't have found a better host for its brand of cigarettes—"the mildest flavor, and no terrible aftertaste," said the spokesman on the show.

And this can describe Perry Como—both his singing and his private life. At first I was surprised at how little had been written about his life, but then I realized that it, like he himself, was utterly lacking in controversy.

At the end of that fifteen-minute television show, which included as musical guests the Fontane Sisters, the Ray Charles Chorus, and the Larks, Como sings one of his hits, "Zing Zing, Zoom Zoom," with children playing behind him, on a seesaw and swing, as if on a playground. But midway through the song, Como forgets a verse. He finishes the song, with a "salut'" to the audience, then apologizes profusely to his listeners; with a finger he casually scratches the side of his face, then rubs his ear.

Since the first great wave of Italian immigrants, the piano had given way to the phonograph and radio, which, in turn, were being pushed aside by television. By the end of the 1940s, there were over ten million TV sets in the United States.

Television offered fresh opportunities for singers to be seen more regularly and in different formats. To see your favorite singers or bands, you no longer had to wait for them to come to town and pay the ticket prices at the Paramount. From here on out, you could do more than just look at photo stills of your favorite singers in *Downbeat*, *Variety*, or *Band Leaders*. Now, for the first time, you could turn a dial and they would be right there with you, in your living room, as you ate dinner with the family.

Magazine and newspaper articles of the time reflect how people saw Como. "How to Relax the Como Way," read one, along with "All He Does Is Sing," "He Got Rich Quick," and "Perry Como: My Philosophy."

In 1950, Como was given his own fifteen-minute program, *The Perry Como Show*. Then, in 1955, with CBS's half-hour sitcom *The Honeymooners*, starring Jackie Gleason, airing on Saturday night, NBC gave Como his own hour-long show and scheduled it against *The Honeymooners*.

The papers hyped the move as the "Battle of the Giants." "The Wildest Saturday Night Fight," read one column, "Gleason (255 lbs.) vs. Como (165 lbs.)." In the latter article, from *TV and Radio Magazine*, the reporter Hy Gardner interviewed both "fighters" about what each thought of the other. Were they contentious? Not with each other, it appeared.

"Ratings can't change a friendship," Gleason responded, seemingly more annoyed with the question than with Como's jump in ratings. "What'd he do, kill my best friend, steal my money or something?"

Como answered: "What can I tell you? My kids are crazy about Gleason. He's the most loveable guy in the world."

Eventually, within a year, the ratings of *The Honeymooners* had dropped to number nineteen. Then the show went off the air altogether, after a total of thirty-nine episodes.

Como bucked the notion that one should perform in a suit. He opted instead for nicely pressed trousers, a neat button-down shirt, and the piece of clothing for which he will always be remembered—a cardigan sweater. He came to be known as the "cardigan crooner," the easygoing singer who "made vanilla popular."

13

"Mam'selle"

FRANK SINATRA

"Ladies and gentlemen, here's some cats that can dance up a storm," Frank Sinatra said, greeting the audience at the sold-out Loew's Capitol Theatre on Broadway and Fifty-first Street in May 1947. "Keep your eye on the little guy in the middle—personal friend of mine."

And with that he introduced the Will Mastin Trio, the little guy being twenty-two-year-old Sammy Davis Jr. The Mastin Trio was hired at a very generous $1,250 a week. The trio seemed to glide onstage, and between the two older black men Sammy wildly tapped out a dance.

Two months later, Sinatra attended the second in a remarkable series of boxing matches—Rocky Graziano versus Tony Zale, which took place in Chicago Stadium on Madison Street on July 16, 1947. In their first fight, the previous year, the rising star Graziano had lost to Zale, a Pole from Gary, Indiana (given name: Anthony Florian Zaleski), who was the reigning middleweight champ. Graziano, who had appeared to be winning that fight, was knocked out in the sixth round. The rumor was that he had thrown the fight. People in his neighborhood—New York City's Lower East Side—sneered at him behind his back.

Sinatra himself must have felt the public pulling away from him, too. At his ringside seat, he surely cheered on the underdog.

Graziano was born in 1919 in Brooklyn, was given the name Thomas Rocco Barbella, and grew up on the Lower East Side. His father, who boxed under the name "Fighting Nick Bob," would put gloves on him and pit the three-year-old Rocky against his six-year-old brother. Neighbors would gather at the house to watch what would often be a bruising beating, with Rocky losing. He grew up a juvenile criminal and neighborhood bully, beating up kids for ice cream, bikes, or even bread. He was in and out of reform schools and Catholic children's services. He was drafted into the Army only to go AWOL after hitting an officer.

While AWOL, he returned to New York to box under the name Graziano. Military police caught up with him, and as punishment he was forced to box for the Army.

The only way for the twenty-eight-year-old Graziano to shake the rumors was to fight Zale again. In a 1969 *Sport* article, John Devaney recalled seeing that second fight, which was not televised but witnessed only by the nineteen thousand people in attendance at the stadium. In the first round the two came out ready to destroy each other. Zale, nicknamed "the Man of Steel," threw powerful body punches; Graziano pummeled his face. Then, with a right hook, Zale connected with Graziano's left eye, opening a deep cut above it. Blood seemed to pour down his face and body onto the canvas. Graziano's cut man stopped the bleeding. In the third round, Zale reopened it. At the bell the referee warned Graziano's camp that if the blood continued, he'd call the fight.

The temperature inside the stadium climbed past a hundred degrees. Two rounds later and unable to drop Graziano, Zale began to weaken. In the sixth round, Graziano, bloodied and with a knot forming under his right eye, cornered Zale against the ropes. With his left hand Graziano stabilized Zale by his neck and pounded his face until he knocked him out. With that, the nearly uneducated New York street kid became the world's middleweight champ.

In all likelihood, Sinatra went to the dressing room after the fight to congratulate Graziano himself.

Graziano's year was also Sinatra's year—the year he released several of the songs for which he is now known, like "I Believe" and "Almost Like Being in Love."

But 1947 also marked the start of Sinatra's decline, which was precipitated by his hot temper as well as some bad, cocky decisions on his part. Yet at the same time, there was a deep-seated anti-Italian-American sentiment in the United States.

That February, Sinatra boarded a plane to Havana with Charlie Fischetti, a known mobster from Bergen County, New Jersey. The thirty-one-year-old Sinatra had accepted an invitation from the gangster and Mob boss Lucky Luciano, who was visiting Havana from Sicily.

Luciano, who was born in Lercara Friddi, Sicily, had been brought to trial in 1936 for running one of the country's largest prostitution rings—thanks in part to Mayor La Guardia, who had assigned the special prosecutor Thomas Dewey (who would later become governor of New York, then candidate for president) to the case. Luciano was convicted and sentenced to thirty to fifty years. In 1944, the U.S. government asked him to assist American and British troops in landing in Sicily. He was released from prison, sent to Italy, and ordered never to return to U.S. soil. After the war, Luciano moved to Cuba—the closest he could get to the United States—to build a gambling mecca.

Sinatra was happy to rub elbows with such a powerful man. He was largely unaware, however, that the fifty-year-old Luciano had called together heads of the various Mafias at the Hotel Nacional. It was an all-star Mob list: Joe Adonis, Tommy Lucchese, Joe Profaci,

Willie Moretti, Albert Anastasia, Joseph Bonanno, and Santo Traffi-
cante, who was the capo of Mob bosses from Tampa, Florida.

"We was all proud of him," Luciano once said, "a skinny kid from
Hoboken with a terrific voice and one hundred percent Italian."

A Scripps-Howard columnist, Robert Ruark, caught sight of
Sinatra and the bosses in Havana and filed a story.

"Sinatra is playing with the strangest people these days," Ruark
wrote. "Mr. Sinatra, the self-confessed savior of the country's small
fry, seems to be setting a most peculiar example for his hordes of
pimply, shrieking slaves." Lee Mortimer of New York's *Daily Mirror*
followed up, contacting the FBI to ask about the nature of Sinatra's
involvement with the Mafia. (A state senator had already decried
Sinatra as a Communist to the House Un-American Activities
Committee due to his film short *The House I Live In*.) In his
columns, Mortimer seemed to enjoy attacking Sinatra personally.
Having attended a performance of the singer and actor Carl Brisson
at the Versailles nightclub, Mortimer wrote: "A middle-aged dame
next to me sighed, 'He's the Sinatra of the mink coats.' Lady, that's a
base libel. It's the other way around. Frankie is the Brisson of the
basement bargains."

Sinatra was enraged by the attacks. In April, he was at Ciro's
restaurant, a celebrity hangout on the Sunset Strip in L.A., when he
spotted Mortimer. The reporter must have felt Sinatra's cold stare; he
finished his drink and headed for the door. Sinatra put down his
whiskey, followed him out, cornered him, and decked him, knocking
him flat on his back.

Mortimer later called the authorities, and the next day, while
Sinatra was in the recording studio, police entered and arrested
him, supposedly while he was singing "Oh! What a Beautiful Morning." Sinatra was initially sued for twenty-five thousand dollars, but
the two settled on nine thousand, provided Sinatra apologize publicly.

Around that time, pictures of Sinatra with, among other actresses,
Lana Turner appeared in the newspapers and fan magazines. Turner

was especially sexy, with blond hair, tight shorts, and a halter top in *The Postman Always Rings Twice*; the tight-fitting, breast-enhancing blue sweater she wore in *They Won't Forget* had earned her the nickname "the Sweater Girl."

None of this helped Frank Sinatra with his fan base.

The boys had always been wary of him. Many soldiers saw his 4-F status during World War II as a clever way to dodge the draft. But more so, he made men jealous. Like Rudolph Valentino and Russ Columbo before him, he was a dangerous lover.

Throughout the war, Sinatra had sung to the young working-class girls whose boyfriends had gone off to battle. He wasn't a typical heartthrob. He was vulnerable, approachable. He was average-looking, his suits draped over his slim frame. He was safe for both the girls and their boyfriends because he was married to an adoring wife and had two kids, with a third on the way.

But by 1947, those bobby-soxers had come of age and married those soldiers who had returned. And now he was seen as the husband cheating on his wife.

His young female fans began to feel slighted, especially his Italian American fans, who, as Catholics, were taught that adultery was sinful. They wore sweaters, but not in the way Lana did. They all had seen themselves in Nancy, and now they were raising children at home just as she was. How could he cheat on Nancy while he was on the road? How could he do this to her—to them?

Sammy Davis Jr. remembered seeing Sinatra in 1948.

Frank was "slowly walking down Broadway with no hat on and his collar up—and not a soul was paying attention to him. This was the man who only a few years ago had tied up traffic all over Times Square . . . Now the same man was walking down the same street and nobody gave a damn."

Davis didn't want to embarrass him, and in any case the twenty-two-year-old didn't know what he could possibly say to the man who had become his idol. So he let Sinatra pass by.

Sinatra's "Mam'selle," which had landed at the top slot on the charts in May 1947, would be his last song to reach that high for nearly seven years. Of course, Sinatra couldn't have known that he was about to fall out of favor, and yet he sang "Mam'selle" like a torch song in a French café after everyone has gone.

A French horn intones the first phrase of the melody, answered by an oboe, and then a bright, bittersweet solo violin floats over lush strings. Sinatra's velvety voice sets the scene: in a small café, he has a rendezvous with a mam'selle who's as warm and sweet as the violins that are playing.

He is trying to make love with his voice—treating each note gently, savoring the moment, respecting it. A guitar strums lazily in the background, like a clock gently ticking.

But as the evening gets later, the mood changes—a change of which Sinatra is all too aware. Their kiss becomes a sigh. The smoke lingers as chairs are stacked on tables and lowball glasses are washed and placed back on the shelves.

When he sings, "And yet I know too well, someday you'll say goodbye," it's as if he were singing goodbye to the young women, grown up now, who once pined for him.

"Then violins will cry, and so will I, mam'selle."

Part Two

The Italian Decade, the 1950s

14

"You're Breaking My Heart"

VIC DAMONE

Vito Farinola was working as an usher at the Paramount Theatre on Broadway.

He had been singing the Ave Maria at his church, St. Finbar's in Bensonhurst, Brooklyn, and performing at various events for school, Lafayette High. His father, an electrician, had been out of work due to an injury, and money was tight for the Farinola family. Even so, Vito's mother, a piano teacher, insisted that her son study music, and had been paying for him to take voice lessons. Vito was afraid that he might be wasting their money.

Perry Como was performing at the Paramount. After a certain amount of time on the job, Paramount ushers were afforded special backstage privileges. And one night, Vito was asked to escort Como, hair still perfectly in place and his suit without a wrinkle, from the stage to the fifth-floor dressing room.

In the elevator, he summoned up his courage and said: "Can I ask your advice?"

"What is it, kid?"

"I'd like to sing a couple bars for you because I want to see if I have talent. 'Cause if I don't, we can't afford the dollar for singing lessons. Would you mind if I sang 'There Must Be a Way'?" It was a song that Como had released the year before.

"No, go ahead."

Vito straightened his red usher's jacket and nervously sang two bars, then, self-conscious that he was singing for Perry Como, stopped.

"Keep going."

Vito sang some more, four or six bars, then stopped again.

"Will you finish the song?"

Vito finished the song, the final note filling the elevator car as it ascended. And when he did, Como said to him, "Oh, no, kid. You have to keep singing. You've got something."

The residents of Bensonhurst in the 1940s could walk out onto Eighteenth Avenue or Bay Parkway and find any number of *salumerie*, vegetable stands, cafés, bakeries, and, in the summer, Italian ice vendors. The neighborhood is still heavily Italian, though now with Russian and Chinese immigrants moving in alongside the grandchildren of Italian immigrants. Eighteenth Avenue has been renamed Cristoforo Colombo Boulevard, and Bensonhurst's streets, neighborhoods, and schools figured prominently in *Welcome Back, Kotter* (set in New Utrecht High School) and parts of *Saturday Night Fever*.

Vito Farinola was the youngest of four children and the only boy. He was part of a bubble of second- and third-generation Italian Americans whose parents or grandparents had emigrated before the quota set by the 1924 U.S. Immigration Act. It was this generation—those born between 1925 and 1935—that produced, with a few exceptions, the next wave of singers. These singers were born during Prohibition, grew up during the Depression, came of age during the war, and sought to make lives for themselves in the postwar years of confidence and prosperity.

The southern Italians who emigrated identified less with Italy than with the region or village they left. Once here, they often lived in pockets with others from that village. And the Italians who settled in Bensonhurst—along with many of the Jewish families who lived there—had moved out of the crowded tenements of the Lower East Side to the less-populated sections of south Brooklyn.

Immigrant Italians had escaped political corruption and centuries of oppression; they escaped starvation from fields that produced few vegetables because of drought and overcultivation. These Italians had little allegiance to the government of the Old Country (though nostalgia for the land and the family they left behind, surely). Those who had fled their Italian villages insisted their children become American.

Third-generation Italian Americans spoke to their parents in English, but to their grandparents they spoke (or were spoken to) in the Italian dialect of their place of origin.

You still ate your macaroni and gravy and pasta fagioli; you still drank Papa's homemade red wine, strong and sparkling; you still had Sunday dinners with your entire extended family; you still listened to Enrico Caruso on the radio or on the Victrola. And every Italian family, it seemed—no matter how poor—made sure there was some form of music in the home, be it an accordion or mandolin, piano or Victrola.

You were expected to work and contribute to the income of *la famiglia*. Many kids Vito's age didn't finish high school; college was an extravagance for young men who could otherwise be making money.

Vito's grandparents had come from the port city of Bari, the capital of Apulia. The relics of Saint Nicholas are housed in the basilica named after him there. It was a cultured city, and its opera house, the Petruzzelli, ranks among the finest in Italy, along with the San Carlo in Naples and Milan's La Scala. It was Vito's mother who encouraged him to sing, and it was her maiden name—Damone—he took when he became a professional singer.

"I mean, my mother was shoving it down my throat," Damone told me. "I wanted to play baseball with the boys. We had a team called the Baysides." But he practiced instead, diligently singing scales with his mother at the piano.

At fifteen, Farinola was listening to a program called *The Battle of the Baritones* on WINS radio when, for the first time, he heard the voice of Frank Sinatra.

"Oh, my God. What's that?" he said to himself. He leaned closer to the radio. The voice was singing "I Don't Stand a Ghost of a Chance with You."

"I really didn't understand Crosby," Damone said. "He was singing 'boo, boo, boo, boo.' But Sinatra . . . he was telling a story. And he had the timbre and style that I could imitate."

It didn't occur to Farinola to wonder whether Sinatra was Italian. After all, he recalled, "everyone I knew in my neighborhood was Italian."

Farinola had quit school and was working at a fruit and vegetable store when, while he was singing at a family wedding, an olive importer from his neighborhood, Lou Capone, heard him and offered to manage him.

"Actually, his wife's brother is married to my father's sister," Damone said in a newspaper interview later. Capone spent his own money to set up Vito with audition recordings, which he delivered to all the record labels. Soon, Vito Farinola took a name that was easier to pronounce and—to his ears at least—more Anglo-sounding. "Vito" became "Vic," and the quadruple-syllable Farinola was exchanged for the two-beat Damone (the final vowel now silent).

In April 1947, just before his nineteenth birthday, Vic Damone auditioned for and won a spot on CBS radio's *Arthur Godfrey's Talent Scouts*—the *American Idol* of its time. *Arthur Godfrey's Talent Scouts* ran on radio for three years before it was simultaneously televised in 1948.

Damone chose to sing "Prisoner of Love"—the song Russ Columbo had made famous in the 1930s and Como the previous summer. In attendance at Damone's audition was Milton Berle, who, impressed with what he heard, took Damone to the William Morris

Agency the next day to get him a gig recording songs for Muzak, which was background music for department stores as well as elevators.

Not long after the Godfrey audition, Berle helped Damone land two weeks at a New York nightclub on Fifty-seventh Street called La Martinique; the gig went so well they extended his contract for another couple of weeks. Either from those performances or from his Muzak recordings, an executive from Mercury Records heard him and signed him to record "I Have But One Heart." Soon, he had a spot on WHN radio in New York. Then it was on to the New York Paramount, where he had been ushering just months before, and to the Metropolitan Opera House.

The New York Times, reporting on Damone's 1948 appearance at the Metropolitan Opera, described a "curly haired kid": "the tall, dark boy who rates only a few pegs behind Bing Crosby in popularity polls sang a brief Italian aria—definitely a classic—then cut back to the soft and low swing melodies that have brought him fame and quite a lot of fortune."

Damone was good-looking—with delicate eyes and mouth, a long, straight Roman nose, and thick, wavy hair atop a high forehead. But like so many Italians of the time, who were described by their curly hair, or dark skin, or swarthy complexion, to *The New York Times* this singer was a "dark boy."

Damone, however, refused to be pigeonholed. "The people who want to hire popular singers are interested in just one thing—can you put your talent over—make it spark," Damone argued in a *New York Herald Tribune* interview. "They don't care anything about how young you are, where you were born, or your race or creed. That's why show business is the most truly democratic business on earth. You wonder why we're willing to work night and day to hit high?"

But reporters were fascinated by the Italian lifestyle, and Damone knew it.

"Mom has a vacuum container, and she packs up everything from breaded veal cutlets and a side order of lasagna, to chicken cacciatore and gnocchi," he told a reporter at the *New York Herald Tribune* in 1948, describing food that was then foreign to most Americans. Even pizza was still a local, ethnic dish.

Yet despite his success, Damone, in the article, admitted that he attended Mass regularly and still lived with his family—in a make-shift bedroom partitioned out of the living room by a curtain.

And like many Italians, he tried to take his family with him, even on tour.

"Sometimes Dad and my sisters come along and we make believe we're home," Damone said. "I want to keep things that way—even some day when I am really in the chips and can take the folks out to Los Angeles and build them a big house."

"One morning the doorbell rang,"Vic Damone told me many years later. We were talking on the telephone, and he was recalling the story behind his second hit. "I answered the door in my bathrobe."

"I'm looking for Vic Damone," a gentleman said.

"How did you find my house?"

"Everyone knows where you live," the man said. The man's name was Pat Genaro, an Italian American songwriter from New York City.

"I wrote a song for you. It's based on an old Italian melody," he said, and handed Damone a sheet of music.

After two years, Damone had had plenty of success, but he hadn't reached as high on the charts as he had with his first record, "I Have But One Heart," which was also inspired by a Neapolitan song. He read the music, recognized the tune, and invited Genaro inside, whereupon his mother offered him something to eat.

The song was called "You're Breaking My Heart" and was adapted from "Mattinata," a song written by Ruggiero Leoncavallo, the same composer who wrote *Pagliacci*—the opera from which Enrico Caruso had had his first million-selling record. Damone's father, who was listening, was pleased that his son would record a tune that he himself often hummed. With this song, part of which was sung in traditional Italian, Damone actually took time to read aloud the lyrics until he got the Italian pronunciation correct.

Damone brought the music to the head of A&R at Mercury Records, Mitch Miller. He recorded four songs in three hours, then recorded two takes of "You're Breaking My Heart" in twenty minutes.

Bright, sweet violins open the recording, with a clarinet adding a bit of color. A piano, imitating a mandolin strum, keeps the rhythm as Damone sings, "You're breaking my heart, 'cause you're leaving."

The meter then changes from 6/8 to a folksy beat-strum-strum waltz—complete with a guitar straight from the Old Country—as he begins the verse in the original Italian:

L'aurora di bianco vestita
Già l'uscio dischiude al gran sol;
Di già con le rosee sue dita
Carezza de' fiori lo stuol.

The dawn is dressed in white
Already opening up to the great sun;
And with its rosy fingers
Caresses the fields of flowers.

Vic Damone sings like a ballroom dancer moving to that waltz—back straight, shoulders square. It's as if he were gently holding his partner's hand (his other hand suggestively, though discreetly, low on her waist) as he directs her, gliding across the ballroom floor. His only vocal extravagance is a bit of vibrato, although one that is lovely and perfectly even.

The song spent twenty-six weeks on the charts, topping at number one in September 1949, above Perry Como's version of "Some Enchanted Evening" from the musical *South Pacific*.

Damone's singing is invariably smooth and precise. One might say almost too precise—he never veers off the beat. Perhaps it's because producing a beautiful tone is so easy for Damone that he doesn't work at putting across the song in other ways. He had Sinatra's baritone timbre and Como's ease. No wonder it's easy to sing along with him.

Singers of that generation wore as a badge of honor any accolade Frank Sinatra bestowed on them. Upon hearing Damone sing, Sinatra said that Damone had "the best pipes in the business."

Within two years of cornering Perry Como in an elevator, Vic Damone went from making eighteen dollars a week as an usher at the Paramount to pulling in $100,000 a year as a Mercury recording artist.

As "You're Breaking My Heart" was released, Damone realized that he had movie opportunities in Los Angeles. He was young, thin, and handsome, but he didn't like his nose. "I couldn't concentrate on the song," he told several reporters. "I was worrying about what the people on my right and left were thinking." So he got a nose job, smaller than the old "Italian one though still straight as an arrow." In photographs, even his "curly" hair seems to have been pomaded into thick waves.

"His new schnozzola, he thinks, will conquer all," John S. Wilson quipped in *Downbeat*. Of course, "Schnozzola"—an Italianized Yiddish word—was the nickname of the bulbous-nosed Italian American vaudeville comedian and singer Jimmy Durante. Over the next decade, Damone would make several movies, but his film career, his new nose notwithstanding, never took off.

15

"That Lucky Old Sun"

FRANKIE LAINE

"I was the first white singer to sound black," Frankie Laine told me on a sunny Saturday morning. It was 2004, and we were sitting in his bright living room in San Diego.

"Before Elvis did, I borrowed from black singers." He was a ninety-year-old man looking back on his life with mild incredulity, as if he thought he should have gotten more notice for it.

He wore a dark blue silk bathrobe, covering what looked to be Snoopy pajamas, and sat sipping tea in the large living room of his multi-level 1980s house. He had a wide, likable face and a huge smile. He wore large black-framed glasses with thick lenses that made his eyes seem open and very alert.

He lounged in a plush leather chair, his slippered feet comfortably crossed on an ottoman. Behind him, light oak bookcases reached from floor to ceiling. On a table next to the couch under a reading light, I noticed a book on the science of evolution written by a good friend of mine.

The house was situated on a cliff, and the wall of windows opposite the bookcases opened out onto San Diego Bay. We might have been on the Amalfi coast, gazing at the Gulf of Salerno.

"Well, maybe I wasn't the first," he corrected himself, pronouncing his *a*'s with a broad Midwestern accent. "But I certainly was before Elvis—a good seven years." I immediately thought of another Italian singer, Louis Prima, who was often taken for black.

"I remember going to a record store in the early fifties on the South Side of Chicago. I was just talking to the clerk, checking how my records were moving," he told me, and went on with the story.

A black man walked in and asked for Frankie Laine's newest record. The clerk said, "Today's your lucky day. Not only do I have Frankie Laine's newest record; I have Frankie Laine standing right here in front of you."

The black man looked at Frankie Laine and said, "That ain't him—Frankie Laine is colored!"

The clerk held up the record cover next to Laine and finally convinced the man that it was Frankie Laine standing before him, and that Frankie Laine was indeed white.

The black man frowned. "I ain't buying a record from a white man who sounds black." Like Prima, Laine was heavily influenced by black singers and musicians. And like Prima, Laine, because of his style of singing, would struggle to find his audience.

Francesco Paolo LoVecchio was born in Chicago in 1913. He would be the eldest of eight brothers and sisters.

His parents had emigrated from Sicily in 1906—from a small town called Monreale, a hillside town south of Sicily's capital city, Palermo. Anyone who hails from Monreale will proudly mention the beautiful twelfth-century Norman cathedral, perched on Monte Caputo, overlooking a valley of olive, orange, and almond trees. The marble entrance, formed by three arches and Doric columns, is flanked by two towers—one unfinished—that can be seen for miles.

In Chicago, the LoVecchios lived at 331 Schiller, a street of tightly packed, mostly two-story wood-frame houses in a predominantly Italian neighborhood on the North Side close to Lincoln Park, though with some Germans, French, and Swedes as neighbors. The neighborhood was called Little Sicily, and in 1942 most of it—beginning a block west of the LoVecchio house—would be razed to make room for what would be called the Frances Cabrini Homes, built for the poor Italian community and named after Mother Cabrini. Although born in Sant'Angelo Lodigiano, Italy, Cabrini became a U.S. citizen and was the first American to be canonized by the Catholic Church. The public housing complex would expand with taller buildings in the late 1950s and early 1960s and be called Cabrini-Green.

But back when the neighborhood was Little Sicily, folks had nicknamed the tall, thin Francesco LoVecchio "Spaghett'."

His father was a barber, well respected in the neighborhood, and Laine later remembered that a couple of large men would often show up at his house or the shop to pick up his father, who would leave with a black leather bag packed with the tools of his trade. His father was Al Capone's personal barber, and Capone, who lived in Park Manor on Chicago's South Side, would send for him whenever he needed a shave or haircut.

But this connection didn't seem to offer the LoVecchios much protection. As a child, Frankie would often visit his grandparents, who lived in the neighborhood above a grocery store. One afternoon, he and his grandmother heard several gunshots coming from the grocery store, and they rushed downstairs to find his grandfather shot dead.

Music was a refuge for Frankie. As a fourth-grader at the Immaculate Conception School, he became a member of the church choir. But it was his father, a music lover himself, who helped shape Frankie's taste in music.

"My father used to take us to Ravinia Park to hear concerts," Frankie Laine told me. "And one time, I actually got to see Enrico Caruso.

"I remember when my father bought our first Victrola. He also brought home two records—one was Caruso, the other Bessie

Smith." The Smith record was "Bleeding Hearted Blues," with "Midnight Blues" on the flip side, which she recorded in 1923. Smith, a black Tennessee-born singer, had a chesty, languid voice and inspired Billie Holiday, Sarah Vaughan, and, later, Janis Joplin. Years later both Caruso and Smith, opera and the blues, Italian and black, would show in Frankie's style.

"One day I ducked out of school to see a movie. It was an Al Jolson movie called *The Singing Fool*." Frankie Laine gave me a big smile. "It was then that I knew what I wanted to do."

Seeing Al Jolson drop to his knees as he sang "Sonny Boy" made Frankie's heart stop. Jolson sang that song in blackface, perhaps further fueling Laine's desire to "sing black."

Laine danced before he sang professionally. He left Chicago in 1930 at the age of seventeen, following his dancing feet to endless, tiring dance marathons. The marathon dance circuit was a popular diversion during the Depression; every town, it seemed, sponsored dance marathons.

Laine traveled to the East Coast, to New York, Pennsylvania, Connecticut. He found an experienced dance partner named Ruthie Smith, and together they hit all the big spots. In Atlantic City, they totaled 3,501 hours in forty-five consecutive days, winning the grand prize, a thousand dollars.

During one marathon, a promoter who had heard Frankie sing to himself backstage encouraged him to fill in for a big-band singer. That evening turned into a ten-year journey in search of his big break as a singer.

Again and again, he got opportunities that came to nothing. Upon hearing Perry Como sing one night in 1937 at Chicago's Merry Garden Ballroom, a hot dance spot in a largely Swedish neighborhood bordering LoVecchio's Little Sicily, Frankie introduced himself. They became friends, and Como, who had changed bands, recommended that Laine audition for a spot with his former bandleader, Freddie Carlone. But during the audition, both Laine and Carlone realized that Laine's rhythmic style of singing didn't match the squarer, more ballad-like sound Carlone was trying to get. In the late 1930s, Frankie was a step ahead of his time, and paid the price for it.

In 1938, with forty dollars in his pocket, LoVecchio left Chicago for New York to audition for radio shows. The money soon ran out, and with no way to pay for a room, he found himself sleeping on benches in Central Park and sneaking into hotel lobbies.

Then a friend in the business told him about an audition that WINS radio was holding. He met the program director, Jack Coombs, and sang three songs, including "Shine," about a shoeshine boy. He won the spot, and Coombs suggested that LoVecchio change his name to the punchier, less-ethnic Frankie Laine.

It was the big break that wasn't. Not until 1946, nearly a decade later, did Laine, by now thirty-three, have a hit record with a standard called "That's My Desire."

"I was kind of a late bloomer," Frankie Laine told me sheepishly. I asked him if he would call himself a crooner.

"No, I'm more of a belter," he responded.

And yet, ironically, "That's My Desire" was a ballad. The song was produced by Mitch Miller, released on Mercury Records—the same label that released Damone's "I Have But One Heart" three months later—and reached number four on the *Billboard* charts. The song begins with a walking bass punctuated by muted trumpets; Laine delivers the lyric easily, in a tightly coiled vibrato.

Laine possesses tremendous energy when he sings, even in slow songs. You get the sense that he's holding back—that he's only hinting at how powerful his voice is. But at the same time, he bends notes, often swooping up a third from under the note, in the same sultry manner as Billie Holiday.

In "On the Sunny Side of the Street," released soon after, Laine sings in a manner as happy as its title suggests. He cannot help but make the song his own, even changing the famous ascending opening line—"Grab your coat and get your hat / Leave your worries on the doorstep"— into a descending one, playfully meandering back and forth across the traditional melody and intersecting with it at key parts. When Laine sings that he's a rover who has crossed over, he makes you feel as if you should be roving too.

He has a dancer's stamina, with an operatic, chesty delivery. "Frankie Laine sings with the virility of a hairy goat and the delicacy of a white flower," said one disc jockey at the time. "And, brother, when you can do that, you're in!"

Laine's first number one hit came in 1949—with another ballad, "That Lucky Old Sun," again produced by Mitch Miller for Mercury.

The record begins with a strum of the guitar, à la Django Reinhardt. Then Frankie Laine's voice hits—and damned if it doesn't sound like Elvis, the crazy top notes quickly descending to deep guttural lows. He punches each syllable as he sings: "Dear Lord above, can't you know I'm pining." He doesn't ease into notes. He swats them.

There's a deep timbre to his voice—and an almost melancholy delivery of the lyric. He's got not a care in the world but to "roll around heaven all day." To me, "That Lucky Old Sun" is the link between Sinatra and Elvis, between the pop standard and rock and roll. Laine sings on the backbeat, as does Sinatra, but his voice rises and falls like that of a blues singer—or like that of the white Tennessee country boy who blended black and country at Sun Studio.

Within a couple of months, Mitch Miller encouraged Frankie Laine to go from black to cracker—from the soulful, spiritual-sounding "That Lucky Old Sun" to the whip-cracking, cowboy-barking ("Hah! Hah!") "Mule Train." Like Prima before him—and several Italian American singers by the end of the 1950s—Laine moved between black and white music, as well as black and white audiences.

Seven years later, Laine, performing in Las Vegas, attended Elvis Presley's first show at the New Frontier Hotel and Casino—just a few months after the release of "Heartbreak Hotel."

A hit on *Ed Sullivan*, Elvis was a flop in Vegas. The critics didn't think much of him, nor did those in the audience, who were a decade or more older than the teenagers buying his records. And because of that, he wasn't a draw to the gambling tables—which didn't set him in good stead with the casino owners either.

After the show, Elvis's manager, Colonel Tom Parker, invited Frankie Laine for dinner and drinks. Laine accepted.

"I'd be happy to do half as well as you, Mr. Laine," Elvis said.

16

"Be My Love"

MARIO LANZA

Back in the Old Country, each city, town, and village had its own saint the people prayed to, a saint who had suffered, had shone with holiness, or had performed a miracle. That saint became a symbol of the community. Naples has San Gennaro, who is to protect the city from volcanic eruptions; Palermo has Santa Rosalia, who looks after hermits and virgins; Bari has San Nicola, who protects sailors, prostitutes, and repentant thieves; my grandparents' tiny village of Gimigliano in Calabria has San Giuseppe, who keeps a watchful eye over workers.

Alfredo Arnold Cocozza was born on January 31, 1921—Enrico Caruso died in August of that year. Alfredo's family members and neighbors came to feel that in a kind of divine intervention, the voice of Caruso had passed to the seven-month-old boy. The Italians of South Philadelphia would soon have Mario Lanza, who would become their patron saint of song.

Like many South Philadelphia Italians, Mario's family had come from Abruzzi e Molise. His mother's father, Salvatore Lanza, emigrated from Tocco da Casauria, Abruzzi, in 1902, and his grandmother and his mother, Maria, then eleven months old, joined him shortly thereafter. In South Philly, Salvatore opened a small grocery and put his family on the two floors above it. Mario's father, Antonio Cocozza, emigrated from Filignano, Molise, in 1905 at the age of nine.

Italians in the city mostly settled in South Philadelphia, a kind of peninsula formed by the Delaware River to its east, which flows into the Schuylkill to its west. South Street separates South Philly from Center City. The Italians formed enclaves among Irish, Polish, and Jewish communities. They settled in streets of mostly two-story houses—a mix of brick row houses and detached wood frames. There seemed to be a greengrocer on every block. Italians would shop in an open-air market on Ninth Street, where by late afternoon the day's rubbish would be burning in garbage cans lining the street. It was in South Philly that two brothers, Pat and Harry Olivieri, invented the cheese steak sandwich. Two rival cheese steak shops still exist—Pat's and Geno's.

Decades later, South Philly served as the setting for *Rocky*, a movie written by and starring Sylvester Stallone about a second-generation Italian American boxer realizing, against all odds, his American dream. You remember him slouching out of a simple, run-down row house; waiting outside the pet store for his girlfriend, Adrian; pumping his fists through the Italian market, garbage cans ablaze, until he reaches the steps of the Philadelphia Museum of Art.

Here in South Philly, Bing Crosby's guitarist Eddie Lang (Salvatore Massaro) was born in 1902; the jazz violinist Joe Venuti grew up around the same time; and the popular singer Eddie Fisher was born to Russian Jewish parents in 1928.

Antonio had been wounded while fighting for the United States during World War I, and so was unable to work, forcing his wife, Maria, to earn money as a seamstress. At home, Antonio filled the household with the music of Enrico Caruso, inspiring Mario—then known as Freddie—to memorize the plots of all the operas and sing along to the family's many records. Freddie's mother, believing her son had true vocal talent, insisted on paying for music lessons.

By the time Freddie was seventeen, he had performed in various local operas. In 1942, when Freddie was twenty-one, his voice instructor, Irene Williams, arranged for him to meet William K. Huff, a prominent arts patron in Philadelphia. Upon hearing Freddie sing, Huff contacted the famed Boston Symphony Orchestra conductor Serge Koussevitzky, who happened to be rehearsing for a concert at the Philadelphia Academy of Music.

Freddie met Koussevitzky, who was in his dressing room stripped to his waist. The conductor pointed Freddie to the rehearsal room across the hall, where he rehearsed "Vesti la giubba" from *Pagliacci*. Koussevitzky heard him, came out, told him he had a great voice, and invited him to the Tanglewood Music Center in the Berkshires. Not long thereafter, Freddie Cocozza changed his name to the shorter, catchier Mario Lanza, which combined a masculine form of his mother's first name, Maria, with her maiden name, Lanza. He left for Massachussetts four months later.

In November 1942, Lanza was called up to the Army. He began service in early 1943 and was eventually assigned to a special services department within the Air Corps, enabling him to perform in various GI musicals in New York City. One musical was *Winged Victory*, written by Moss Hart, which made it to Broadway, then toured to Los Angeles.

On August 28, 1947, Lanza filled in for the well-known Italian opera singer Ferruccio Tagliavini, who had canceled an appearance at the Hollywood Bowl at the last minute. Word had gotten around about his big voice, and the Hollywood Bowl appearance would set the course for the rest of his life. With Frances Yeend, the famous soprano with the New York City Opera, he sang the love song from the first act of *La Bohème*, "O soave fanciulla"; as an encore, he performed the first song Caruso recorded, "E lucevan le stelle."

On the warm, dry summer night, Lanza's voice resonated within the desert hills of Los Angeles—very similar to the arid mountains of southern Italy, and to those of Caruso's Naples and Lanza's familial Abruzzi—and reached Louis B. Mayer, the impresario who had founded Metro-Goldwyn-Mayer and who was sitting in the audience. Shortly afterward, he signed Mario Lanza to MGM.

So it was that I, like most everybody else, became aware of Mario Lanza through a movie. It was not one of his own pictures, though; it was a film from 1994 called *Heavenly Creatures* that I saw in an art theater in Tampa, Florida, with my then girlfriend, Martha, and my parents, based on a true story of two teenage girls living in Christchurch, New Zealand, in 1954.

The girls, Pauline Parker and Juliet Hulme (played by a young Kate Winslet), formed a tight bond through their love of storytelling and of their favorite singer, Mario Lanza. They invented fantastic medieval stories, placing their pop idols in roles of knighted saviors, as they swooned and sang along with each other to Lanza's "Be My Love."

They became so close that their parents feared they were lesbians and decided to separate the two by having one of the girls move with her family. The two decide to run away together to America—the homeland of Mario Lanza. But before doing so, they decide the ultimate escape is to kill Pauline's mother, the person most disturbed by their relationship.

This they did, and when the movie was released, it became known that Juliet Hulme was alive and well and, under the name Anne Perry, had become a popular writer of murder mysteries.

My mother told me years later that she herself adored Lanza as a girl in Montreal. In the film, they showed a video of Lanza singing "Be My Love," and as I watched, I could understand why. Everything about him was big—his voice, his smile, his charm. Perhaps my mother found some of Lanza's characteristics in my father, who approaches the most simple tasks with grand flourishes.

It was through *The Toast of New Orleans*, released in 1950, that people—as far away as New Zealand, apparently—first encountered Mario Lanza. In most of his nine films, Lanza plays either an unknown opera singer discovered in the unlikeliest of places or a famous opera singer who falls upon hardship. In *The Toast of New Orleans*, he plays a Cajun fisherman living in the bayous, where he and his fellow villagers speak in accented English that could be derived from any European (southern or eastern) dialect. There he is discovered by a New Orleans opera impresario during a duet of "Be My Love" with Kathryn Grayson (who five years earlier had appeared in a movie with Frank Sinatra and Gene Kelly called *Anchors Aweigh*). Grayson is singing for the audience of villagers, when, to her surprise and annoyance, Lanza joins her onstage. His eyes sparkle, and his smile is infectious, and you know by movie's end he will have won her over.

The movie opened in New York City at the Loew's State Theatre on September 19, 1950. Three months later, a recording of Lanza singing "Be My Love" was released by RCA as a single. It went to number one on March 3, 1951, and stayed on the charts for thirty-four weeks. It was the biggest-selling record in RCA history and was the first operatic record to sell over a million copies since Enrico Caruso.

Lanza was an opera singer who used the instrument of the crooner—the microphone. And the stage for this opera singer was not the Metropolitan Opera House but MGM studios.

If Frankie Laine was a bronco ready to bust through the gates in 1949, in 1950 Mario Lanza was the bull—in both voice and stature—triumphantly poised at the center of the ring.

"Be my love," Lanza cried out. "For no one else can end this yearning." The song was a ballad, but Lanza sang it as an opera aria. His delivery was tender—as if he were singing for you and you alone—yet powerful, as if he were announcing to the world his love for you.

Four months later, another movie would put his voice in the ears of mainstream America. *The Great Caruso* opened on May 10, 1951, in Radio City Music Hall, with Lanza playing his idol in this fictionalized film in which Caruso makes his way from Naples, as a horse-and-wagon deliveryman, to the stage of the Metropolitan Opera House. While the girls loved Lanza, the movie also inspired budding opera singers such as Placido Domingo and José Carreras, who were children at the time. Domingo once said, "If I am an opera singer, it's because of Mario Lanza."

At five feet seven, Lanza was not a tall man and he tended to put on weight, often weighing over two hundred pounds, but the studio insisted that he stay slim for screen appeal, which he found difficult owing to his tremendous appetite for food and drink. (His appetite for food, apparently, was rivaled only by that for sex with various women, although he was married and had four children).

After *The Great Caruso*, Lanza's reputation with MGM began to slide. His increasing weight, fueled by alcohol, and his growing belligerent attitude toward the studio's demands caused MGM to let him go. On the recording side, though, Lanza was still RCA's best-selling artist in 1954 and 1955. In late 1955, though, RCA bought Elvis Presley's contract from Sun Records, and in 1956 Presley had an extraordinary ten Top 20 hits, putting Lanza in the shadow. It's as if Caruso had passed the torch to Lanza, who in turn passed it to Elvis.

The next year, Mario Lanza visited Italy. Like so many children and grandchildren of Italian immigrants, he was drawn to discover his ancestral homeland, ultimately deciding to move his family to Rome. There he would make two movies at Cinecittà, Italy's Hollywood, a studio complex outside of Rome.

The first of them, in 1958, was titled *Arrivederci Roma*, released in English as *Seven Hills of Rome*. In the film, Lanza plays an Italian American singer named Marc Revere (even in film, the Italian American has Anglicized his name) who travels to Rome searching for his fiancée, who has left him. Although he's a star back in the States, no one in Italy knows who he is. He moves into an apartment with his cousin Pepe Bonelli, an artist and musician who lives on a piazza in what appears to be the Trastevere section of Rome.

In one of the movie's more memorable scenes—set at the fountain at the Piazza Navona—Lanza sings the title song of the film,

"Arrivederci, Roma," with a young girl, someone who, in reality, Lanza had discovered while walking through Rome. The song was written by the Italians Renato Rascel, Pietro Garinei, and Sandro Giovannini in 1955, but had its first popular release in the film. Versions of it were later recorded by Dean Martin, Perry Como, Connie Francis, Vic Damone, and Nat "King" Cole, to name just a few.

But to me, the most memorable scene is one that is a paean to Italian American popular song. Lanza as Marc Revere has been performing at a theater and is in his cousin's apartment rehearsing an aria entitled "M'appari tutt'amor." It is from the opera *Martha* by Friedrich von Flotow, and although the opera's libretto is in German, this particular aria is sung in Italian.

Revere's rehearsal is interrupted by music coming from the piazza outside. He stops singing and walks to the doors on his terrace. The piazza is filled with Italian teenagers dancing to a rock-and-roll combo of guitar, saxophone, trombone, and stand-up bass playing rockabilly style. When the song ends, Revere stands at his balcony, smiling and clapping.

One young man sees him and says, "Tu sei americano?"

"Yes," Revere says. "And that's a real good beat you got there."

The young man says in broken English, "Do you know the barberi singer?"

"Do you mean *The Barber of Seville*?" Revere asks.

"No, the barber singer—Perry Como!"

"Sure, I know—the Italian boy," Revere says.

At the word "Italian" the crowd cheers, and Revere does an imitation of Perry Como singing one of his hit songs, "Temptation," nailing Como's easy mannerisms, complete with a mock golf swing (golf being a favorite pastime of Como's) and a scratch with his finger under the eye.

After applause, Revere asks the crowd: "Do you know Frankie Laine?" The crowd responds in the affirmative.

"He's an Italian boy, too. His name is LoVecchio."

"Ah, sì, LoVecchio!" one of the kids says.

Revere sings "Jezebel" and makes the grand gestures with his arms that Laine was known for, complete with a showstopping end.

A girl walks from the back and says in Italian-accented English, "Hey, man, you're real good."

"So, do you know Dino?" Revere asks.

"Sure, he's a god."

"He should be; he's Italian, too!" And with that, Revere sings "Memories Are Made of This," feigning drunkenness, as Martin often did during his show. The kids accompany Revere as they sing the background vocals.

Finally another girl shouts out: "What about Louis Armstrong?"

"Sure," Revere says. "He's one of my favorites."

"But he's not Italian," she says.

"Honey," Revere says in Satchmo's gravelly voice, "he doesn't have to be!" And he sings "When the Saints Go Marching In."

Lanza died of a heart attack nearly two years later. His drinking had affected his liver, and the fluctuations in his weight had taxed his body, giving him arteriosclerosis, high blood pressure, phlebitis, and gout. He had admitted himself to a sanatorium in Rome in order to lose weight and get some rest. Within days of checking himself in, he was dead at age thirty-eight.

There were thoughts of having Mario Lanza buried in the Enrico Caruso family plot in Naples, but Lanza's widow, Betty, had his body sent to the States. He was buried in Los Angeles, but first the body was sent to Philadelphia, where fifteen thousand people filed past the closed casket at the Leonetti Funeral Home, paying their respects. The next morning, there was a Mass at the St. Mary Magdalen de Pazzi Church, which Lanza attended as a boy.

Next to St. Mary Magdalen de Pazzi Church in South Philly stands a museum. It's so close to the church, in fact, that it could be an adjoining prayer chapel.

There is no admission charge, only a suggested donation. A

woman in her seventies greets you at the counter. She has close-cropped gray hair and wears a starched white blouse and a black skirt that falls just below the knee. Arranged on the glass counter are bumper stickers, ready-to-be-framed photographs, and heart-shaped "Be My Love" key chains. The woman lets you inside the next room, which is bigger than it appears from the outside.

In the middle of the room, glass cases display Mario Lanza's movie costumes from *The Great Caruso* and *The Toast of New Orleans* alongside his everyday clothes. Film posters from around the world line the walls. Turning to your left, you see a time line of his life story in photographs—from youth to Army service and from film to film—and you follow them as if following the stations of the cross on a church wall.

The last time I was there, another elderly lady was giving a tour to two women my mother's age—the age the girls in *Heavenly Creatures* would have been now. The visitors spoke in accented English—British, or possibly Australian. I assumed that they wouldn't have come all the way to the United States just to visit the Mario Lanza Museum. Still, they knew about it, and had made a point of stopping here. They were making a pilgrimage.

The museum is run by the Mario Lanza Institute, which was founded in 1962, three years after Mario's death. Its mandate is not only to keep the memory of Mario Lanza alive but also to offer scholarships—four a year—to promising vocal students from around the world.

On my way out, the same woman who greeted me accompanied me outside and down the street. On her thick-soled black shoes she proceeded, slightly hunched, down the block of brick and limestone buildings.

"This is where the grocery store used to be," she said, pointing to a three-story brick building. The ground floor—once the store Lanza's grandfather owned when he first came to America—was now an apartment.

"Up there," she said, pointing to a window, "is where everyone could hear Mario singing out to the neighborhood."

17

"Here In My Heart"

AL MARTINO

Alfred Cini had been wounded at Iwo Jima. Now, at age twenty-four, he was working as a bricklayer like his father—like the thousands of other Italian American bricklayers who had built up the cities of America, and the stonemasons who had constructed the stone Catholic churches of Philadelphia, Newark, New York, and New Haven.

Bricklaying drew Italian immigrants, who took pride in creating something tangible—something they could see and show to their children and grandchildren. It was hard labor, but it nevertheless required a certain amount of craft. It shows up in some of the best Italian American literature, including books by John Fante and Pietro Di Donato, each an American born to immigrants from the Abruzzi.

In *Christ in Concrete* (1939), Di Donato, who grew up in West Hoboken (now Union City), New Jersey, tells the wrenching story of a ten-year-old boy, Paul, whose father, Geremio, falls to his death on Good Friday while laying brick and pouring concrete for an office building on New York City's Lower East Side. In Fante's novels *Wait Until Spring, Bandini* (1938), and *Ask the Dust* (1939), set in Boulder, Colorado, the teenage Arturo Bandini leaves his family and hard-drinking, bricklaying father for Los Angeles to become a writer. Paul sees bricklaying and manual labor as a literal death sentence; Arturo views it as a psychological one. In *Christ in Concrete*, Geremio's son Paul contemplates his fate: "The men are driven. They prefer death or injury to loss of work. Work and die. Today I did not die. I have been let to live today and must be thankful that tomorrow I may return to work—to die."

His back stiff and aching from hours spent bent over bricks and cement, trowel in hand, Alfred Cini, too, dreamed of another line of work, even as he sang in neighborhood bars and saloons at night.

In 1948 Mario Lanza, Cini's childhood friend, encouraged him to move to New York City. There he changed his name and took an apartment with Guy Mitchell from Detroit, and his fellow Philadelphian Eddie Fisher—two young singers whose careers were on the rise after their appearances on *Arthur Godfrey's Talent Scouts*. Martino, too, auditioned for the show; like Vic Damone before him, he borrowed from Perry Como (a recent hit called "If") and came in first place. While Frank Sinatra might have been nearly every Italian American singer's idol, Como's grace and ease evidently inspired them to think that they, too, could croon. You could imitate Como's fluid phrasing in ways that you couldn't Sinatra's. Sinatra was the greater singer, but Como had as big an influence. Just then, Como was more popular, too. For the next four years, Martino performed in various nightclubs in the city.

In 1952, Rosemary Clooney was telling every young man to kiss her with "Botch-A-Me," an American transliteration of *baciami*, Italian for "kiss me." That same year, Al Martino recorded "Here in My Heart," which became his first hit. The song was written by Pat Genaro—the same songwriter who showed up on Vic Damone's doorstep with "You're Breaking My Heart." Mario Lanza considered recording it, but Martino, sure that the song would be a hit, asked his friend to let him have it instead. Lanza, happy to help him out, obliged.

The song begins with the strings swirling upward around a brass crescendo. Martino cries out impetuously, "Here in my heart, I'm alone and so lonely." In a lush, heavenly effect, a harp plucks gently under his singing.

Lanza's influence on Martino is obvious. Martino approaches the song like an opera singer, delivering it like an aria, adding a plaintive turn on the word "alone." At the end of the first two phrases he begins to croon. It is a romantically hopeful yearning. He knows— and you knew, and any girl who listened knew—that he is going to get it his way.

"Here in My Heart" hit number one—in both the United States and the U.K.—and stayed on the charts for nineteen weeks. Just a couple of weeks after its release, Mercury came out with Vic Damone's version of the song, and it charted at number eight; a version by a relative newcomer named Tony Bennett, an Italian kid from Queens with two hits of his own, reached number fifteen.

Two more Al Martino recordings—ballads also sung in a quasi-operatic style—made it onto the charts the following year: "Rachel" and "Take My Heart," the latter written by Pat Genaro.

Then, on November 8, 1953, Al Martino disappeared.

"Martino Missing on Boston Tour," read the headline of one tabloid article after a nightclub performance.

United Press International quoted the owner of the nightclub, saying that Martino "seemed to go pale" onstage—"he was definitely nervous and upset."

A letter was found that read, "I am tired, finished, through, disgusted."

The article described Martino as a "onetime Philadelphia bricklayer"—a light-complected Italian who stood five feet nine, weighed 131 pounds, with brown hair and brown eyes. It mentions a three-inch tattoo of a Hawaiian girl that Martino most likely had had inked on his upper right arm sometime during the war.

In the newspaper photographs, Martino has a sharp nose and chin, with well-defined eyes and, at twenty-six, a prematurely receding hairline. He has a warm smile, but his angular features and stern gaze hint at a toughness inside. He had been wounded in the war, had worked hard labor, probably had hung with a tough crowd back home.

And indeed, offstage—behind the scenes—things could get dangerous for a singer. Of course, if you played along with the Mob, all would be fine. They were your best friends. After all, they had let you sing in this club; all you had to do was give them a month's commitment, say, and a night or two without pay. The mobsters wanted something in return for investing in you. No problem, you were still making good money. But if you decided to go your own way without their consent, then your life was at stake.

You could be Italian, Jewish, or Irish—and so could the mobsters. In 1927, the comedian Joe E. Lewis was approached by "Machine Gun" Jack McGurn and asked to renew a contract at the Green Mill Cocktail Lounge in Chicago, whose backers included Al Capone. Lewis had already accepted an offer at the Rendezvous from a rival gang. Early in the run of his new show, thugs broke into his hotel room, beat him up, slashed his throat, and left him for dead. He survived, but his ability to speak didn't fully return for a few years.

Apparently, Al Martino's manager had been muscled by the Mob and had committed Martino to paying $75,000 to his new "managers." The official reason given by his management for his disappearance was exhaustion. A newspaper reported that he had announced to the sold-out room, "Nine out of every ten nightclub openings are a flop. I am a flop too."

This all came to light just days after he left for England, where "Here in My Heart" was also big, along with a couple of his other songs. For the rest of the decade he lived in London (having sent for his wife and young son), performing at the Palladium, London's equivalent of the New York Paramount, as well as in various nightclubs and cabarets.

Martino's new "manager" was Albert Anastasia, who became one of the most powerful organized crime bosses in New York. Anastasia (given name: Umberto Anastasio) was a native of Tropea, a cliff-side town in Calabria overlooking the Tyrrhenian Sea, with a clear view of the island of Stromboli. He moved to New York in 1919 at age seventeen. His gang of contract killers became known in the press as Murder Inc. and was the precursor to the Gambino crime family.

Apparently, Martino refused to acknowledge his new management and didn't pay the $75,000 (some accounts say it was more like $100,000). Rumors say that Martino was beaten up so badly the night he disappeared that it took him years to recover from the broken bones. Perhaps he, too, had made a deal with the Mob and couldn't pay back his debts.

In 1957, while getting a shave at a barbershop in Manhattan's Park Sheraton Hotel, Anastasia was shot dead by members of the rival Genovese family. Shortly afterward, with the help of a family friend, Martino cleared his debts with the Mob and returned to the United States.

This time he steered clear of New York, settling in Los Angeles. He sought work as a bricklayer but found none. Then he started singing in nightclubs again. It wasn't until 1963 that he had another hit—really a string of hits, beginning with "I Love You Because" and "I Love You More and More Every Day," followed by the song he would become best known for, "Spanish Eyes," released in 1965.

And he achieved a brief rebirth when, in 1972, he was tapped by Francis Ford Coppola to play Johnny Fontane in *The Godfather*, the crooner who sings at the wedding of Vito Corleone's daughter. In a later scene, Fontane meets the Godfather in his dark study, which overlooks the festivities below. He asks the don to help him land a role in a movie, then breaks down in tears. Corleone slaps him, telling him to act like a man.

Many believed this scene was a reference to the lore of Frank Sinatra's career, as interpreted by Mario Puzo, the novel's author. The scene also brings to mind that Tony Bennett had once performed at the wedding of the crime boss Joseph Bonanno's son. In fact, this scene links many Italian singers: Vic Damone was also asked to play the role of Fontane, as was another popular singer named Don Cornell.

Now Al Martino, once beholden to the Mob, was playing a singer who would soon be indebted in the same way. Martino knew the downside of such a deal. He sang the theme from *The Godfather*, a love song that could also represent the laws of *omertà*, the Mafia's code of secrecy—"Speak Softly Love."

Looking back years later, Martino said matter-of-factly about the mobsters, "We befriended them, we worked for them, they owned the nightclubs."

As I became more familiar with their music, I wanted to see these crooners before they stopped singing, and I saw Al Martino first.

While visiting my wife's family for Easter in rural central New York State, west of Utica, I opened the local paper to read that Al Martino was performing at the Turning Stone Casino, a nightclub on the Oneida Indian reservation. And so on Holy Saturday, Martha and I drove out to the casino—a construction of concrete and bright lights that rose from cornfields. Men and women wearing jeans and flannel shirts—old farmers—lined up in front of the one-armed bandits and crowded the poker tables of the main hall. A red carpet led to the concert hall, where a hostess directed us to our reserved table. I had half thought that Martha and I would be the only ones there, so I was surprised to see that almost every table was taken— many by people in their early thirties, as we were. The waitress, a bleached-blond woman in her fifties, took our order.

"I'd like a Manhattan," I said.

"Sorry, honey, but we're a dry casino," she said in the voice of a lifelong smoker.

"A dry casino? How could there be a show in a dry casino?" I said. I had images of tall glasses of martinis sloshing over their edges and bowls topped with bar nuts. At least I had a waitress who called me "honey."

The curtains rose to reveal a twenty-two-piece orchestra, and as the music began, Al Martino came onstage—trim in tux and carnation boutonniere—singing his 1965 hit "Spanish Eyes." We were immediately transported back in time. Gone was the denim, gone were the fields, gone was rural New York State. All that was missing was a cocktail.

People at the show were dressed up a little more than the rest of the casino-goers; the men wore sport coats, the women wore dresses. One guy there, probably in his forties, told me that he had come because it had reminded him of his father, who himself had seen Martino in concert decades earlier. The man was Italian, and from the area. Only later did it occur to me how many Italians had wound up in cities in upstate New York—many having settled there from my own ancestral Calabria.

I went to hear Martino a few years later in the maze of casinos that is Connecticut's Mohegan Sun. That night he sang to a sold-out cabaret room of about two hundred people. It was a mixed audience—young and old, black, white, Hispanic—though predominantly Italian American, it seemed to me. Martino acknowledged a woman wearing a red-velvet pantsuit as a member of his fan club; a buxom woman in her sixties, sporting sparkling gold earrings and a black dress with a plunging neckline, brought up roses after his song "Tears and Roses."

A woman sitting at my table leaned over and said, "They are like Deadheads for this guy!" She seemed to be in her late forties, wearing a maroon cocktail dress, with her hair pulled back in a tight ponytail. She told me that she was a cabaret singer, part Jewish, part Neapolitan. She was happy to have gotten the chance to see Al Martino, to whom both her parents had listened. She had dragged along her boyfriend, a slightly older African American saxophonist. During a break in a song, he turned to me and asked, "Does your wife give you shit about listening to this music?"

Once again, I was surprised to see a couple of guys my age there with their wives. One said, "I remember my old man listening to this." He, too, was connecting with his Italian American past.

From the stage, Al Martino thanked his onetime music director

Ray Sinatra—Frank's cousin—and recalled Mario Lanza as his greatest early influence.

"All my life I had a desire to travel," he said in a raspy, tired voice, introducing his next number. "And this song let me go all the places I wanted to."

The violins came in, then the horns. Martino held the microphone, his pinkie ring—part of the Italian crooning uniform—glinting in the spotlight. In a voice full and ageless, he sang that first operatic ballad from 1952, "Here in My Heart."

18

"Because of You"

TONY BENNETT

In October 1952, Tony Bennett was just coming off a successful year of hits, including two with Columbia Records: "Because of You" and "Cold, Cold Heart," a remake of a song the great country music singer Hank Williams had written and recorded.

Bennett had already played the Paramount, filled with screaming bobby-soxers. He had played at the El Rancho hotel in Vegas. But now he was to appear at the Copacabana, where Dean Martin and Jerry Lewis had first made it, where his early favorite Jimmy Durante had performed, and where his idol ruled: Frank Sinatra.

On the same bill was the comedian Joe E. Lewis.

The Copacabana opened its doors at 10 East Sixtieth Street in New York City in 1940. It was modeled after a nightclub in Rio de Janeiro, and the Copa was first-class all the way. Palm trees lined the stage, which faced out to a 650-seat room of cozy red-leather banquettes and rows of lamp-lit cocktail tables. Waiters served cocktails and star-quality food from one of two kitchens—you could order a fillet of lemon sole or baby lamb steak béarnaise from the French menu, or, from the Chinese menu, chicken chow mein or pepper steak with bamboo shoots, water chestnuts, and mushrooms.

There were three shows a night, the last one beginning at 2:00 a.m. Twenty-plus long-legged showgirls in feather and plume costumes danced between acts. By all accounts, this really was the hottest club north of Havana.

The Copa was known to be owned by Frank Costello. Costello—Francesco Castiglia, born in Lauropoli, a mountain village outside the city of Cosenza, Calabria—was known as "the prime minister of the underworld." And his saloon, the Copa, was managed by the iron fist of a Jewish immigrant named Jules Podell.

That night, Bennett was on top of his game—or so he thought. At age twenty-six, he was about to walk onto the most glamorous stage in New York. The place was packed; Lewis had the audience roaring with laughter.

Bennett knew what good showmanship meant. When he was a boy, his uncle Dick, a onetime hoofer on the vaudeville circuit, took him to the Waldorf-Astoria to see Maurice Chevalier, the French singer and vaudevillian, easily identifiable by the straw boater hat that he always wore onstage. He sang such songs as "Louise" in his unmistakable thickly French-accented English. A musicians' strike was going on, but instead of canceling, Chevalier sang the entire show a cappella, without his band. In later years, Bennett's act would recall that evening; he would often end his shows by singing "Fly Me to the Moon" a cappella and without a microphone.

After Lewis finished, Bennett took the stage and sang his first number. But he was intimidated. "I couldn't handle the crowd at the Copa," he recalled in his autobiography, *The Good Life*. "They never stopped talking, and I didn't yet know how to hold a difficult audience like that." Eventually, the audience members put their drinks down and listened.

There's a photograph of Tony Bennett that I particularly love, taken shortly after World War II. He's leaning against a railing at the edge of the East River; rising above him is the Triborough Bridge. His sleeves are rolled up to his forearms and his white shirt is unbuttoned to mid-chest, revealing a T-shirt underneath. He's wearing stylish high-waisted pants. A nice thick wave of black hair caps his head; his prominent nose gives him the look of an Italian movie star. Not your typical all-American heartthrob, Tony Bennett looks ethnic, looks Italian.

The photograph was taken at a turning point in his life. He had just returned from the war to his hometown of Astoria, Queens, in an Italian neighborhood that happened to be blocks away from Steinway Village—a part of Astoria originally populated by Germans, who, in the nineteenth century, worked as piano makers at Steinway & Sons.

The Triborough Bridge, which connects Queens to the Bronx and uptown Manhattan, is an apt symbol of change: a link between Old World and New; Italian and black; the comfortable and the exciting; pop standard, swing, and jazz.

The bridge opened in July 1936, when Bennett was almost ten years old. Mayor La Guardia presided over the ribbon-cutting ceremony, and Anthony Benedetto, Bennett's given name, was selected as part of a group to sing "Marching Along Together" at the event. At the end, La Guardia walked to the group for a photograph, placing his hand on young Anthony's shoulder.

Anthony's parents had emigrated from a village called Podargoni, nestled in the foothills of the remote Aspromonte above Reggio Calabria. Like so many other Italian American families, the Benedettos listened to Enrico Caruso, simply, Bennett later recalled, because "that's the only music everyone in the family could agree on."

Anthony's father died of congestive heart failure within months of the Triborough Bridge event; his mother took a job as a seamstress and, with the help of both sets of grandparents, raised Anthony and his brother and sister.

At the age of sixteen, a year after the Japanese bombed Pearl Harbor, Anthony dropped out of the School of Industrial Art to find work to help his mother pay the bills. He started entering amateur shows to make money. He sang at bars and saloons all over Queens, performing at such restaurants as Ricardo's just below the Triborough Bridge, where a booking agent he met suggested he use a stage name, which Anthony did, as Joe Bari.

While it may seem that his name was taken from Bari, the capital of Apulia, in his memoir Bennett explains, "I had been told that Anthony Dominick Benedetto, or even just Anthony Benedetto, was too long and sounded too ethnic. I had come up with the last name 'Bari' because it was short and it was the name of both a province and city in Italy, as well as an anagram of the last part of my grandparents' birthplace, Calabria. And to my ears 'Joe' sounded pretty American."

Two years later, the Army drafted Anthony, who was eager to go, hoping to join his older brother, who had been drafted shortly after Pearl Harbor. Anthony was sent to Le Havre, France, and then to the front lines in Germany, where he rose to the rank of corporal. The Battle of the Bulge had just been fought, and the French and American troops were pushing the Germans back.

It was in France that Anthony learned what the rest of America was really like. It's hard to imagine the insulation that city neighborhoods provided for Italian Americans. I remember my father, who grew up in Danbury, Connecticut, saying that really it wasn't until he enlisted in the Navy that he realized how racist the rest of the world was. It was the first time he got called a wop or a dago with any regularity. Of course, there were also "micks," "niggers," and "spics." But Italian Americans made up the largest percentage of "ethnics" in U.S. forces during World War II—more than 500,000 served. The Army segregated black troops from white ones, but as Bennett recalled, he often befriended black soldiers and once was punished for buddying too much with a black friend from Queens.

About this time, Glenn Miller, as captain, was an active service member, and his Army Air Force Band had entertained troops throughout the war. In December 1944, his Air Force plane, carrying himself and several other passengers, disappeared while crossing the English Channel. A few months later, the war ended, and Benedetto, who had only been in Europe for four months, stayed on to finish his service.

The Army needed a replacement for Miller, so in late 1945 a pop-jazz orchestra was formed. Like America itself, the Army switched from big band to jazz. Benedetto heard that the Army Air Force Band was being replaced with another band; he contacted the officer in charge and was brought on as orchestra librarian—that is, until someone heard him sing. He started performing, and over the American Forces Network the band broadcast a show weekly in Germany called *It's All Yours*. Benedetto remained in Europe for another several months to serve out his tour of duty.

Benedetto returned from the war a man of the city—and a jazz musician. He began hanging out at the clubs on Fifty-second Street and listening to Charlie Parker at Birdland. Big band was over; the sound was now bebop. He traveled uptown to the Apollo on 125th Street and the Savoy on Lenox Avenue to hear Count Basie and Billie Holiday.

He resumed performing at local nightclubs and restaurants, singing first at an Astoria saloon called the Nestle because it was "nestled" in a crook below Hell Gate Bridge, which, when completed in 1916, was the world's longest steel-arch bridge. He also did a stint as a singing waiter at the Red Door in Queens—as Frank Sinatra had done a decade earlier across the Hudson at the Rustic Cabin in New Jersey.

Benedetto had been studying voice, and at some point one of his instructors told him not to emulate other singers but to listen to instrumentalists instead. He began studying Stan Getz and Lester Young. Jazz influenced his croon.

At one point, he found work with a couple of songwriters as a "demonstrator." When songs were recorded on shellac—before tape—songwriters would hire people to perform or "demonstrate" their music scores to potential singers. One time Benedetto "demonstrated" for Frankie Laine, who, after a pause, said: "You should be the one making records and singing here on this stage."

In 1949, performing under the name Joe Bari, Benedetto got a spot on *Arthur Godfrey's Talent Scouts*. He made the final round, but lost to a young Irish American woman from the Ohio River valley named Rosemary Clooney, who sang a song called "Golden Earrings."

During a "Joe Bari" stint at the Village Inn, the comedian Bob Hope, who had spent World War II entertaining military troops on his USO tours, stopped by for a listen. Hope heard the singer's talent, the raw but powerful voice just reaching the upper levels of his register. He took Benedetto aside and guaranteed him a night at the Paramount.

"But you've got to get rid of the name," Hope said. Joe Bari sounded hokey—even for an Italian. Bob Hope asked Joe Bari his full name.

"Anthony Dominick Benedetto."

"Oh, no, too long for the marquee," he said. "We'll call you Tony Bennett."

After Bennett's Paramount appearance, Hope asked him to join him on a six-city tour.

Mitch Miller had heard a demo disc that Bennett had made and signed him to Columbia Records in 1950. Miller had just signed Rosemary Clooney to sing an ersatz-Italian song called "Come On-A My House." She had doubts about the song, but recorded it at Miller's insistence, and it became a huge hit for her.

The music for the first song Bennett recorded, "The Boulevard of Broken Dreams," was written by an Italian American Broadway and film composer from Brooklyn named Harry Warren. Warren, whose family had emigrated from Cosenza, Calabria, in the 1890s, grew up as Salvatore Guaragna.

On the recording, the song starts with a single guitar strummed; Bennett's voice bursts through, "I walk along the street of sorrow"; then the orchestra breaks out into a slow grinding tango as he sings about the romance of Gigolo and Gigolette (two Italianate names). His voice is raspy. His style is already formed—bombastic, holding nothing back. As he walks along the street of sorrow, he delivers the final line, "along the boulevard of broken dreams," as if pushing a last bit of air through his throat.

Upon listening to the record, released on June 12, 1950, Frank Sinatra was heard by the drummer Mickey Scrima to say, "That kid's got four sets of balls." Sinatra knew a great song when he heard it—even if crooning fans and bobby-soxers weren't quick to buy up Bennett's records yet.

They would soon enough. "Because of You," which Bennett recorded with Percy Faith and His Orchestra, known for his large, lush arrangements, hit number one in 1951 and stayed on the charts for thirty-two weeks. It sold a million copies.

Bennett's voice sounds as if cigarettes and whiskey had burned his vocal cords. His voice can be an acquired taste—a passionate cry to some, a strained affect to others. Even then, it took listeners and critics a while to adjust to an instrument that was not as crisp and bell-like as those of other singers of the era. In 1952, a critic in *Time* magazine wrote:

> Tony makes his stage entrance in a breathless vaudeville lope . . . When he belts and writhes a tune, he sounds like Frankie Laine; he uses Frank Sinatra's phrasing and slurring methods; he occasionally adds a few scale slides reminiscent of Billy Eckstine; at times he seems to be contemplating Bing Crosby's nonchalance, as through a dark glass enviously.
>
> Bennett's voice, however, is distinctly his own; it has a diffused, No.-00-sandpaper sound, a quality which he feels has endeared him to his fans.

In 1953, Bennett recorded what would become a signature song for him. "I know I'd go from rags to riches," he sings to his inamorata, if only she would say she cared. He does a turn on the word "rags," which, back in Italy, was typical of many Neapolitan singers. It's a kind of trill that is thought to exhibit a singer's virility. The song has a showstopping end—in which he holds the final note for three and a half measures—like "The Boulevard of Broken Dreams," for which Bennett would become known as he sings, "My fate is up to you."

Bennett's first long-playing album, *Cloud 7*, recorded in 1954, is one of my favorite recordings; it is understated and feels intimate, with him singing "I Fall in Love Too Easily" and "My Baby Just Cares for Me."

Like the Triborough Bridge, Tony Bennett here bridges Old World and New: the safe, close-knit Italian neighborhood of Astoria and the mysterious Harlem; swinging pop standards and the cool jazz sound.

19

"Your Cheatin' Heart"

JONI JAMES

Tony Bennett's recording of "Cold, Cold Heart" went to number one in 1951. Two years later, Joni James, a twenty-two-year-old Italian American woman from the McKinley Park section of Chicago, had a number two hit with "Your Cheatin' Heart," another song by Hank Williams, who had died of an apparent drug and alcohol overdose at age twenty-nine, a month before its release.

"I had never heard him sing it," Joni James told me on the phone. "I just read the lyrics and fell in love with them—pop singers just weren't singing songs like that in the early fifties."

James's recording features her ethereal voice, which seems to float above the string accompaniment. It's a voice well suited to blending in with others, a style she must have developed as a member of the church choir at SS. Peter and Paul in McKinley Park.

"We sang Kyrie Eleison every morning," she told me forty-five years later. She was exuberant and had a bubbly, positive personality. And when she recalled her childhood, she began speaking in Italian, addressing me in a motherly way as *caro*, or dear.

Her mother had come from Abruzzi, and her father from Calabria. As a teenager during World War I, he had served in the Italian army in Libya. He died of stomach cancer when Joni was four and a half years old.

Giovanna Carmella Babbo and her younger sister and two brothers were raised by her mother and grandparents, but lived on welfare. SS. Peter and Paul took them in and gave them a free education, and Joni was taught music by Sister Tarcisius. "When you think about it," James said, "she was my voice instructor."

She studied ballet and modeled, and it was while working as a shoe model that she changed her name to Joni James. Joni was an Americanization of her first name; James she simply picked from the phone book.

Her love was ballet, and just as she was planning to move to New York to study with the American Ballet Theatre School, she was struck by appendicitis. She had her appendix removed, but she wasn't able to regain her full abdominal strength, and her prospects for a ballet career were over.

"Like Sarah Vaughan, like Doris Day," James told me, "I was a dancer who ended up as a singer."

She began singing for local radio stations—and even sang duets regularly with the then-unknown Johnnie Ray, who would soon have a hit with "Cry." She felt her voice was nothing special, because singing was all around her: "Italians—they cook, sing, and make babies."

And yet she recorded a few songs and had a hit in 1952 with "Why Don't You Believe Me?" It's the cry of an Italian girl.

"Why don't you believe me?" she asks what must be her jealous Italian boyfriend, then placates him: "It's you I adore, for ever and ever."

The record went to number one nationally. James was shocked that she could gain popularity through her voice—"without someone ever seeing me in person." For she was used to dancing and modeling, and indeed she was beautiful. An early album cover shows her hair in a brown bob, and she has delicate eyebrows, almond-shaped brown eyes, and full lips.

After this surprise first hit, she met Frankie Laine, who had grown up in another Italian neighborhood close-by. He advised her, above all, to "just be yourself."

She was working with a composer and conductor named Nick Acquaviva, and in 1956, at age twenty-six, she married him. To mark the occasion of when they first met, he wrote "When We Come of Age," a song about two young lovers who promise to wed when they are older. In ways, the song evokes an Italian arranged marriage, old-school-style.

With big bands in decline, James found work as a studio singer. She wasn't the only Italian American woman singing at the time: Antoinette Ardizzone from Greenwich Village—renamed Toni Arden—had a hit in 1949 with "I Can Dream, Can't I?" and followed up a couple years later with "Too Young," "Kiss of Fire," and "I'm Yours." The voice of Chiquita Banana commercials in the 1950s was the Bronx-born June Valli, who, in a 1953 single, admitted to "crying in the chapel."

Between 1952 and 1961, Joni James would have sixteen Top 40 hits; seven were in the Top 10.

20

"That's Amore"

DEAN MARTIN

President Truman had signed a cease-fire agreement with North Korea; the U.S. troops were being sent home; the Soviet Union had announced that it had developed its own hydrogen bomb. For the past twenty years, the Democrats had held the presidency, and America, it seemed, was tired of a president still tied to the New Deal. Dwight D. Eisenhower, former commander of Allied forces in World War II and then president of Columbia University, ran for the U.S. presidency, becoming the country's first Republican chief executive since 1933. Times were good—at least on the surface.

Suddenly many Americans could afford to buy their own houses, a car if not two, and a television set.

The middle class was growing. Men made a decent living; women stayed at home and raised the kids. A man sat down with a cocktail as soon as he walked in the door.

Yet there was unease, as America was afraid of the Soviet Union, afraid of another potential war. In this climate, the Italian American singers helped Americans enjoy the good life—and, in effect, took their minds off their mounting problems.

In the 1953 film *The Caddy*, Dean Martin played Joe Anthony, a layabout who takes golf lessons from Harvey Miller (played by Jerry Lewis), the son of a professional golfer who himself suffers from stage fright. Joe turns out to be an extraordinary golfer. The two team up and find themselves on the professional circuit—with Joe as the pro and Harvey as the caddy.

In one scene at the clubhouse, a Waspy young man asks Joe what line of business his family is in.

Joe responds, "Fish."

"Importing or exporting?" the lock-jawed WASP asks.

"Catching," Joe replies.

At one point in the film, Joe and Harvey visit Joe's family, who live in a fishing village in what appears to be Monterey, California. The two are greeted by hysterical parents, who pull out all the stops with a celebration welcoming their now-successful son.

Mrs. Anthony whisks them to the ground-floor restaurant they own, where the entire family and local friends await them. A bounty of Italian food—pasta, pizza, fish—appears in succession on the table, which is covered with a checkered tablecloth and set with bread sticks. Glasses are filled from jugs of red wine.

Enter a trio of musicians playing violin, accordion, and guitar. The family encourages Joe to stand up and sing. He obliges, and with a smirk and a wink he joins the musicians:

When the moon hits your eye like a big pizza pie
That's amore . . .

In a single scene, the image of Italian Americans is fixed as if forever.

The Caddy seems to draw on aspects of the life of Joe DiMaggio—the Sicilian father who is a fisherman living in San Francisco, and the famous son who never joined the family business because he suffered from seasickness. Art imitates life: even in the film, the successful son of Italian American immigrants goes by an Americanized name, Joe Anthony.

For many Americans, Dean Martin is the quintessential—the stereo-typical—Italian singer: dreamy good looks, cocktail in hand. The girls love him, but he sings for the guys—"They're the ones who pay for the drinks, and they're the ones who will take the girls to the shows. Might be a different broad next time."

By the time *The Caddy* came out, Dean Martin was thirty-six years old—not exactly a youngster, especially in those days.

He had come from Steubenville, a steel town overlooking a bend in the Ohio River. Populated by Italian and Greek factory workers, the town was only thirty miles from Pittsburgh. It was a place known for gambling—and it was the birthplace of Dimetrios Georgios Synodinos, the sports commentator and Vegas bookie known as Jimmy the Greek.

Gaetano and Angela Crocetti had come to Steubenville from Abruzzi. They named their second son Dino Paul.

While Pierino Como enjoyed being a barber, Dino Crocetti turned his back on the barbershop, and work in general, and faced instead the world of dice, whiskey, and cigars.

His looks and confidence got him by. His first language was Italian—the language the family spoke at home. And it wasn't until he got to first grade that he realized no one else was speaking the same language.

My father remembers his own first day as a first-grader at St. Peter's school in Danbury. The nun, an older woman named Sister Walburga, wearing a white band and wimple typical of the Sisters of Mercy order, stood above him, yelling in a language he couldn't understand. My father looked up at her silent, with a terrified stare. When he didn't respond to a question or command—something my father obviously didn't understand—she lifted him by one ear and dragged him to the front corner of the classroom.

My father learned English quickly, as did Dino Crocetti, though he admittedly didn't speak it well. As Crocetti told it later, he was embarrassed by how he spoke, a feeling that followed him into adulthood. But he learned to hide it. He spoke sparingly, in short sentences, though with a sharp wit.

He made up for his Italian-tinged English with his comic antics and his big smile.

At home, the Crocettis listened to all the traditional Italian music on an Italian radio station, but it was Bing Crosby and Russ Columbo who most inspired Dino. His family remembered him slouching around the house, singing the hits he heard on the radio or on the family Victrola.

Hanging out at the cigar stores and illegal gambling halls was much more fun than the tenth grade. Dino saw how money changed hands at those places. He wanted to make a quick buck himself, so he briefly tried his hand at boxing, fighting under the name Kid Crochet.

"I fought twelve fights . . . and won all but eleven," he would joke.

Listening to Dino's voice now, you can almost imagine him singing to himself, humming along to life's pleasures. You can see him behind the crap and poker tables; he seemed just as relaxed as if he were lounging in his own living room.

While hanging out at a roadside saloon called Walker's, Dino was encouraged to sing a couple of songs. In the audience was a bandleader named Ernie McKay. Once onstage, Dino realized the only songs he knew by heart were Italian songs. He was cool and relaxed just the same as he started singing "Oh, Marie." McKay hired him on the spot.

Dino Crocetti briefly became the flashier Dino Martini, then Dean Martin.

While performing with McKay's band in Cleveland, Martin saw a blue-eyed brunette beaming in the audience. Opposites attract, and Dino loved the blue-eyed, ivory-skinned white girls, so different from the Italian and Greek girls he'd grown up with. White was exotic; white was American. Her name was Elizabeth McDonald, and she was an eighteen-year-old student at Swarthmore, the tony WASP college on Philadelphia's Main Line. They married. She helped him with his diction and learned how to cook Italian food for him.

Then, in 1943, Martin filled in for Frank Sinatra at the Riobamba on East Fifty-seventh Street—five blocks uptown from Louis Prima's Swing Street. At the time the Riobamba was a hot nightclub, though not as hot as the Copacabana. In a review for *The New York Daily Mirror*, the critic Lee Mortimer wrote that "Dean looks a lot like Sinatra, the man whom he replaced." Of course, they looked nothing alike, but, as advertised, Dean Martin was "tall, dark, and handsome."

Two years later, Martin formed a novelty act with a Jewish kid from Newark named Jerry Lewis, the son of vaudevillians who first settled in Manhattan's Lower East Side. Lewis was a lonely kid, about ten years younger than Martin. In their act, Martin was the straight man, Jerry the clown.

Their big break came at the 500 Club in Atlantic City. The 500 Club, owned by Paul "Skinny" D'Amato, was becoming one of the most popular venues on the East Coast. And D'Amato, who was born into a poor Atlantic City Italian family, with no education, worked his way, like Martin, from hustling in back-room gambling halls to owning one of the biggest clubs in what was then the East Coast's best-known gambling town.

In 1946, Dean signed with Diamond Records, the same label on which decades earlier Nick Lucas was heard, and recorded standards such as "All of Me," "Which Way Did My Heart Go?" and "I Got the Sun in the Morning." Earlier that year, Musicraft Records had released *Phil Brito Sings Songs of Italy*, which had caught Martin's ear.

It wouldn't be the first time that Martin would draw inspiration from this now-forgotten singer and guitarist, Phil Brito, another Ohio Valley Italian, who had shortened his name from Colombrito. Brito was born in 1915 in the coal-mining town of Boomer, West Virginia. He was a guitarist and vocalist with the Al Donahue band from 1939 to 1942, and had two hits on his own that came in just below the Top 20 on the charts: "I Don't Want to Love You (Like I

Do)" and "You Belong to My Heart (Solamente una vez)." His biggest song was "The Sweetheart of Sigma Chi."

"That's Amore"—a song Martin claimed he never really liked—was his first big hit, reaching the number two spot and staying on *Billboard*'s pop charts for twenty-two weeks. The song was co-written by Harry Warren, whose song "The Boulevard of Broken Dreams" Tony Bennett had made famous. With the lyricist Al Dubin, the Brooklyn-born Warren had written the music for such classics as "You're Getting to Be a Habit with Me," "I Only Have Eyes for You," and "Lullaby of Broadway."

With Mack Gordon, he was responsible for "Chattanooga Choo Choo," "(I've Got a Gal in) Kalamazoo," and "Serenade in Blue"— all performed by Glenn Miller and His Orchestra. And with Johnny Mercer, he wrote "Jeepers Creepers" and "You Must Have Been a Beautiful Baby."

It was around the time of "That's Amore" that pizza became an American staple. The popularity of pizza began growing after World War II, in part due to the returning American soldiers who had been stationed in Italy. Having developed a taste for pizza in Naples or elsewhere, they visited Italian pizzerias when they returned home, taking their families along.

"Booming Popularity of the Pizza Pie Puts Cheese in Limelight Overnight," read the headline of one *New York Times* article from 1958 written by the food columnist June Owen. G. William Calascione, the secretary of the Italian Fresh Cheese Association, she wrote, declared that "pizza had replaced the hot dog as a national institution."

"Americans see Italian films, they wear Italian fashion . . . Why not *eat* Italian too?" Jane Nickerson wrote in another *Times* article; she went on to explain how to find Italian foods in various cities, and how to translate the labels.

In 1958, the first U.S. edition of *Italian Food* by the English cooking author Elizabeth David was published; it became the first major Italian cookbook in America.

Pizza quickly made its way from local pizzerias to fast-food chains. The first two pizza chains, neither owned by Italian Americans, opened in the unlikeliest of places—Shakey's in California in 1954, and Pizza Hut in Kansas in 1958.

21

"*Eh, cumpari!*"

JULIUS LA ROSA

Julius La Rosa had been a guest on *Arthur Godfrey's Talent Scouts* for two years the night he sang a ballad called "Manhattan."

La Rosa, who was twenty-three, went offstage to thunderous applause. Then Arthur Godfrey announced to the audience: "That was Julie's swan song with us. He goes out on his own now, as his own star, soon to be seen on his own program, and I know you wish him Godspeed, the same as I do."

It sounded gracious—but Julius La Rosa is best remembered today as the only singer fired on national TV.

Arthur Godfrey, at fifty years old, had a fatherly way about him. But he always had to be in control, and those who appeared on his stage knew that he was the paterfamilias. He began cultivating certain performers who would appear on his show at regular intervals—the McGuire Sisters and Julius La Rosa—and called them "the Little Godfreys."

Godfrey discovered La Rosa while the latter, a Sicilian from New York City, was stationed in Pensacola, Florida, and performing for the Navy. Word had reached Godfrey about this "natural" singing sensation, so one night Godfrey—who, as a naval reserve officer, was visiting the Pensacola base—went to hear the kid sing at an enlisted men's club. After hearing La Rosa perform "The Song Is You," which Frank Sinatra had recorded in 1942, Godfrey invited La Rosa to come on his show when he got out of the Navy. Six months later, on November 19, 1951, La Rosa, now twenty-one, entered America's living rooms via Godfrey's CBS show, which was broadcast simultaneously on the radio (the TV show ran an hour, while the radio show aired for three hours).

For two years Julius—or Julie, as he was affectionately called—was Godfrey's golden boy. Broad-shouldered and thick-haired, he had wide-set eyes and a large generous smile. In press photographs from those years, the square-jawed singer resembles a Latin Matt Damon. Every week he sang a number or two.

When Archie Bleyer, who led the orchestra and arranged music for many of Godfrey's artists, started a label, Cadence, Julius La Rosa was his first artist.

La Rosa had his first hit in February 1953—"Anywhere I Wander," a ballad from the film *Hans Christian Andersen*, which got up to number four and stayed on the charts for a modest nine weeks. "This Is Heaven" and "My Lady Loves to Dance" followed. On these records, La Rosa's voice is smooth and familiar with fairly straight delivery and a uniform, modulated vibrato. He's easy to sing along with. Like Sinatra, he enunciates each word.

La Rosa was becoming more popular than ever, but his collaboration with Bleyer upset Arthur Godfrey. And many say Godfrey was worried about being upstaged by La Rosa. Also, La Rosa had started dating Dorothy McGuire—and some suggested that Godfrey was jealous.

One incident especially infuriated Godfrey—the proverbial "last straw." Godfrey generally had his singers dance a few steps as they sang. One day, when it was his turn to do a dance number, Julius had a family emergency and asked permission to miss a rehearsal.

Godfrey took this as a slap in the face. The next day he left a note for La Rosa saying that since he had missed rehearsal, he wouldn't be

needed on that week's show. La Rosa went out to find an agent—
something that Godfrey forbade his performers to do.

"Do you believe that little guinea?" Godfrey was heard to say, a
remark that filtered down to La Rosa.

"Maybe I was arrogant, a little cocky," Julius La Rosa told me, recalling the incident. He smiled, then took a sip of coffee. "I was young."

We were having a brunch buffet at a hotel restaurant in Tarry-
town, New York, not far from his home.

"I was what you would call an overnight success," he said. He
wasn't bragging, simply explaining the course his life had taken just
ten days out of the Navy when he had gone on national television.
Even in his seventies, La Rosa was fit and trim in his blue polo shirt.
And when he spoke, he looked directly at me through his horn-
rimmed glasses, choosing his words carefully, delivering sentences as
clearly and thoughtfully as he sang them. He was one for whom, he
explains, the lyric is more important than the melody.

He told me about growing up in a Sicilian family in Bushwick,
a historically German part of Brooklyn that then had a growing
population of Italians. In 1885, Bushwick was the terminus of the
borough's first elevated railroad and at that time was home to
Rheingold and dozens of other breweries.

As a boy growing up there, La Rosa and his family and friends
would take the Sea Beach subway line to Coney Island for an afternoon in the sun. The kids would crowd into the first car, close to the
engineer, and they would sing "Eh, cumpari!" the entire way down.
"Before we knew it, everyone in the car was singing the song."

After the success of his first song, "Anywhere I Wander," Archie
Bleyer insisted La Rosa record "Eh, cumpari!" (Hey, friends!). And it
was shortly after this, on October 19, 1953, that Godfrey fired La
Rosa from the show. Two days later, "Eh, cumpari!" became a hit. It
reached the second spot and slowly moved down the charts for
twenty weeks, eventually selling two million copies. It is a Sicilian
novelty song, a kind of Italian "Old MacDonald Had a Farm"—but

instead of ducks quacking, it is about the sounds musical instruments make.

"Eh, cumpare, ci vo suonare," he sings. "Chi si suona? U friscalettu. E come si suona u friscalettu?" Hey, friend, something is playing. What is playing? A whistle. And what does a whistle sound like?

La Rosa makes the sound of the whistle. After the whistle follows the saxophone, then the mandolin, and after each verse, all the aforementioned instruments are sung and heard.

After the Godfrey show, Julius La Rosa appeared several times on *The Ed Sullivan Show*. In time, he would serve as a guest host on *The Perry Como Show*, filling in for Como during the summers. It was on this show in 1956 that La Rosa met the woman who would later become his wife, Como's twenty-four-year-old secretary, Rory Meyer, who had once won an Ava Gardner look-alike contest. That year he followed up "Eh, cumpari!" with another Italian number— a "silly little song," La Rosa said—called "Domani," which means "tomorrow" in Italian. "Maybe you'll fall in love with me domani . . . I'll change my name from Johnny to Giovanni."

Julius La Rosa was the first Italian American singer to earn a following entirely on television. When he tried to break into live singing for audiences at nightclubs, he was struck dumb with terror.

"I was spoiled because I started on radio and television, where, when you walked out, everyone paid attention to you," he told me. "But when you walk onto the stage at a saloon—the Copa, the Stork Club, whatever—unless you have any authority on that stage, they're going to walk all over you. Which is what they did with me for twenty years until I got enough confidence to say, 'I'm here; I'm working for you.'"

He told me about the first time he performed at the El Rancho casino in Las Vegas.

"There were two guys in the back corner talking throughout the first two numbers. I stopped in the middle of the song and said to them, 'If you don't shut up, I'm going to come over and whop you right in the mouth.'"

When the set was over, La Rosa walked out to the hall to make good on his promise. The manager darted out, screaming: "Do you know who those guys were?"

They were mafiosi apparently; but as the manager yelled at La Rosa, one of them walked up behind him and said, "Leave the kid alone; he's got balls."

La Rosa took another sip of his coffee. This was the man who Ella Fitzgerald had said back in 1955 was the most underrated singer in America.

"You know," Julius said to me, "I actually was never fired on TV."

I wondered what he meant. It seemed that everyone I had talked to remembered watching the program on which he was fired. I asked him to explain it.

"The TV program ended just as I finished my song. But the radio show continued, and it was on radio—not television—that Godfrey said it was my swan song."

Julius La Rosa was such a fixture on *Arthur Godfrey's Talent Scouts*, his audience was so shocked at his dismissal, that it seemed as if they had really witnessed it. It was important for La Rosa to clarify that he wasn't fired on the medium—television—that created him.

22

"Darktown Strutters' Ball (Italian-Style)"

LOU MONTE

"What did George Washington say when he crossed the Delaware?" Joe Maselli asked me.

I was in New Orleans for a conference when I met Joseph Maselli. He was born in Newark, but after a stint in the Navy he moved to New Orleans, where he got a degree in accounting at Tulane University and worked as an accountant for various bars on Bourbon Street. He asked himself why he was working as an accountant for these bars when he saw how easy it was to distribute liquor. Which is what he ended up doing. Until his death in 2009, he was president of the American Italian Renaissance Foundation in New Orleans. When I met Maselli in 2004, he was eighty years old and stood maybe five feet five. He had a low, raspy voice and carried himself like the former boxer he was—that is, like a boxer who wears nicely tailored suits and drives a white Mercedes.

Maselli offered to give me a tour of Italian American New Orleans, and he told me to wait for him outside my hotel the next morning. Then he gave me a fake boxer's weave and jab to the jaw.

He barely touched me, but I nevertheless felt the power coming from that fake jab. It rattled my brains. I felt the way I used to feel with my father's brothers, who were always joking around with me and didn't know their own strength. I felt like a wimp.

He picked me up in his white Mercedes the next morning, and throughout our day together—during which he showed me the sculpture on the waterfront that he commissioned of Italian immigrants seeing America for the first time—we bonded on things Italian of his generation.

He showed me the restaurants where he ate—and had eaten for decades. They were all French or old New Orleans–style restaurants and coffee shops, but many, he proudly told me, were owned—either then or now—by Italian Americans. The legendary New Orleans establishment Antoine's, for example, was opened in 1840 by Antoine Alciatore, an Italian-born chef who grew up in Marseilles.

At one point he turned to me and asked, "What did George Washington say when he crossed the Delaware?" He smiled and gave me a nudge.

"I don't know, what did he say?"

He laughed. "You know, if you were to ask any Italian guy that question—anyone about sixty-five or older—he'd know the answer."

"What is it?"

"It's just a little joke. Ask your father; he'll know. I guarantee it."

He began telling me of a time when a restaurateur he had just met was talking up his Neapolitan background. They were about the same age, Joe reckoned, and this guy was using all the Italian American terms and pronunciations. "He looked Italian, even darker than either one of us," he said. "But something seemed a bit off—a bit too much."

So he posed him the question about George Washington. The man shrugged his shoulders, waiting for the punch line with an anticipatory smile on his face.

"You're not Italian," Joe said.

"Of course I am," the man said, twitching.

"You're not," Joe said. "Or else you would have known the answer."

"Okay, okay," the man said. "But don't tell anyone; my business will be ruined. I'm Jewish."

I asked Joe again. "Okay, so what did George Washington say when he crossed the Delaware?"

He clapped me on the back and said to me in his dialect, "Fa gia nu cazzu a friddu." It's fucking cold out here.

A couple of days later I called my father and, just as we were about to say goodbye, I said, "Hey, Pa, what did George Washington say when he crossed the Delaware?"

There was a pause, then a burst of laughter. I could tell that it was something he hadn't thought about in decades—that the pause was him retrieving from his past this link to all those Italian-born and first-generation Italian Americans.

He responded in the same way, but in his own Calabrese dialect.

For Italian Americans it was their joke, a way of laughing at themselves and laughing at the Americans, at the myths and legends surrounding their founding fathers. What a scream that America's founding father spoke Italian, and had the Italian outrage at cold temperatures.

A week or so later, my father tried the joke out on my sister's father-in-law, a third-generation Sicilian, born in Tampa, Florida, but of my father's generation.

He responded in his Sicilian dialect—the joke was the same, be it Neapolitan, Calabrian, or Sicilian—and then added: "And what did Christoforo Colombo say when he saw the Indians once he landed?"

My father said, "Tu sei pure italian'." So you, too, are Italian.

And that reminded me of Lou Monte, who was known for his Italian-language novelty songs. Many of them retold American stories with Italian characters—or with a predominantly Italian take.

"Please, Mr. Columbus," a sailor named Luigi says, begging Columbus to return to Spain.

"Why you tell-a Isabella that-a the world is round. Please, Mr. Columbus, turn-a the ship around."

But when they reach the shore, you can hear Luigi cry when he sees the Indians—"Hey, there's Italians all around!"

Louis Scaglione, or Lou Monte as he became known, was born to Calabrese parents in Manhattan in 1917. After serving in World War II, many Italians started moving out of the cities to the suburbs, eager to finally have their own houses and land.

When Monte returned from the army after World War II, he settled in Lyndhurst, New Jersey, at the time a town of ten thousand people that today claims one of the highest percentages of Italian Americans in the country (38 percent of its current population is of Italian descent). While living there, he performed throughout the state, doing a mix of singing and Italian comedy at various nightclubs. He was the Migliaccio—the Farfariello—of the 1950s, making Italians laugh at themselves through novelty songs. It was a way for them to brush off stereotypes and to wink to one another about what they all knew—that Italians had come to this country first.

When the Italians, often second-generation, moved to the suburbs, they moved one step farther away from their ancestors' Italian villages. These Italian novelty songs expressed the nostalgia they felt for them.

As with "Please Mr. Columbus," in 1962 Monte placed Italians in the midst of America's forefathers, making Paul Revere's horse Ba-Cha-Ca-Loop—*baciagalupo* being a term Italian Americans use to make fun of themselves and their own words. (Julius La Rosa referred to the Italian-accented English they spoke as "bacciagalup' English.") It was a way of beating the *'merican'*—anyone living in America not of Italian heritage—to the stereotype.

The song tells a story about Paul Revere trying to keep the horse—an Italian horse—from drinking wine. Revere worries that if the horse goes into the tavern, he will drink and pass out with a pepperoni in his hand and an ice pack on his head.

The horse does manage to get a drink in the tavern, but to the opposite effect: "Just because he drank, the British thought he couldn't last; but it's that nice Italian wine that made him run so fast."

In 1954, Monte carried on the commedia dell'arte tradition of Migliaccio, Durante, Louis Prima, and Dean Martin with an Italian version of an old standard first recorded in 1917 by Nick LaRocca and the Original Dixieland Jass Band: "Darktown Strutters' Ball (Italian-Style)." It's a fun, upbeat number about a man who is hurrying his girl to the dance. The song opens with a mandolin playing "O sole mio," then Monte sings, "I'll be down to get you with the pushcart, honey, you better be ready about a half past eight." Monte is nonchalant, tossing off phrases. He alternates verses in English, then in Italian—and even a little Italo-English (Itaglish): "Abbiamo un 'puntament, sotto bash-a-ment." We have an appointment in the basement.

The Italian served to disguise the song's sexual overtones, and it put the thirty-seven-year-old singer on the charts.

My father understands Monte's Calabrese dialect; but when a Milanese friend of mine visited me in New York, I put on the song, and he shook his head, genuinely confused: "Is that even Italian?"

Monte went on to give an Italian twist to popular songs such as "Italian Huckle-Buck," which Frank Sinatra and Tommy Dorsey had recorded in 1949 as "The Hucklebuck," and "Somewhere There Is Someone" and a version of "The Sheik of Araby" subtitled "The Sheik of Napoli."

His biggest hit came in 1962, "Pepino the Italian Mouse," about a rodent who's running around and scaring off Monte's girlfriend. It's sung in a mix of Calabrese and Neapolitan dialect. "Tu sei sicilian'?" the mouse asks. To which Monte responds, "No, I'm a Calabrese, you nut."

The song Monte is best known for is his version of the classic Italian American song "Luna mezza mare" (Moon Halfway over the Sea), which he recorded under the title "Lazy Mary."

In the opening scene of *The Godfather*, a brass band starts up a tune that brings all the old folks and kids to the floor. It's "Luna mezzo mare." There's the fun version, and the nasty version—which Italian Americans know, even today.

"C'è la luna mezz'o mare," there's a moon in the middle of the sea, the song begins. And the daughter begs her mother to find someone for her to marry.

Lou Monte sings the lyrics in Italian, then says on the record, "And now for you nice ladies and gentlemen out there who don't understand the Eye-talian language, I'd like to do two choruses in British"—not quite as risqué, but suggestive nonetheless.

"You'd better marry a fireman," sings Monte. "With his hose he'll come and go, go and come—*zemba la boom.*" The last phrase is a kind of gibberish in dialect that hints at what might come next sexually.

At that point in *The Godfather* an old man at the Corleone wedding gets up and starts singing and makes a gesture to his crotch. You catch the Corleone mother turning red and laughing as she sings the song as well. (The actress who plays Don Vito Corleone's wife is a jazz singer from the 1950s and 1960s, Morgana King, née Maria Grazia Morgana Messina DeBerardinis.)

Monte's version of the song reached number twelve on the *Billboard* pop charts in March 1958, and today it's hard to find an Italian American who doesn't remember his or her parents—or especially grandparents—singing it at a wedding, during Christmas, or at Sunday dinner.

23

"(The Gang That Sang) Heart of My Heart"

DON CORNELL AND JOHNNY DESMOND

Call them the "three baritones," if you will. In December 1953, three Italian American crooners put their mark on a 1926 song entitled "(The Gang That Sang) Heart of My Heart," which was itself an echo of an Irish ballad called "Heart of My Heart." They were Don Cornell, Johnny Desmond, and Alan Dale, and their recording reached number ten.

Later the same week, another vocal group called the Four Aces had a hit with the same song, reaching number seven. As it happened, three members of the Four Aces, who came from Chester, Pennsylvania, a city between Philadelphia and Wilmington, were also Italian American—Al Alberts (Albertini), Lou Silvestri, and Rosario Vaccaro (the fourth, Dave Mahoney, was Irish and met Albertini while in the Navy). Their best-known song came in 1955, "Love Is a Many Splendored Thing."

The three baritones were in their early thirties and had strong individual followings and fan clubs of their own. To look at photographs of them placed side by side, you see three faces of Italian

American men: Don, the larger-than-life romancer; Johnny, the suave ladies' man; and Alan, the enigmatic and aloof introvert.

Johnny Desmond (Giovanni Alfredo de Simone before he changed his name) was born in Detroit in 1919. Desmond first sang with the big band of Bob Crosby (Bing's brother) in 1940, which brought him to New York, where he joined Gene Krupa's band and performed at the Paramount. World War II interrupted his career. But while he was in the Air Corps, Glenn Miller heard the voice and brought him on board. Johnny Desmond became known as the GI Sinatra.

He began recording in 1947, releasing such songs as "Guilty" and "C'est Si Bon." It wasn't until 1951 that he hit number thirteen with a song that would make Tony Bennett big—"Because of You." In 1954, Johnny Desmond had another hit with "East Side, West Side," paired with a twenty-eight-year-old Italian American singer and pianist from Philadelphia, Buddy Greco.

Meanwhile, in 1952, Don Cornell had three Top 10 hits: "I'll Walk Alone," "I'm Yours," and "I (Serenade)." Bronx-born Cornell got his first bit of recognition when, as a kid named Luigi Francisco Varlaro, he appeared on the radio show *Major Bowes' Original Amateur Hour*. All his neighbors tuned in. Upon realizing Varlaro's success, his father made him promise one thing: "No matter what happens, don't ever change your name."

In his late teens, he had begun playing guitar and singing for the bandleader and trumpeter Red Nichols. He also boxed, but called it quits after twenty or so fights. In 1941, the bandleader Sammy Kaye had heard his singing, hired him, and put the twenty-two-year-old singer out front.

I spoke with Don Cornell's widow, Iris, shortly after he died in 2004. Iris, who now lives in North Miami Beach, Florida, remembers stories of Luigi Varlaro playing small theaters and clubs. It was just as the United States entered World War II, and Mussolini was America's enemy. When he walked onstage with Sammy Kaye's band and introduced himself with his obvious Italian name, the boos and hisses would cut through the air. One night, when Varlaro came onstage after the first musical number, Sammy Kaye introduced him as Don Cornell. The crowd applauded. And Luigi Varlaro had a new name—although, to keep his promise to his father, he never changed it legally.

His biggest hit came in 1954: "Hold My Hand." It was featured in a movie, *Susan Slept Here*, with Dick Powell and Debbie Reynolds. The ballad opens with a swirl of sweet strings; Cornell exudes confidence as he sings in short phrases with absolute rhythmic freedom and swagger. His style of singing—from the back of the throat—harks back to earlier crooners. He was a big-band crooner, perhaps a little behind his time.

In "(The Gang That Sang) Heart of My Heart," the three Italians, brought together by Coral Records, took the Irish song to their own neighborhood. Hearing it, I can't help but think of a few teens standing in a city piazza in Italy—or, a bit later, on a street corner in the Bronx—crooning together under a streetlight, especially as the three sing in unison.

The harmonies sound straight out of a barbershop. The three call out to one another by name, each getting a chorus of singers to join in a call-and-response. Then Don, Johnny, and Alan end with one line each, displaying their distinct and magnificent voices.

"I know a tear would glisten," sings Don Cornell in his signature delivery—that of an opera singer.

"If once more I could listen," Johnny Desmond sings as he continues the lyric with a light, mellifluous swing and sway.

"To the gang that sang 'Heart of My Heart,'" croons Alan Dale, finishing the verse in a voice that sounds as if sung through a muted trumpet. He sounds a lot like Russ Columbo.

Alan Dale was the youngest of the gang by nearly a decade, and although he had already made a name for himself in the late forties—with his own radio and TV show—his biggest hits were yet to come.

24

"Sweet and Gentle"

ALAN DALE

"A performer is never certain about his performance," Alan Dale remarked in his memoir, *The Spider and the Marionettes*, offering a glimpse into the mind of a singer as he's performing. "The mind works every second on stage to say the right thing. The pacing must be right. The hands must be right. His eyes! Which side of the room is he favoring? Is he taking advantage of every situation and covering every mistake? His own, the band's, the light man's? Is the mike OK? With all this, he must always smile and communicate his joy to the fifteen hundred strangers who came to have fun and forget their own problems."

For Dale—Aldo Sigismondi—performing was second nature. He was born in Bensonhurst, Brooklyn, in 1928, an only child in a theatrical family. His mother, Kate (Agata), who was born in Messina, Sicily, was a piano teacher. His father, Aristide, who came from Abruzzi, worked in various theaters in Little Italy as a *macchiettista*, around the same time as Eduardo "Farfariello" Migliaccio. Aristide Sigismondi was best known for his sketch "La Morte di Festa a Mulberry Street" (The Death of the Mulberry Street Festival); Italian Americans throughout New York City listened to him on the radio and later saw him on TV.

It was odd to think, at first, that my introduction to Alan Dale was through his memoir rather than his music. He was a singer who initially wanted to be a writer but because of his family background found it easier to follow a life onstage. But then I realized perhaps it's not so strange; I am simply the opposite, a writer who, had I lived a few decades earlier, would have yearned to sing onstage.

Of course, it wasn't long after I began reading Dale's memoir that I found a CD of his music and listened to it as I read.

Sigismondi was only fifteen when he walked into the Club Atlantis in Coney Island in 1943 and auditioned for an orchestra led by the bandleader Eddie Small, delivering a belting version of Sinatra's "All or Nothing At All." He got the job, and within months was seen and hired away by the bandleader Carmen Cavallaro, who, on a tip, had stopped off to hear one of his performances. He took the name Alan Dale, inspired by the minstral character Allan-a-Dale who joined Robin Hood's legendary gang of outlaws.

By 1945, he was the voice for George Paxton and His Orchestra, performing at various nightclubs and hotel bars and at the Roseland Ballroom at Broadway and Fifty-first Street in New York. In 1948, WINS radio station in New York held one of many regularly aired "Battle of the Baritones" programs. Frank Sinatra came in at number one, but Dale came in second, ahead of Perry Como and Bing Crosby.

CBS gave him his own show, first on radio, then on TV: *The Alan Dale Show.* Television viewers warmed to his good looks, just as they had to Perry Como's. In a photograph of him from that time, his light brown hair, combed up in a kind of pompadour, matches his theatrically thick eyebrows. Below his straight, smooth nose, he gives a delicate thin-lipped smile.

"(The Gang That Sang) Heart of My Heart" with Don Cornell and Johnny Desmond was his biggest *Billboard* hit until 1955, when he helped popularize the mambo in America with a recording of "Cherry Pink (and Apple Blossom White)." The King of Mambo, the Cuban Pérez Prado, had already had a hit with an instrumental version, but Dale was the first to put a voice to it.

On the record, the opening trumpet bends on the fourth note of the intro. "It's cherry pink and apple blossom white," Dale sings, mimicking the trumpet's bend but in a deep croon, "when your true lover comes your way." His fluttering vibrato makes his voice seem simultaneously full and ethereal. Brass, xylophones, and drums break into the smooth down–down, up–up, down–down, up–up of the mambo.

Within months he came out with "Sweet and Gentle," about a man transformed after dancing the cha-cha with a woman.

"Oh, I was sweet and gentle, and kind of sentimental," Dale sings, hiccuping the "and" to match the cha-cha rhythm. "And then one magic night I learned to do the cha-cha," and now he'll never be the same. You can almost see him dancing in place as he sings, his feet gently tapping the floor. The song reached number ten. Disc jockeys soon referred to him as "the Sweet and Gentle Crooner."

His manager was Lou Capone, the first manager of Vic Damone (who had attended Lafayette High School in Bensonhurst a few years after Dale). Soon Alan Dale was Prince of the Baritones and Dreamboat of the Airwaves.

Successful but searching for stardom, Dale tried rock and roll. In 1955, a film was released about rebellious youth and inner-city schools. It was called *Blackboard Jungle*, and it featured a song by a band from Warwick, Pennsylvania, named Bill Haley and His Comets, "Rock Around the Clock." The movie and song marked the beginning of the rock-and-roll generation. The next year, Columbia Pictures followed up with a movie called *Don't Knock the Rock*, which featured the DJ and music promoter Alan Freed as well as Alan Dale in the role of a rock-and-roll singer who returns to his hometown. In effect, the movie (not nearly as successful or shocking as the first) brings rock and roll from the city to the suburbs. Dale seemed out of place singing Haley's title song, "Don't Knock the Rock": the music was rocking, but he couldn't fight the impulse to croon. Nevertheless, the role introduced him to a new audience.

On May 19, 1958, his career came to a halt.

"Spurned Suitor Hurls Dale Down Stairs of Nightclub," one newspaper headline read.

He had been performing at the Latin Quarter in New York, a nightclub owned by a man named Lou Walters, who also owned clubs in Boston and Miami. Some say a stranger came out of the crowd when the show was over and threw Alan Dale down a steep staircase to the street. At the bottom was a plate-glass display case. Hoping to break his fall—and save his face—Dale sacrificed his hands, putting them through the glass case, cutting them up and disfiguring them for life.

Sure, he might have been flirting with another guy's girl—though he might have just been singing to her. But insiders mumbled sotto voce to one another the more likely reason: "the Mob."

A photograph from the tabloid *Confidential* pictures a delirious Dale on a hospital cot, his hand bandaged up. He looks directly at the camera.

And that was one of the last public photographs to be seen of Alan Dale. Once he recovered, he continued to perform in small nightclubs—and seven years later he returned to his first love, writing, and told his story in a bitter 1965 memoir.

"I wanted to do it my way," he wrote, explaining how he saw himself as the spider. ("My subconscious wove another strand until I was watching them from within a web. I made the web my home and stayed alone—rather than join the marionettes!")

"Now I sing in the many cafes that feature name talent on weekends in and around New York," Dale writes. "This will not make me a star. No producers there to see me; no columnists, no celebrities. Only ordinary people . . . [but] I work there on my own terms." That is, he has no manager. He is controlled by no one—not promoters, not critics, not gossip columnists, not even fans. He sings only when the mood strikes him.

25

"I've Got the World on a String"

FRANK SINATRA

It was a film, rather than a song, that provided the comeback for the greatest American singer.

If Frank Sinatra's career had ended in 1947, he would have been remembered as a first-class singer but not a legend. It was only after he got knocked out cold that he found his soul—like a fighter realizing his own fallibility for the first time. Sinatra's early songs were filled with romantic yearning. His later songs were the musings of an experienced man.

While Sinatra's career never spiraled to the depths of Alan Dale's—performing at no-name clubs—at one point he surely must have felt that he was heading there.

With the sultry brunette actress from the South, Ava Gardner, Sinatra was incapable of hiding his love. Everyone in the industry had known he was having an affair, but in 1949 it was confirmed for the public, who, until then, could turn a blind eye, hoping it was just hearsay, just gossip. Sinatra asked his wife for a divorce.

On March 28, 1950, Sinatra returned to the Copa for the first time in a few years. A month into his engagement, he began to feel the effects of the Copa's grueling schedule that required singers to perform three shows a night. During the first few minutes he felt a bit off, exhausted. Then, halfway through his set, it happened; as he tried hitting a note, nothing came out. "The Voice" was gone.

The story has often been told: the cigarettes and the booze and the late nights out, the low record sales, the weak film reviews, the battles with the press—they had all sucked the life out of him, and killed the one thing that got him there. He had ruptured his vocal cords.

But that was just the beginning of his woes. Sinatra took a combination of hits, and his own cockiness left him open for retribution.

On March 1, 1951, the Democratic senator Estes Kefauver, chairman of the Special Committee on Organized Crime in Interstate Commerce, called Sinatra to testify in what would become known as the Kefauver hearings into illegal activities such as gambling and organized crime. Because so many of the people accused had Italian surnames, many Italian Americans saw these hearings as another black mark against them.

The hearings were televised live from the federal courthouse in downtown Manhattan, and watching them, for people of the era, was an unforgettable experience. The most indelible impression was made by Frank Costello, who asked that the camera not show his face. The camera focused instead on his hands, tightly wringing and rolling over each other.

Sinatra's testimony wasn't broadcast. He was questioned at Rockefeller Center, where he denied having dealings with the mobsters Meyer Lansky, Lucky Luciano, and Willie Moretti.

"Hell, you go into show business and you meet a lot of people. And you don't know who they are or what they do," he responded.

For his outspokenness and his film on racial intolerance, he was deemed a Commie; for his bursts of anger toward the press, he was deemed dangerous; for his failure to serve during World War II, he was unpatriotic; and for his acquaintance with mobsters, he was a Mafia affiliate.

To this day, many Americans still can't allow an Italian to be successful on his own. He must have some backing, some support, and that support must be the Mob. Try telling a friend that you have an uncle who works in construction, as I did. His eyebrows will rise knowingly.

As if that weren't enough, Sinatra's agent, Lew Wasserman at MCA, dropped him. Since the beginning, he had been unfaithful to Nancy; now Ava Gardner, whom he had just married, was unfaithful to him.

In the end, it was Ava Gardner who taught Frank humility. Nelson Riddle said it was a woman "who taught him how to sing a torch song," by breaking his spirit.

Columbia records dropped him and MGM didn't renew his film contract. He was thirty-seven years old and on the verge of being a has-been.

Sinatra had read James Jones's novel *From Here to Eternity* when it came out in 1951, about a company of soldiers stationed at Pearl Harbor just before the Japanese attacked. When he heard that Columbia was going to make a movie based on it, he knew immediately the role that would be perfect for him: Private Angelo Maggio, a tough, slightly built Italian guy from New Jersey. He tried contacting both the head of Columbia, Harry Cohn, and the film's director, Fred Zinnemann, but they were already considering Eli Wallach for the role.

That November, Gardner, who was making a movie for MGM, *Mogambo*, sent a plea through Cohn wife's, begging him to consider Frank Sinatra for Maggio.

He got an audition, and a month later he learned he got the role.

Sinatra was putting his career back in place. He knew he had to start at the bottom. To get back into film, he accepted a mere $8,000 fee—a huge drop from the $130,000 he had been paid for his role in *Anchors Aweigh*.

As if pulling himself further up on the ropes, he would revive his

music career. Next was Capitol Records at KHJ studios in Hollywood—a onetime radio station, now Capitol's recording studios—
where he met the executive Alan Livingston.

Al Martino remembered seeing Frank Sinatra waiting for Livingston—the only man then willing to take a chance on him: "He
was waiting in the lobby; I felt he was too big of a star to be waiting
for anyone."

Lucey's was a Mexican restaurant on Melrose Avenue right
across from the KHJ studios. Its baroque setting with white chairs
and deep red velvet walls must only have highlighted for Frank
the absurdity of what he was about to agree to. After all, just a few
years before, he had been untouchable, but he was determined to
start somewhere. For "a scale deal"—a deal that only unknown
musicians and singers were given—he signed with Capitol. And Livingston set the course for his rebirth by bringing in Nelson Riddle
as arranger. It's hard to imagine Sinatra's comeback without his pair-
ing with the genius arranger. The essential components were all
coming together.

Nelson Riddle, a fellow New Jerseyan born in Oradell, had made
his name a few years earlier with a lush, sweet setting of Nat "King"
Cole singing "Mona Lisa." He was six years Sinatra's junior, and he
would arrange the songs that would come to define Sinatra's rebirth.
They were light and airy, despite an orchestration heavy on brass and
a symphony of full strings.

The first two songs Sinatra and Riddle recorded were "I've Got
the World on a String" and "My One and Only Love." The first was
a kind of autobiography for Sinatra, the story of the resurgence of
his career. And no stranger to marionettes—the wooden figures featured in the puppet shows he would certainly have seen growing up
in his Italian neighborhood—Frank Sinatra didn't merely want to be
a spider, wrapped up in his own cozy web as Alan Dale had wished
for himself. Sinatra wanted to control those marionettes.

It was at this time that Frank Sinatra began wearing his now-
iconic black felt Cavanaugh hat. Perhaps it was to cover his receding
hairline, but the effect gave him an air of authority.

Sheet music for "Core 'ngrato," written for the opera singer Enrico Caruso, America's first pop recording artist (above: Courtesy Enrico Caruso Museum of America; right: photograph by Buyenlarge/Getty Images)

LEFT: Eduardo "Farfariello" Migliaccio, playing a stereotypical Italian immigrant (Courtesy John D. Calandra Italian American Institute, Queens College/CUNY); ABOVE: Nic Lucas, one of the first performers for who Gibson built a special guitar (not the one pictured here) (Sasha/Hulton Archive/Getty Images); BELOW: crooner Russ Columbo wit June Knight, his co-star in the 1934 movi musical *Wake Up and Dream* (Hulton Archiv Getty Images)

In October 1944, bobby-soxers besieged the Paramount Theatre in Times Square, where Frank Sinatra sang "All or Nothing at All" and other hits. (right: Hulton Archive/Getty Images; below: photograph by NY Daily News Archive/Getty Images)

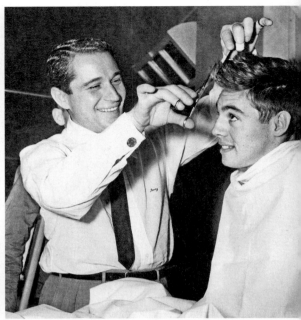

The saloon singers: ABOVE LEFT: eighteen-year-old Vic Damone (Metronome/Getty Images); ABOVE RIGHT: Perry Como, who had been a barber (Pictorial Parade/Hulton Archive/Getty Images); BELOW LEFT: Mario Lanza, whose opera stages were the movie studios of Hollywood (GAB Archive/Redferns/Getty Images); BELOW RIGHT: Jerry Vale, whose voice was suited to classic Neapolitan music (Michael Ochs Archives/Getty Images)

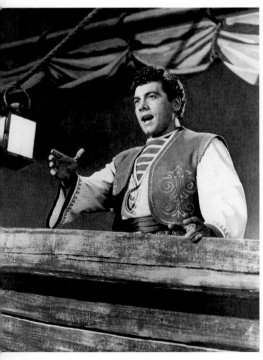

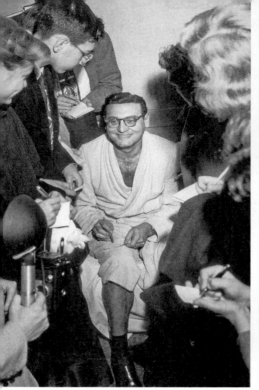

ABOVE LEFT: Frankie Laine signing autographs backstage (Metronome/Getty Images); ABOVE RIGHT: Tony Bennett at the Copacabana (Sony BMG Music Entertainment/Getty Images); RIGHT: Louis Prima giving it his all, with saxophonist Sam Butera playing above him and Prima's wife, Keely Smith, onstage (John Bryson/Time & Life Pictures/Getty Images)

The vocal harmony groups:
ABOVE: Dion and the Belmonts (Dion DiMucci at far left) (Frank Driggs Collection/Getty Images); LEFT: the Cre (Michael Ochs Archives/Getty Images); BELOW: the Four Seasons (Frankie Va is third from left) (Gems/Redferns/Ge Images)

LEFT: Young lovers Connie Francis and Bobby Darin singing together on *The Ed Sullivan Show*, 1960 (CBS Photo Archive/Getty Images); BELOW: Sammy Davis Jr., Frank Sinatra, and Dean Martin at Rat Pack headquarters, the Copa Room at the Sands Hotel in Las Vegas (Michael Ochs Archives/Getty Images)

LEFT: Frank Sinatra welcomes Elvis Presley back from the Army, 1960 (Michael Ochs Archive Getty Images); BELOW: Tony Bennett and Bruce Springsteen, paesans, at the Grammy Awards in 2006 (Larry Busacca/WireImage for Sony BMG Music Entertainment/Getty Images)

In August 1953, *From Here to Eternity* premiered at the Capitol Theatre on Fifty-first Street in Manhattan. Sinatra's co-stars were Montgomery Clift, Burt Lancaster, Deborah Kerr, and Donna Reed.

Burt Lancaster plays the role of Sergeant Milton Warden, who is
in love with Captain Dana Holmes's wife, played by Deborah Kerr.
Montgomery Clift plays Private Robert E. Lee Prewitt, a bugler and
former boxer. The Army wants Prewitt to box for them, but he
refuses—as he once accidentally killed a man in the ring. The pla-
toon dislikes him for being a loner; Maggio becomes his only friend,
and together they go into town on the weekends and spend the
nights drinking and carousing with women.

The movie was released in the face of McCarthyism. With many
of the characters refusing to do what the Army demanded, the
movie spurned authority in favor of individualism.

In this role, Frank Sinatra came back triumphant. He *was* Maggio.
He was the guy whom everyone bet against but who wouldn't go
down without a fight. There was no mistaking he was Italian. Like
Maggio, Sinatra held the rebellious attitude almost as if it were a
badge of honor.

In one scene, a bigoted sergeant named Judson, played by Ernest
Borgnine (an Italian American playing an Anglo-Saxon), eggs on
Maggio, calling him "a little wop."

"Only my friends call me a wop," Maggio responds.

The antagonism continues until Maggio, who goes AWOL, is
arrested by Judson, an MP, and brought to jail, where he is severely
beaten by the sergeant. He escapes and finds Prewitt to tell him
what he has been through.

"And when Judson beat me the last time, I smiled and spat in his
face," says Maggio, just before bleeding to death.

Sinatra's portrayal of Maggio is full of hints of Rocky Graziano—
his street toughness, his cockiness, his punching an officer, and his
going AWOL. Graziano himself was in search of a comeback at this
time. He and Tony Zale met again in the ring, this time with

Graziano defending his championship; he was knocked out cold in the third round. In 1952, hoping to regain the title, he fought and lost to Sugar Ray Robinson, also in the third round. After one more fight, he retired.

A kind of rebirth came for Graziano in 1954, when he was invited to become a regular on *The Martha Raye Show* as the awkward boyfriend to the quick-tongued Raye. In one episode, Raye refers to him as her "goombah"—Italian American slang for the southern Italian *cumpare*, or friend. Graziano does a double take, surprised that this Irish girl from Butte, Montana, has used a word from his background. From then on he would refer to himself on the show as "goombah," popularizing the word for non–Italian American audiences.

Sinatra's reinvention, too, was nearly complete. He came to embody a certain kind of Italian American man. Any Italian American has someone in his family like him. A man who's sure of what it means to be a man.

My uncle Frank, who never finished high school, became a prosperous contractor and developer in Danbury and Bethel, Connecticut. He and my aunt Terry did not have children; during my childhood I was the only boy in the extended family, and I was always afraid of him. He was gentle and gracious with the girls, but severe with me, as if wanting to "toughen me up" and teach me, an Italian American boy, how to be a man. He would grill me on the chemical properties of cement or wood, for example, and then be genuinely displeased when I didn't know the answer.

I felt others were intimidated by Uncle Frank as well; yet he was generous, too, always looking out for his family and friends no matter what else was going on in his life.

From time to time I would go with Uncle Frank to the Sycamore Diner in Bethel. We would sit at the counter, and one by one contractors and foremen would sit at the empty stool next to Uncle Frank and chat over coffee and dry toast; each left with a new assignment, or the possibility of one.

Sinatra came to the rescue of many of his friends. In 1954, he helped Sammy Davis Jr. land some shows in Las Vegas. One night, while driving from Vegas back to L.A., Davis slammed into a stalled car on the highway. He lost his eye, and his face was disfigured. Sinatra visited him in the hospital and offered his house in Palm Springs for Davis to recuperate in when he got out of the hospital.

Sinatra himself was back at the Sands, the hottest nightclub in Vegas. An early moment during this comeback was captured on video.

Frank Sinatra walks onstage to thunderous applause. He seems as comfortable as if he were walking into his own living room, albeit full of guests. He gives a half smile, almost a smirk. His black tuxedo is impeccably pressed, but he moves with ease in it as others might in a familiar pair of jeans—he wouldn't have thought to perform in anything else. With his right hand he takes the microphone from the stand, the gold from his Sicilian-crested pinkie ring glistening.

His blue eyes shoot a look out at the audience that is simultaneously inviting and threatening.

"Ladies and gentlemen, as vice president in charge of entertainment, I hereby welcome you to this saloon."

The saloon was the Copa Room at the Sands in 1953, just a year after it opened. Sinatra was part of a tradition of Italian American singers who began their careers in neighborhood saloons, singing to longshoremen, bricklayers, firemen, anyone who had been busting his back. He was there to entertain. To get minds off muscles aching from hauling carts off ships, backs sore from hours of hunching over perfectly placed bricks. The people who sang at these bars and taverns were saloon singers.

Sinatra referred to himself as a saloon singer; it was his highest compliment if he called you one too.

From high school dances, Sinatra had moved on to weddings and first Communions, any place where there was a gathering of people who wanted to celebrate. He graduated to steak houses and nightclubs. In these saloons you had to fight for attention, to be heard above the drinking, above the eating, above the talking.

It was in a saloon that you proved your worth. You had to make them want to listen to you. But once you did, the reward was a small room of devoted listeners—a place where you could sing your heart out and people would feel it.

Sure, there was a thrill in singing to large audiences at the Paramount and Carnegie Hall, but it was the saloon that offered the closest contact with your audience. Even as their careers advanced and they hit the big time at the Copacabana, the El Morocco, the Flamingo, Ciro's, or Mocambo, singers still had to fight to keep the audience's attention. You couldn't take anything for granted—just because you got booked into the Copa didn't mean the people there would listen to you. You had to have technique, you had to connect with the audience, you had to put on a good show. You had to be cool; you had to have style. You had to earn the respect of everyone there.

With a slight wave of the hand Sinatra cues the brass for "I've Got the World on a String." His blue eyes glisten, focusing right on you. They are cool, severe; then the smile warms them. The orchestra is at his attention, as are the waiters, and especially the men and women in the audience, who begin to set down their forks and knives and rest their hands on their cocktail glasses.

Sinatra had been humbled by his bad luck. He was the scrappy underdog, the one who had been beaten down. He was like that Italian immigrant who had made it to America and found that first job, but realized he was still looked upon as the dregs of society.

But at this moment, this saloon is his. He is going to give up his heart. He is going to sing for them.

In an interview with *Metronome* magazine, he defined his style, the bel canto style of singing: "You don't have to sing loud and raucously and belt them over the head all the time. You can use a little restraint and try to create a mood that you and they can both feel sort of like being in a small room, and if you really mean it, and show that you mean it, you can register all night."

By now, his voice had taken on weight. It was fuller, and it had the hint of a rasp that would define his singing after 1954. He explored the deeper tones; the high notes were not as high.

In March, the Oscars were awarded and Sinatra won Best Supporting Actor, an accolade that solidified his reputation as an actor. That month his song "Young at Heart" hit number two—and stayed on the charts for twenty-two weeks.

Songs for Young Lovers, his first LP with Nelson Riddle, which came out in February 1954, included "My Funny Valentine," "I Get a Kick Out of You," and "They Can't Take That Away from Me."

If not the first "concept album," it was one of the most successful and enduring. The intent was to focus on a single theme—in this case, songs to which a young man might romance a woman. On the jacket cover, a hand-painted illustration (the style of which would continue through the next three Sinatra/Riddle albums) features a young couple intimately talking during an evening stroll. Sinatra, wearing a suit and his soon-to-be iconic hat, leans against a lamppost, as if setting the mood for the night. And he was also setting the mode of how records would be listened to—for *Songs for Young Lovers* would signal the transition from 45s to long-playing records.

Frank Sinatra chose the songs that he could relate to. He chose the songs that he had lived. And from the way he sang the lyric—his phrasing—it was almost as if he had written them himself.

You can hear the ease, the confidence of his mature style in "I've Got the World on a String." One of Sinatra's first collaborations with Riddle, the song was recorded in April 1953 and released that July, a month before *From Here to Eternity* appeared in movie theaters nationwide. It's a confidence born out of experience, not youthful cockiness. He's triumphant; with just a movement of his finger, he can make the rain disappear.

He has been beaten down, but now he's back up. And in his voice he's not asking for forgiveness or acceptance. He's telling you to listen to him. There are no apologies. He had hit bottom and survived. No one could tell him what to do now.

Sinatra sings the first line, holding on to the opening note for a couple of beats. The song is a celebration, yet at the same time he's singing with a wink in his eye, as if daring you to knock the string out of his hand.

"Life is a beautiful thing, as long as I hold the string," he sings, as if swooping up the girl, transporting her to exotic places. There's no wooing in his voice, just a confident swagger. His audience has changed, and so has his tone.

Sure, he's singing to the girl; but now he's singing *for* the men.

26

"Just a Gigolo"

LOUIS PRIMA

Frank Sinatra, it is said, discovered Las Vegas. But Louis Prima put the city on the map. He made the desert town a destination.

While Sinatra was enjoying a rebirth, Prima was going through a dry spell; what's more, he realized he couldn't afford to tour and pay his big jazz band anymore. In 1954 he called up Bill Miller, a friend who managed the Sahara Hotel, which had been built two years earlier. Miller said he couldn't give Prima and his band any gigs in the main showroom, but he could hire them on a trial basis for the Casbar Lounge.

When Prima and his wife, the singer Keely Smith, arrived that November, Las Vegas was booming, having grown from about sixteen thousand people in 1945 to nearly fifty thousand.

The stage of the Casbar Lounge was small, only twenty feet across with a low ceiling; and it opened up directly onto the gambling floor, where slot machines rang, croupiers called out, and patrons drank and smoked incessantly. It was not a good venue for real musicians. To make matters worse, Prima and Smith were given the desolate midnight slot.

And yet they made the stage a place of spectacle. Watching black-and-white film footage of their act, you see Prima jumping up and down and jiving with the band members, who are just as animated. The camera pans to Keely Smith, who is simply standing at the back of the stage, her face framed by a pageboy haircut; she stands so far away from them that she's almost offstage. Prima hops and skips over to her, sings a phrase or two, cuddles with her. She remains deadpan, the perfect foil for the cartoonish Prima.

"I didn't know what to do," Smith later recalled. "So I just stood there, and it worked."

Their first week in late November drew better audiences than Miller had expected, so he extended their contract through the New Year, for the same time slot. But Prima wasn't getting the sound he wanted. He needed more jump, more juice. So he immediately called a friend from New Orleans, the tenor saxophonist Sam Butera, asking him to join them on Christmas Day and to bring a couple more musicians, which at the beginning would include the trombonist Lou Sino and the drummer Paul Ferrara. Butera fused Italian melodies into his sax riffs, and they, as much as Prima's voice and trumpet, became the hallmarks of the Prima sound.

Together, Prima, Smith, Butera, and the Witnesses mixed it all up—Dixieland jazz, standards, boogie-woogie, scat-singing. The result sounded like a tarantella played by a combo on amphetamines.

"Until Prima had Sam," Smith recalled, "the group didn't really cook."

They packed the Casbar, performing five shows a night. Soon, movie stars, ballplayers, and other entertainers began dropping by. Sinatra, Dean Martin, and Sammy Davis Jr. would watch in awe. Prima was doing in Vegas what he had done on Fifty-second Street—working the post-theater shift.

The group's first LP was released in 1956: *The Wildest!* with "Just a Gigolo," "Buona Sera," "Jump, Jive, an' Wail," and "The Lip."

The record "Just a Gigolo" begins with a shuffle beat, then segues into "I Ain't Got Nobody," before the tempo gradually builds with Prima's trumpet dueling with Butera's sax. The joint was jumping, as they say. Prima named the band Sam Butera and the Witnesses, a kind of play on a Christian evangelical church assembly that has experienced God. Whatever they did, they looked as if they were having a blast. They were the original lounge act.

On "Oh, Marie," Prima and Butera engage in a call-and-response. Prima sings the lyric in English, then scats in Italian. Butera responds on his sax.

"Quando sono, c'e desa per te," sings Prima. Sammy riffs and tries to follow, riffing wildly, but can't.

"Una nota," Prima says, encouraging him, "come on, boy. Bracia te." One note—c'mon, get it.

But Butera can't get it. He gives up. Prima, laughing, now says, "What's the matter, Sam? You can't play in Italian?"

Butera was nearly two decades younger than the forty-six-year-old Prima, and with his dark curly hair and broad olive-complected face he could have been taken for Prima's son. He called Prima "chief"; Prima called him "boy."

Like most people under forty-five, I first encountered Louis Prima through *The Jungle Book*. The movie came out in 1967, the year I was born, but I first saw it when I was seven years old. Prima did the voice for King Louie the Orangutan, and the orangutan's "I Wan'na Be Like You" was the catchiest song of the whole movie. Prima as King Louis sings: "Now I'm the king of the swingers, oh, the jungle VIP." He's almost reached the top of the primate order, but now he wants to be a man. Prima continues to scat, "Oobeedo, I wanna be like you-u-u."

Prima's voice was rough and powerful, yet fun.

Thirty years later, I had planned a trip to Las Vegas to meet a friend to celebrate his upcoming wedding. I figured I would visit the Sahara Hotel while I was there, and when I realized that Sam Butera still lived in Vegas, I thought I'd try to contact him. I managed to get his home number through friends of friends.

I was told that whoever had worked for Prima was going to be tough. Prima ran his band strictly, controlling everything, every note; everything was rehearsed and rehearsed. He even controlled the lighting onstage, subtly signaling with his hands to the lighting guy.

I called around five o'clock in the afternoon. I introduced myself and asked if we could meet when I came to town.

"Boy, whatcha doing calling me so late; it's my bath time," he said gruffly. He had a thick New Orleans accent and spoke in cool-cat jazz-speak.

I apologized and offered to call him earlier the next day, say 3:00 p.m.?

"Boy, that's when I eat dinner!" Butera seemed nothing like the playful saxophonist I had recalled from videos and CDs. But he did agree to meet me in person when I came to Vegas and told me to give him a call.

I stayed at the Flamingo, built by Bugsy Siegel in 1946 and now one of the last of the original hotels standing. I walked up the Strip to the Sahara to see if any of that Prima energy still existed. I worked my way through the maze of interconnecting casinos, filled with cigarette smoke and sanitizer, which was meant to mask the smoke odor but instead smelled like cheap perfume.

I didn't get far, so I decided to take the Monorail, which connected the rear entrances of several hotels along the Strip, up to the Sahara Hotel to find the spot where the Casbar Lounge had originally stood (it had moved due to hotel renovations over the decades). I walked inside the hotel and asked some of the dealers, but no one could tell me. I walked all the way to the far north end of the Sahara, which was becoming less and less populated. Ready to give up, I sat at an empty bar and ordered a drink.

I asked the bartender about the Casbar Lounge. He was my age, and at the question his face brightened. He had grown up in Vegas, he told me. He was the only one I'd spoken to at the Sahara who had even heard of Louis Prima.

"Right there, behind you," he said. "It's not exactly as it was, though it's been pretty much replicated."

I turned around to see it. The stage was even smaller than I had imagined, and the seats were pushed incredibly close together. I could see Prima and Butera and the Witnesses jumping about, and I could understand how the energy emanating from such a tight space would become infectious, stirring the crowd to get up and move.

I left the Sahara and headed down the Strip back to the Flamingo. I ducked into a couple of places, hoping to give Sam Butera a call to set up a time to get together. But there was not a single place on the Strip where music wasn't playing or slot machine bells ringing, drowning out my mobile phone. Even outside, hotels pumped music to their outdoor cafés. The quietest place was on a traffic island in the middle of the Strip. The afternoon heat beat down.

"Hello, Mr. Butera?" I said, and asked when we could get together.

"Not now, boy, I got work to do," he said. "I gotta water my lawn."

I suggested another time.

"No, man, let's do this thing now," he said. Here I was in the middle of the Las Vegas Strip, on a cell phone, suffocating in the dry desert heat, with no recorder, no chair. Luckily, I had brought a notepad and pen. So I knelt down and took notes.

I asked him who influenced him musically. He muttered something I couldn't understand, then, for some reason, changed the conversation to memories of the Cajun food his housekeeper had cooked when he was growing up. Hoping to follow up recollections on food, I asked him about what food his mom might have cooked.

"Why you askin' me that, man?"

I quickly changed my line of questioning again: "So what was it like growing up Italian in New Orleans?"

"Eye-talian? Who you calling Eye-talian, boy?!" he shouted. My heart stopped. I thought for a moment about how Prima had always been mistaken for being black. Perhaps, I thought, Butera wasn't actually Italian but black, and had passed as Italian all those forty years because he looked like Prima.

"I ain't no Eye-talian," he said. "I'm Sicilian."

27

"Innamorata"

JERRY VALE

It's the famous shot from *Goodfellas*—the camera enters the back door of a nightclub and goes through a commercial kitchen, working its way past the hot table, the ovens, the bar station, and through swinging doors into the plush, velvety red-walled interior of the Copacabana. Couples are seated at lamp-topped round tables, each only inches from the next table. The mobsters of the movie sit with their girlfriends at the front table drinking (this is Friday night, after all; their wives are at home). You see the back of a white-haired singer in a tux. He sings in a tenor that often reaches F-sharp above middle C, delivering a ballad full of heartache and lamentation, telling himself, "Pretend you don't need her, my heart, but smile and pretend to be gay."

The song is framed by the Italian attitude—never let people know they've got you down. But this singer can't do it. His heart is broken, and he's going to tell the world. He encourages himself to lift his chin up if the "tears start to fall." But his voice tells you that he's already past that point; the only thing he can do is to look somewhere above her, trying to convince himself that he doesn't love her, and in fact he doesn't even see her.

I first heard Jerry Vale sing live several years ago at a banquet hall in Bensonhurst. It wasn't quite the Copa, but once inside you felt the grandness of the place—water fountain, gold chandeliers, white Roman columns.

Together with two friends, I sat down at a communal table, where we were served a five-course Italian meal, along with endless carafes of cheap Chianti that tasted better as the evening went on.

When Vale took the stage, women squealed as their husbands heartily applauded. People set aside their ziti and chicken parmigiana to turn their attention to the stage.

His thick white hair is one of the first things you notice. It had started going gray by his late twenties, and it lent him the nickname the Silver Fox. He responded to song requests from the audience. Sitting at our table were two sisters in their late fifties who grabbed each other's hand and made their way to the dance floor; their husbands sat back and drank wine, each with a cigarette in hand.

Vale sang a classic Italian song called "Mala femmina" (Evil Woman); one verse he sang repeated in Neapolitan, Calabrian, and Sicilian dialects. Each verse was met with cheers by those who spoke the dialect.

He sang his signature song, "Innamorata" (Sweetheart), from the 1955 film *Artists and Models*, starring Dean Martin (who sang the song in the film) and Jerry Lewis. Released in March 1956, it was Vale's biggest hit.

Vale delivered his Italian songs in pure Neapolitan fashion, with trills and frills: "If our lips should meet, innamorata, kiss me, kiss me, sweet innamorata," turning over the second-to-last syllable of the song title. On high notes he modulated his voice, bending and warbling.

———

For Neapolitans, the number of times a singer can turn on a note is a sign of athleticism and virility.

At this time another American-born singer, Jimmy Roselli, was singing real Neapolitan saloon songs in nightclubs attended by Italian Americans. He sang in their language; he brought them back to the Old Country.

People in the audience—who lived for the most part within the tristate area of New York, New Jersey, and Connecticut—would cheer Roselli on to turn the note over. He seemed to perform vocal acrobatics—something particular to Neapolitan singing, which is almost like watching an athlete perform an amazing feat. At the opera, when the tenor or soprano holds the note endlessly, the audience holds its breath. But the Neapolitans, in their street style, added to this feat an elongated trill between two adjacent notes.

Jimmy Roselli was born in Hoboken in December 1925, ten years after (almost to the day) Frank Sinatra, and he was often referred to as "the other singer from Hoboken." He was born to Phil Roselli, whose parents came from outside of Naples, and Anna Bernadette Lavella, who came from Avellino, between Rome and Naples. The newborn was affectionately called Mickey.

Within days of his birth, his mother died, and after a time his father, a fighter who boxed under the name Fighting Phil, left the young Mickey in the care of his father, Michael, a longshoreman, who made his own wine and bread and would speak to Mickey in Neapolitan.

By age eight, Jimmy was singing at church Mass and shining shoes to make a buck. Within a couple of years, he moved his shoeshine business into the saloons. He soon realized that if he sang some of those old Neapolitan songs, his tips would double. The sentiment of this ten-year-old boy hit the rough longshoremen in the heart.

When he was thirteen, he won first prize on *Major Bowes' Original Amateur Hour*. At fourteen years old, he took a job at the Club Rhumba in Keansburg, New Jersey. For years, he toiled in various jobs—as a restaurant manager, a construction worker, and a bookmaker—while landing minor singing gigs. For Roselli, it wouldn't be until 1965—when he was nearly forty years old—that he got his first big break.

That year, he recorded an album for United Artists records, and the title song from that record was "Mala femmena," which reached number 43 on the *Billboard* easy-listening charts. But it's another one of his Italian songs—"Innamorata," released a couple years later—that grabs me.

"If our lips should meet, innamorata," Roselli sings, ahead of the beat. The key modulates and the orchestra builds in swirls, and just as it reaches its pinnacle, with violin flourishes, Roselli switches to Italian. His singing is pure testosterone; he barely checks the power. One more modulation, and Roselli reaches even higher; his voice breaks at one point, sounding like the clown's cry from *Pagliacci*. On the final word, "innamorata," he turns the note over again, and again.

In complete opposite form, Dean Martin, in his 1956 recording, sounds as if he's lounging back on a sofa, singing, "Kiss me, kiss me, sweet innamorata." It's like he's beckoning her to the couch. Martin is having fun.

Meanwhile, Jerry Vale's arrangement features sweet violins and a full chorus. His singing is direct, almost triumphant, utilizing a vibrato that is wide, consistent, and warm.

Nearly a decade after that performance at the banquet hall in Brooklyn, I met Vale at his home in Palm Desert, California, with his wife, Rita.

At age seventy-four, he had a handsome pear-shaped face, with cheeks that pushed up when he smiled. There was something about Vale, his posture, his smile, that said this man is a nice guy—very much like his idol Perry Como.

His clothes and full head of hair reminded me a bit of my father, as did his and Rita's taste in furniture—all contemporary and light-colored.

Rita served sushi, out of concern for her husband, who had suffered a heart attack the previous year, as well as a selection of Italian meats and cheeses for me, the guest. She interjected comments and witty jokes from the bar that separated the kitchen and the living room. We spoke throughout the afternoon.

"I'm just a singer," he said. "It's a job."

"Seriously, Jerry?" Rita said. "You are one of the great singers."

Vale took me into his den to show me his records and the various photographs of friends. As he pointed, I noticed a pinkie ring on his hand and a gold bracelet dangling from his wrist. In his mind he was just doing his job by singing. But it was a job he did well.

Jerry Vale was a link between opera, Italian popular song, and American pop standard. He was born in 1932 in the northeast corner of the Bronx, a part of the borough, with tree-lined streets, that can feel more suburban than urban. Until his voice teacher changed his name in his teens, he was Genaro Louis Vitaliano. His mother and father, Fanny and Louis, had parents who had emigrated from Naples and Calabria. They called their son, simply, Sonny.

Like so many of the crooners before him, he first sang at church and at parties. While in high school, he got a part-time job at the local barbershops, where he would sweep the floor and shine shoes for customers, singing as he did so. Then he went to work with his father, oiling the steam shovel that his father maneuvered through the streets, digging up the surface for repairs.

Meanwhile, he did the small dinner theater and nightclub circuit, until, in 1952, at the urging of the singer Guy Mitchell, he auditioned for and got a contract with Mitch Miller at Columbia Records. His first records, "And No One Knows" and "You Can Never Give Me Back My Heart," did modestly well. His first hit came two years later with "Two Purple Shadows," which reached number ten on the *Billboard* charts.

In 1956, Vale would chart again with both "You Don't Know Me," backed by Percy Faith and His Orchestra, and his first Italian hit, "Innamorata," written by Harry Warren.

The thrill of his success was tempered a few months later when the Italian ocean liner *Andrea Doria* was hit by another ship, the *Stockholm*, and sank off the coast of Nantucket, Massachusetts. Forty-six people died, including Vale's grandmother, who was returning from a visit to Italy.

After a show one day in 1958, Vale glanced down at an entertainment magazine and set his eyes on a picture of the woman who would become his wife—Rita Grapel, a Jewish girl from Brooklyn who was working as a nightclub dancer.

Vale performed all over the New York area—the San Su San club on Long Island, Paddock in the Bronx, and Ben Maksik's Town and Country in Brooklyn—then all over the country. In 1959, at last, he was invited to perform at the Copa.

There, he recalled, he sang his tearjerker "Mama," about the day he will be reunited in heaven with his mother. But no one in the audience seemed to notice or care—they continued eating and drinking.

Like Tony Bennett and Julius La Rosa, Vale admitted, "I didn't have the know-how or experience to manage myself in such a venue like the Copa. I couldn't deliver a joke or make light of situations to calm an audience or silence a heckler. I really didn't have an organized 'show,' which was necessary in order to succeed." Vale got to work on putting together his stage routine.

It was with the help of Frank Sinatra that he later landed his first gig at the Sands; and upon hearing Vale perform, the owner, Jack Entratter, told him he could extend his engagement, which he did for another twenty-two weeks.

Sinatra had given Vale a leg up, but with Dean Martin, Vale was not so lucky. In 1965, Vale had agreed to go on *The Ed Sullivan Show*, and then Dean Martin asked him to appear on his show. The problem was an exclusivity agreement Vale's manager had signed with Sullivan, stipulating that he couldn't appear on any other national TV shows within twenty-three days of Sullivan's show. The two shows were only twenty days apart. Sullivan's people wouldn't budge, and Vale decided to cancel with Sullivan and go on Martin's show—for a lower fee and paying his own travel expenses.

Vale and the orchestra rehearsed a couple of numbers, but just afterward the producer informed him that the show had gotten too long and that they would have to cut Vale's song. Vale went to Dean Martin and asked him to work it out, but Martin, who was nearly two decades older, simply replied, "Hey, kid, that's show business."

The root of Vale's appeal to his now-nostalgic audience is that he himself is drawn to songs of past decades. His biggest vocal influence was Perry Como ("I liked his easygoing style," he told me), and among the recordings that most affected him were Como's covers of Russ Columbo songs such as "Prisoner of Love."

In 1958, Vale paid homage to Columbo and Como in one stroke with *I Remember Russ*, a set of his interpretations of the songs of Russ Columbo. Vale sings in the same key as Columbo, yet unlike Columbo or Como he shoots his voice out and anticipates notes. By staying ahead of the beat, his version feels more dramatic.

More than those of many of these singers, Vale's songs—produced with sweet, sometimes saccharine orchestration—are distinctly of an era.

During my wife Martha's illness, "Innamorata" was one song that stood out for me—all three versions. But Vale's singing in particular appeals to me. While it was Sinatra who let me know it was all right to feel what I was feeling, Vale lulled me to another world, transporting me to another time.

28

"Volare"

DEAN MARTIN

In 1958, an Italian singer named Domenico Modugno, straight from Bari, Apulia, came out with "Nel blu dipinto di blu (Volare)"— which, roughly translated, means "to fly in the blue sky, painted blue." It was already a hit in Italy and Europe, and although he sang the song entirely in Italian, it landed on the U.S. pop charts at number one and floated around there for thirteen weeks.

The song starts with a twinkling of strings, before Domenico recites the poetic first verse, "Penso che un sogno così non ritorni mai più, mi dipingevo le mani e la faccia di blu." I think that a dream will never again return, I paint the hands and face blue. As he finishes the verse, a Hammond organ colors the tune as a stand-up bass provides the rhythm along with the light tap of a cymbal and a snare drum.

Never mind that only a few people can understand the Italian lyrics, obsessed *Time* magazine; no one can escape the tune, "the freshness of his singing, the unfettered freedom of his song."

For Americans, the thirty-year-old Modugno, with his dark hair and pencil-thin mustache, could have been a caricature of a baker or pizza maker.

"The swarthy, mop-headed Sicilian followed his voice to the U.S.," said the same *Time* article, not realizing he wasn't from Sicily. "And as soon as he alighted at New York's Idlewild Airport exuberantly sliding down the banister of the landing steps, Domenico treated his welcoming committee to a rendering of 'Nel Blu.' "

Kind of reminds you of the comic exuberance displayed by the Italian actor Roberto Benigni at the Academy Awards, when he jumped up from his chair and walked on the seat backs all the way to the stage to accept the Oscar for Best Actor for his film *Life Is Beautiful* (*La vita è bella*), released in the United States in 1998.

The next year, Modugno followed up "Volare" with another hit, "Piove (Ciao, ciao, bambina)"—"Cry," he sings, "bye, bye, baby." One review at the time noted that Modugno could easily maneuver between a suave Perry Como croon and a rock-and-roll beat.

Only a week after Modugno's "Volare" was released, Dean Martin, who was now forty-one years old, released his own version (which reached only as high as number twelve). Martin's Italian repertoire included "On an Evening in Roma," "Mambo Italiano," "Ritorna Me," and, of course, "Innamorata," from the film *Artists and Models*.

From 1956 to 1959 there were more Italian American singers on the *Billboard* charts than at any time before or since. Not only were they Italian Americans, but their songs were sung, if only in part, in Italian: "That's Amore," "Volare," "Mama," "Angelina," "Mala femmina," "Pepino the Italian Mouse," "Eh, Cumpari!," "Piove," "Come Prima," "Al di La," "Innamorata."

When Sinatra had his comeback in 1954, my father was fifteen. He was eager to join the service as a way to see the world, as a way to make a living, as a way to get out of Danbury. Not that Danbury was bad. It was just small, too familiar.

Danbury was a working-class city, and not to be confused with tony Greenwich or Stamford. Danbury was an ethnic melting pot.

An Anglo owned the Stetson hat company there, among others, and there were society and country clubs. But next down on the informal socioeconomic hierarchy, as my father recalls it, were the Irish— the police officers, firemen, priests, and nuns—if only because they had the benefit of speaking English. Below the Irish were the Italians, the Polish, the Lebanese, the Spanish, and the Portuguese.

There were three Catholic churches in Danbury: St. Peter's, St. Joseph's, and Sacred Heart. The Italians and Portuguese in my father's neighborhood went to the closest church, either Sacred Heart, which had a largely Polish congregation, or the largely Irish church St. Peter's. Each ethnic community had its own grocery or bar. My father remembers the Lebanese grocery store nearby called Lahoud's, as well as Catano's Portuguese bar, which was across the street from the Portuguese American Club. On the way home from the hat factory, his father might stop off at McNamara's Irish pub on Wildman Street. The one place that served pizza in Danbury was the Old Oak pizzeria on Liberty Street.

In the house my father grew up in, music was heard mostly on the Italian radio stations, usually Sundays—weekdays were for working, Saturdays were for doing chores around the house. His father played the concertina at family gatherings, and they listened to Caruso on the radio.

My father heard Italian music when they had people over for Sunday dinner and at Salerno's on White Street, a combination of Italian grocer and *salumeria*. It was here that he heard music from behind the counter on the radio while he discreetly plucked olives from wood casks. These Italian-language radio stations, airing in the urban areas of the Northeast, would play a combination of opera and popular Italian songs.

My mother, Murielle LaFontaine, born in Montreal, came from the right side of the tracks—or so her parents believed. Her father was an amateur violinist, and she recalls hearing him occasionally on the radio in Montreal. After a car accident injured her father, Hubert, preventing him from ever playing the violin, the family moved to

Danbury, where Hubert found work at an electronics factory called Doran Brothers, which employed ten other French-Canadian families. In Danbury, the LaFontaines originally moved to a two-family house on Rowan Street; their landlord was an Italian named La Rosa. My mother was reserved, blond, and blue-eyed. When my parents met, she was still at Danbury High School; my father, at age twenty-one, was just out of the Navy. They met at a record hop.

Italians from the Old Country brought with them the idea of *passa tempo*. It's the beautiful way in which Italians pass time. More than any Italian song, one, to my mind, defines *passa tempo*: "Standing on the Corner." It came from the 1956 Broadway musical *The Most Happy Fella*, composed by Frank Loesser, who also wrote the scores for *Guys and Dolls* and *How to Succeed in Business Without Really Trying*. I have never seen the musical, but based on descriptions and reviews it seems to me to be a kind of Italian *Song of the South*. In place of the happy-go-lucky, though wise, "Negro" is a happy Italian who speaks with a funny accent.

Dean Martin released a version of the song.

"Standing on the corner," Martin sang as he and his friends watched all the girls go by. "Brother, you don't know a nicer occupation." He doesn't have a girl, but, standing on Main Street, he can dream about any number of them.

In "Standing on the Corner," Martin delivers the lyric with a nudge, like the guys hanging out on the piazza at a typical pre-dinner *passeggiata*, or evening stroll, in any Italian city or village. Ogling women to pass the time was an open secret among men, a fantasy at a time when there was little time for fantasy, a moment of lightheartedness in a not-so-light workday.

The writer Nick Tosches, whose family comes from the Abruzzi and an Albanian enclave in Apulia, characterized Dean Martin as a *menefreghista*, someone who doesn't give a damn. He described Martin's singing style and delivery as *lontano*, that is, distant or aloof.

These insights are apt. Jeanne, Martin's second wife, once said, "I didn't know Dean very well before I married him. And after twenty-four years of marriage, I didn't know him any better." She once said that "between women and playing golf, Dean would probably choose golf."

29

"Mama"

CONNIE FRANCIS

Connie Francis was eighteen years old when she first met nineteen-year-old Bobby Darin at the office of her manager, George Scheck, at 1697 Broadway. She knew that he was playing bongos at the time for a Spanish snake dancer, an older woman, and was probably involved with her.

Francis was a daddy's girl born in Newark, New Jersey, and Darin was a rough, opinionated kid from the Bronx. But she was intrigued; they were, after all, both singers, both ambitious, and both Italian. For his part Darin saw Francis as a girl he could impress.

At first Darin accosted Francis with insults. When he learned that Francis lived in Belleville, New Jersey, Darin, who could often be cantankerous, responded: "Belleville, huh? Don't you mean Squaresville?" He talked in hipster-speak, which to Francis seemed like an entirely different language. Eventually he softened and began to woo her, becoming protective of her. He told his friends, Francis recalled in her book, that she wasn't like the other girls: "It's not that she's not smart—she's easily shocked."

It was 1956, and already the lingo had started to change. Kids were referring to others as "hip" or "square."

"Girls tossed off their bobby socks for Capri pants," Connie Francis said to me on the telephone.

Fifty years later, she still sounds sweet and still has a little-girl voice, which can be disarming as she reels off dates and accurately sums up the rock-and-roll scene of half a century ago. In ways, she's like the smart girl in high school who is afraid that her intelligence might intimidate boys—and therefore plays up a cute flirtatiousness.

Francis's father, George Franconero, who worked shoveling coal on barges (he was hired only after adopting the Irish name Frank Connors), oversaw every aspect of her life—what she ate, what songs she would sing, the boys she would date, or would not be allowed to date, which was almost everyone. She went along with this, ever the good daughter.

Bobby Darin, who had written several songs and had been shopping them to various singers, was looking for a manager. Don Kirshner, Darin's classmate from the Bronx High School of Science—who was also working as a songwriter (and would later become a music producer)—introduced his friend to George Scheck, who took Darin on. Upon hearing Darin's song "My First Real Love," he introduced him to Connie. She loved the song, and recorded it.

The song didn't go anywhere, but while they were working on it together, the two fell in love. Darin would take a bus out to the Franconero house on Greylock Parkway and Forest Street in Belleville, to hang out. Darin's interest was obvious, and when George Franconero saw that Connie's was too, he became determined to split up the two—no one was going to get in the way of his daughter's success. He convinced George Scheck to drop Bobby Darin. Scheck was resistant, but Connie was on the verge of becoming a hit, and he wanted to keep her father happy.

Several months later, Francis was taping an appearance on *The Jackie Gleason Show* at the CBS studios. Darin decided to attend the rehearsal, and when they saw each other backstage, they embraced like reunited lovers. Francis's father, who always kept her in sight, saw them. While his daughter rehearsed, George Franconero, to everyone's surprise, went after Darin with a gun, chasing him out of the studio.

Francis was born in 1938 in her maternal grandparents' house in the Ironbound section of Newark, one of the city's Little Italys before Portuguese immigrants began settling there in the 1950s. Her paternal grandparents had emigrated from Reggio Calabria and Naples in 1905, and had originally lived on a farm on land that now lies beneath Newark Airport. Her maternal grandparents emigrated the same year, but from a town outside Naples.

At the time she was born, her parents were living in Red Hook, Brooklyn, where her father was working on the shipping docks (her mother happened to be visiting her parents in Newark when she delivered). Her father and paternal grandfather played the concertina, and Connie herself studied accordion. Francis ruminates in her autobiography, *Who's Sorry Now?*: "Sometimes I think my father wanted me to be an accordion player so much because it was second only to the bassoon as the most asexual instrument ever known to man."

The family moved to Belleville, where she attended high school and sang along with Perry Como's "Prisoner of Love" as well as Frankie Laine's "That's My Desire," which were hits at the time.

Her father was very focused on the life he had planned for his daughter. She wasn't going to be a wife and spend her life cooking and cleaning. She was going to sing professionally and make money.

"Don't try to act sexy," he warned her. "Because you will turn off all the girls, and they're the ones who go to concerts and buy records."

Barely thirteen, Concetta Franconero auditioned for and won an appearance on *Arthur Godfrey's Talent Scouts*, and it was Godfrey who suggested she change her name. At age sixteen, she graduated early from Belleville High School, landed a recording contract with MGM, and was accepted on scholarship to New York University. But by then her singing career had started taking hold.

There weren't many women rock-and-roll singers at the time from whom she could draw influence, but she lists Kay Starr, Jo Stafford, and the fellow Italian American Joni James ("She had a beautiful voice," Francis recalls, "young and sincere").

In 1958, Connie would appear on a show broadcast from Philadelphia, Dick Clark's *American Bandstand*—which sought to be the rock-and-roll equivalent of *Arthur Godfrey's Talent Scouts*. With her thick dark hair, and dark, thickly penciled arched eyebrows, she looked, at different moments, like a pretty teenage girl on her way to a prom and an adoring wife ready to greet her husband at the door.

The song she sang was "Who's Sorry Now?" On the record, which came out that same year, she has a sweet, gentle voice that breaks at certain notes, making it sound as if she's sobbing—even in a song that would be one of her more up-tempo numbers, a song about getting even with a boyfriend who broke her heart (songs of *dispetto*). "Who's sad and blue, who's crying too? Just like I cried over you."

Dick Clark would later introduce her as the girl with the "million-dollar cry."

"The fact that a girl would sing rock and roll then was outrageous," Francis told me. She seems very well aware of her place in music history, and is able to take a step back and look objectively.

Francis was the first woman to have two consecutive number one hits, "Everybody's Somebody's Fool" and "My Heart has a Mind of Its Own," both in 1960. She was also the first woman in five years to hit the Top 10 pop charts. In her voice you hear an Italian city girl from Newark singing in a southern-accented whimper.

She's that quintessential girl from 1958. The one every father loved, the daughter every mother wished she had. She was the girl her girlfriends could talk to; she was the girl you wanted to marry, not just make out with. I wonder how difficult it must have been for her to live up to all that.

She benefited from both talent discoverers—Arthur Godfrey and Dick Clark. Suddenly Godfrey was old (and his singers were the singers your parents listened to). Dick Clark was for your generation.

For the next four years, teenagers would dance to Connie Francis's powerful though childlike voice. She would follow up "Who's Sorry Now?" with "My Happiness," "Lipstick on Your Collar," "Among My Souvenirs," "Mama," "Everybody's Somebody's Fool," and "My Heart Has a Mind of Its Own"—all Top 10 hits.

One of her biggest recordings was the title song of the movie *Where the Boys Are*, composed by her friend Neil Sedaka—who as a teenager had hung out at her house and who was now becoming an accomplished songwriter, known for the Brill Building sound.

"Where the boys are," Francis sings slowly over a bed of steady triplets. The song has a slow doo-wop rhythm. Wherever they are, someone's waiting for her. And when she sings the final verse of "Till he holds me, I'll wait impatiently," her voice cracks on the word "holds," making you want to rush and hold her before she collapses from heartbreak.

In 1959, Connie Francis's father urged her to record an entire album in Italian.

Francis expressed to her father her reluctance to sing so many old-time songs—in Italian no less.

Francis described his response: "Look, stupid, there are thirty-five million Italian Americans in this country. They will buy your record."

She recorded the album in London with a seventy-two-piece orchestra led by Tony Osborne.

"No pop singer had ever recorded an entire Italian album at that point," Francis explained. Of course, Jerry Vale and Dean Martin had put out singles, as had Rosemary Clooney. And Francis's song selection was inspired by the guitarist, bandleader, and singer Phil Brito's 1946 album, *Phil Brito Sings Songs of Italy*—the same record from which Dean Martin had gathered his Italian material a decade earlier.

Francis's album features a song that would become one of her best-known numbers, one that still tugs at the heartstrings of every Italian of a certain generation. "Mama" was released in 1960; the English lyrics were written by Phil Brito. In English, then in Italian, Connie Francis sings, with her angelic girl's voice, to a mother who has died. Nothing, for Francis, could replace the warmth of her mother's embrace. She then sings two verses in Italian.

The song was full of yearning as she sobs, "I'll live in these memories until the day that we're together once more."

Francis had a wide cross-cultural appeal, but her Italian album became a bestseller because Italian Americans had become a consumer force in their own right.

30

"*Dream Lover*"

BOBBY DARIN

"Splish, splash, I was taking a bath," Bobby Darin sings on *American Bandstand*.

The cameras follow as Darin, dressed in a slick sharkskin suit, walks down a flight of stairs alongside the audience to the stage. And like Connie Francis with her country-influenced singing style, the Bronx-born Darin cops a Jerry Lee Lewis southern accent. At one point, as Darin sings "we was a rollin' and a strollin'," you feel as if he could just as easily yell out, "Great balls of fire!" After all, rock and roll was still a southern thing; Elvis, the Big Bopper, and all those early rock and rollers were from U.S. states far south of the Bronx and Philadelphia.

Darin snaps his fingers and walks as if gliding across the stage. At one point he lets loose some fancy footwork, a little side-to-side jig with a 360-degree turn. His hands, though, sway, palms down, on either side of his waist—he strikes a saloon-singer pose.

"Splish Splash" was his first hit—just three months after his ex-girlfriend appeared on Dick Clark's *American Bandstand*—which he wrote on a bet with Don Kirshner.

Darin was twenty-two years old, but with his prematurely receding hairline he looked easily a decade older. Like Connie Francis, he could look like a kid one moment and a worldly young adult the next. With his puffy eyes, big nose, and narrow mouth and chin, he wasn't great-looking, but he more than made up for it with confidence and charisma.

A baritone sax honks while a solo high-hat and piano kick out the R&B beat, but Darin swings and sashays, snapping his fingers as if Dick Clark's stage were a nightclub.

Darin recorded "Splish Splash" for an Atlantic Records subsidiary called Atco. He was one of the first white singers to be signed by Atlantic Records, then known as an R&B label. One of the founders was the Turkish-born Ahmet Ertegun, who had been having great success with Ray Charles. Darin had just appeared on Alan Freed's rock show at the Apollo Theater in Harlem and on his program *The Big Beat*.

His next hit was a rock-and-roll song called "Queen of the Hop." Here was Darin, on a black label, singing rock and roll that was more rhythm-and-bluesy than even Chuck Berry's. But although he was singing rock and roll, from the music he had listened to as a kid— Sinatra, Crosby, Durante—Darin knew he wanted to croon. He knew he wanted to swing. And soon he would.

Bobby Darin was born in 1936 in Bellevue Hospital in Manhattan. He was named Walden Robert Cassotto. He was raised by his grandmother Polly, whom he believed to be his mother; the woman he thought of as his sister, Nina, was actually his mother. (Their true relationships wouldn't be revealed to Bobby until he was in his mid-thirties.)

His grandmother—Vivian Fern Walden, or Polly—was a former vaudeville singer who married Saverio Cassotto, an immigrant who worked—it is said—for Frank Costello, the American head of the Luciano crime family. He was known as Big Sam Curly. They had a daughter they named Vanina Juliette Cassotto, or Nina. Frank

204 **The Italian Decade, the 1950s**

Costello and his wife were witnesses to Sam and Polly's wedding in 1912. When Prohibition went into effect in 1920, Sam began running rum from Canada for Costello.

The facts are hazy, but in 1934 Big Sam Curly was arrested for picking pockets, convicted, and sent to Sing Sing prison, where, shortly after his arrival, he died of pneumonia. Years later Darin would perform at the Copa, the bar owned by the man for whom his grandfather had worked.

The year Sam died, Nina, at age seventeen, began dating a young man who she said was a college student, and became pregnant. She desperately wanted to keep the baby, but Polly was worried about her daughter's reputation. Because Nina was overweight, she was able to hide the pregnancy, so Polly moved them from East 117th Street—Italian Harlem—to 125th Street, where they knew no one. They lived there for a while after Nina had the baby. To protect Nina, Polly, who was in her early forties, took on the baby as her own.

The next year Nina met a truck driver named Charlie Maffia, who eventually moved into the house. Shortly thereafter they moved to a poor part of the Bronx as far south as Jerry Vale's neighborhood was north: East 135th Street, below what is now Interstate 87 across from the Harlem River.

Bobby had been born with a weak heart. Doctors didn't think he would live. Even when he survived, the doctors continued to be doubtful about his prognosis. The entire family doted on him, giving him everything he needed, spending extra for hospital care. In this poor Italian family living on welfare in the Bronx, he was treated like a prince.

Bobby grew up in a house run by his Irish-German grandmother and his own mother, who was half Italian. This meant that Darin was one-quarter Italian (three-quarters or half if that college student happened to have Italian ancestors), but he identified solely with his Italian heritage, if only because of his last name. On one occasion he told Connie Francis, "Someday we'll be the Italian Nelson Eddy and Jeannette McDonald." (I myself am half French Canadian, and my wife, who is of Dutch-English extraction, often joked that when we had children, they would only be a quarter Italian, but would consider themselves full-blooded Italians.)

Darin possessed an IQ of 137 and attended the prestigious Bronx High School of Science; upon graduation, he received a scholarship to Hunter College, a competitive public college in Manhattan, but dropped out after a year. His desire to sing was strong, and college would only get in the way. He had been singing in small nightclubs as well as in resorts in the Catskills, but Darin felt destined for greatness. To get there, he felt he had to change his last name. One story is that he picked the name Darin by thumbing through a phone book. Another is that he took it one night while walking past a Chinese restaurant sign that advertised "Mandarin"-style cooking, but with the first three letters of the neon sign blacked out. However he came up with it, Bobby Cassotto took the American-sounding Darin as his last name.

It was in the Atlantic Records studio, located above Patsy's Italian restaurant on West Fifty-sixth Street, close to Carnegie Hall, that Bobby Darin would solidify his status with another song he wrote, "Dream Lover."

It's got a rock beat, with girl backup singers, but it moves at a slower pace—more of a rock ballad. Bobby Darin was a singer in constant flux, and "Dream Lover" would be his bridge between rock and roll and saloon croon.

One day he passed the Copacabana in midtown and saw on the marquee that his idol Frank Sinatra was performing. "One day, I'm going to sing here," Darin told Francis. It was a sentiment similar to Frank Sinatra whispering in Nancy's ear that he wanted to be onstage like Bing Crosby.

But before the Copa, Darin performed at various record hops with other young rock and rollers such as Buddy Holly, Ritchie Valens, and Dion and the Belmonts, as well as a group of Italian boys coming off the streets of Philadelphia and onto the stage of *American Bandstand*, singing teenybop rock and roll—Fabian, Frankie Avalon, and Bobby Rydell.

31

"Lightnin' Strikes"

LOU CHRISTIE

The song "Lightnin' Strikes" didn't actually come out until 1966, and Lou Christie was one of the last of a group of Italian American singers managed by Bob Marcucci—a list that included Frankie Avalon and Fabian.

In 1959, the music scene changed—a culmination of events of the previous two years. It is said that 1959 was the year the music died (as Don McLean sang in "American Pie"). Buddy Holly, Ritchie Valens, and the Big Bopper died when their private plane crashed in an Iowa cornfield; Chuck Berry was jailed for violation of the Mann Act—transporting a minor across state lines for illicit purposes (in this case it was a fourteen-year-old coat-check girl at a club he owned); Jerry Lee Lewis shocked his fans when he married a thirteen-year-old cousin, a fact that became public in 1958; Little Richard saw the Lord in 1957, became convinced that rock and roll was evil and, after releasing his last rock album in 1959, began singing only gospel; and Elvis Presley, drafted into the Army in 1958 and serving in Germany, had his last "rock" record released in 1959.

There was one more significant factor: Alan Freed—the man

who coined the term "rock and roll" and promoted many black artists in his various concerts and his radio shows—was sued for participating in payola, that is, playing songs on the air because their promoters had paid him to do so. Freed's show was canceled from WINS radio.

Taking his place as the rock-and-roll promoter was Dick Clark with his *American Bandstand*. The show was based in Philadelphia, and many of the artists he featured came from the area. (Clark, who was a shareholder in a record distribution company, was investigated for payola but not charged. He divested himself from the company.)

Many of the show's "white" performers were Italian—dark enough to be edgy and "different" to white viewers, though white enough to be nonthreatening. And one man responsible for bringing several of these kids to the public eye was a Philadelphia music promoter named Bob Marcucci, on whom the movie *The Idolmaker* was based. In fact, many of the audience members were themselves of Italian descent.

"He wanted us all in the Italian mold," said Lou Christie of the manager who had "discovered" the new sound coming from Philadelphia: Fabian and Frankie Avalon.

"He wanted an Italian look—the shirt unbuttoned, the collar pulled up. Dark, sexy, good-looking boys."

I was sitting with Lou Christie in the dining room of his Manhattan duplex. He had cooked a *pasta con le sarde*, with sardines, pine nuts, fennel, and raisins—a traditional Sicilian dish—and we drank a deep red Italian wine from Calabria that I had brought.

Frankie Avalon—the eighteen-year-old Philadelphia-born Francis Avallone—landed on the charts in January 1958 with "De De Dinah" and a few months later with "A Boy Without a Girl" and "Bobby Sox to Stockings." His biggest hit, the next year, was "Venus."

Fabiano Forte—Fabian—sang "Turn Me Loose," "Tiger," and "Hound Dog Man," the last an obvious play on Elvis's hit. Bob Marcucci discovered him, at the suggestion of Frankie Avalon, outside

Fabiano Forte's house. Fabian's father had suffered a stroke, and the teen was sitting on the front steps, crying, just after the ambulance had taken him away.

One other singer from Philadelphia, though not managed by Marcucci, was eighteen-year-old Robert Ridarelli, whose light brown, almost blond, hair crowned his head in a pompadour. Bobby Rydell had hits with "We Got Love," followed by "Wild One" in 1960, as well as a version of "Volare."

Fabian was the teen idol; Frankie Avalon had the charming personality that translated well to film: notably, the various beach party movies that paired him with Annette Funicello, once a Mouseketeer. Rydell was the only one who was a trained musician and singer. After his hits "Wild One" and "Sway," he appeared in the 1963 movie *Bye Bye Birdie*, co-starring with the sexy twenty-two-year-old redhead Ann-Margret.

They all came from the old South Philadelphia neighborhood that had given birth to Mario Lanza, Al Martino, and Buddy Greco.

A few years ago, I tried getting in touch with Dion. I tracked down his manager, Dick Fox, and called him, thinking Dion would be happy to talk with me.

I quickly learned that Dick Fox was an old-style, hard-edged manager.

"So you want to talk with Dion about your book?"

"That'd be great," I said.

"How much do you plan to pay him?"

"Pay him?"

"Yeah. I mean, he's giving you his life story. He should get something in return, don't you think?"

When I explained that I didn't plan to pay, he said, "Then you don't get to talk to Dion. And you also don't get to talk to Fabian, Bobby Rydell, Frankie Avalon, or Lou Christie, because I manage them all."

I nevertheless left my number, should he change his mind. Was it all about the money? I wondered if it was instead a strategy, a way to protect his artists from getting hounded.

I had tried for years to get in touch with Tony Bennett, but after I spoke with his publicist, she told me that Bennett is careful not to speak with anyone who might try to tarnish his reputation—and that of Italian Americans—by connecting him with the Mafia. Bennett was also particular about the reputation of Frank Sinatra, and worried that someone would sully his name. Bennett's manager was his son, Danny, and his organization was very protective of him—like a tight Italian family, mistrustful of outsiders.

A couple of months after being rebuffed by Dick Fox, I got a message on my answering machine.

"Hello, Mark, this is Lou Christie. I just read your book, *Stolen Figs*, and I absolutely loved it. I am Calabrese, too, from a village close to your family's."

He was calling from an airport and left a number where I could reach him.

I called him right back. I learned that he had no idea I had tried contacting him through Dick Fox. It was by chance that he had read the book I had written, about taking my father back to Italy and exploring Calabria both on my own and with him. He invited me to his apartment for dinner.

During that dinner of pasta and sardines and Calabrese red wine, he told me how he went from being Lugee Alfredo Giovanni Sacco of Glenwillard, a suburb northwest of Pittsburgh on the Ohio River, to being the teen idol Lou Christie.

In person, Lou Christie, now in his mid-sixties, is tall and solidly built, good-looking with brooding, heavy-lidded eyes. Even when dressed casually, he still favors shirts with high starched collars, unbuttoned to mid-chest. He's theatrical when he talks, conveying a range of emotions with his hands.

He cut a record in Pittsburgh in 1962, on the C&C label, and the A-side featured a song he co-wrote (with his longtime collaborator

Twyla Herbert) called "The Gypsy Cried." The name on the record, he discovered to his surprise when the first pressing arrived, was Lou Christie. It reached number twenty-four in January 1963.

"I was so angry that they had changed my name without telling me," Christie said. "I wanted to have a one-word name—Lugee. Like Dion, like Fabian." He then admitted that his father didn't mind the name he ended up with because it had "Christ" in it.

Christie sang in a falsetto, which would become his signature sound (and would often get him confused with Frankie Valli of the Four Seasons).

"My father wanted me to sing like Perry Como or Nat 'King' Cole," Christie said. "I decided to sing that song in falsetto to get the DJs' attention—knowing that a record's fate is determined in the first fifteen seconds."

The falsetto worked for Christie, so he used the same technique with his next single called "Two Faces Have I," which was released two months later and reached number six on the charts.

Christie proudly told me that he co-wrote all his songs—unlike most of the other teen-idol singers. And he's retained (or at least bought back) the rights to all of them.

His biggest hit came in 1966: "Lightnin' Strikes." The song went to number one at a time when the English bands—the Beatles, the Rolling Stones, the Animals—were dominating the pop charts.

The song is almost three songs in one, with each section in a different key. It goes from a happy E-flat major, to C major, to F minor. Depending on how you look at it, it's either wacky or sophisticated. No matter what, it was genius. Christie had definitely tapped into the energy of the moment—that of Motown, for instance—with women backup singers with a Ronettes or Supremes sound. It was arranged by Charles Calello, a onetime member of the Four Seasons.

"When I see lips beggin' to be kissed," Christie sings. He can't stop, he can't stop himself. The rhythm marches inexorably toward misbehavior. "Lightnin' striking again," he sings, his voice rising to a falsetto.

Just after the song made the charts, Christie, following his teenage dream, hired Bob Marcucci to manage him and moved to Los Angeles.

After Christie and I had finished dinner and emptied the bottle of wine, I told him about my conversation with his current manager, Dick Fox.

Lou smiled. "I know! Isn't he great?"

"Great?"

"Singers are drained, psychologically," Christie explained. "Hardly any of us do interviews anymore, because people always want to go back and have you answer the same questions you've been asked for the past forty years."

32

"I Wonder Why"

DION AND THE BELMONTS

The bass line that seems to come out of Carlo Mastrangelo's nose—
"dun dun dun, duh-dun dun-duh dun"—feels like the revving pulse
of a very loud, very powerful Corvette. Then Freddie Milano, Angelo D'Aleo, and Dion DiMucci pick up the harmonization, singing
in falsettos each word, "know—why—I," then all three join for "love
you like I do."

They harmonize one more verse, just in case they didn't get your
attention. Then the lyrical tenor lead voice of Dion floats over the
top of the rhythm.

"I had never heard that before," remembered "Cousin Brucie"
Morrow, who was a disc jockey of Top 40 music at WINS in 1959
(after Freed's show was canceled) and who promoted and emceed
many live shows for vocal harmony groups. "That sound was so raw,
so edgy. That sound marked the beginning of Italian—or white—
doo-wop."

The Laurie label released that Dion and the Belmonts record in
1958, the year my father, at twenty-one (a year older than Dion),
would cruise with his friends in Danbury, Connecticut, stopping off

for a bite to eat at the Sycamore Diner, a carhop restaurant that still hosts vintage-car shows yearly.

I remember a picture from the 1950s of my father and his brothers Frank and Tom. They are wearing white T-shirts with chinos, and their hair is slicked back in pompadours. Out of my uncle Frank's mouth dangles a cigarette, most likely taken from the package rolled up in my father's left sleeve. My uncle Tom's obsession with cars would begin at this time—he was a Chevrolet man. His car was the 1957 Chevy, painted pearl blue with white insets and whitewall tires. Later, in the 1960s, he would drag race a 1956 Corvette he had painted yellow with black details and named the Stinger. He had sponsorship from oil companies, and on the side, below the car's name, was painted "The Rotella Brothers."

Drag racing is the urban equivalent of stock-car racing. While stock-car racing came from bootleggers trying to outrun police over long distances on rural southern roads, the thrill of drag racing basically lasted the length of a city block from one light to another (or drivers would perhaps race on a less traveled road, though still for only a short distance). The Rotella brothers cruised the strip, through Danbury and Bethel, until they ended up at the Sycamore. I can picture them in movies such as James Dean's *Rebel Without a Cause* and Marlon Brando's *The Wild One*. Boys dressed in chinos and loafers with a button-down short-sleeve shirt, the shirt opened to the third button. Or wearing jeans rolled up around black boots and white T-shirts. Whether the shirts were T's or button-downs, the sleeves were rolled up. Hair slicked back in a confident DA, just so, like a cock strutting his stuff.

The girls would have been dressed in pleated skirts and white socks. Tight blouses covered bras formed in perfectly circular, cone-shaped cups—sleek and a bit severe, like the bullet-shaped tail fins of the Cadillacs or Chevys.

Everything is fast, served to your convenience—malt shops, TV dinners, and drive-in restaurants where the girl carhops ride roller skates.

The term "doo-wop" did not come into use until the late 1960s or early 1970s. No one knows for certain where it came from, but credit is often given to a music producer named Richard Nader. Until then, the music was simply referred to as vocal harmony or rock and roll. In effect, it was vocal harmonies based on rhythm and blues and gospel. It was the urban rock-and-roll cousin of rockabilly. Kids and teenagers would escape their cramped apartment buildings and tenements and housing projects and go to the streets where, under a streetlamp, in a vestibule, or in a subway station, they harmonized, even competing with one another—a kind of one-upmanship. It was the music of poor kids—after all, they didn't have to save up to buy instruments.

The first doo-wop group was the Ravens, four African Americans from Harlem. Before them, groups such as the Ink Spots and the Mills Brothers sang for white audiences; the Orioles were the first to incorporate obvious gospel and R&B into their vocalizations with "It's Too Soon to Know," which landed on what was then *Billboard*'s race-record charts in 1948. (The next year *Billboard* would change the "race record" designation to "rhythm and blues.")

The Orioles evidently spurred many other bird-name groups—the Crows, the Flamingos, the Penguins, and the Wrens. A group from Harlem calling themselves the Cadillacs, led by the singer Earl "Speedo" Carroll, released "Gloria," a feat of harmonization that would become the measuring stick for vocal harmony groups to come.

"Glo-or-ee-a," sings Carroll, standing far from the microphone. He repeats the name, this time walking closer, which gives the song a strolling feeling. Then the bass comes in, also as if he's walking toward the mic. The rest of the group joins in the harmonization.

One of the first bands to cross over from the race charts to pop were the Harlem-based Teenagers, a group of African Americans and Puerto Ricans, led by thirteen-year-old Frankie Lymon. They sang "Why Do Fools Fall in Love," which was written in part by Lymon. The song hit number one in 1956, and two weeks later the group

made its first national television appearance on *Frankie Laine Time,*
which had replaced *Arthur Godfrey's Talent Scouts.*

It's not surprising that Frankie Laine, who prided himself on his
"black"-influenced singing style, invited this group to appear on his
show.

I found a video of that appearance on YouTube. Frankie Laine,
wearing thick, black-framed glasses, introduces the Teenagers, who
bound onto the stage by leaping over a wall behind Laine. They
wore shirts with bow ties, over which were white sweaters with the
letter *T* sewn on. They all had their hair pulled to a side part with
pomade ("Blacks used pomade," my father once told me, "while Italians used Brylcreem"; pomade is a strong petroleum product in a tin,
Brylcreem is a cream from a tube). Both blacks and Italians felt a
need to make their dark thick curls appealing to a straight-haired
white America.

Laine referred to the music of this younger generation as rock
and roll, and seemed very cool and hip in his banter with the group,
who were eager to sing.

Laine asks Frankie Lymon about the inspiration for his writing
the song.

"What does a thirteen-year-old boy know about love?"

"Well, Mr. Laine," Lymon says, hamming it up for the audience.
"I've been falling in love since I was only five. But I've been a fool
about it since I was eleven."

After more banter, Laine decides it's time for the group to sing.

"So are you ready to rock and roll?" Laine asks with a smile.

"That's right," Lymon replies.

"That means I ought to get lost, huh?" Laine says.

"That's about it," Lyman retorts, and with his arm directs Laine
offstage.

The music begins, and the Teenagers start clapping as they get in
position to sing—"ooh wah, ooh wah." The smoothness, confidence,
and charm with which Frankie Lymon carries himself as he talks
and sings and dances bring to mind a young Sammy Davis Jr.

The following year, Nat "King" Cole was the first black performer to be given a TV show, but the public wasn't yet ready for a black TV host. To help boost his friend's ratings, Frankie Laine—then at the height of his popularity—became the first white entertainer to appear on the show.

When Dion and the Belmonts had their hit with "I Wonder Why," white vocal groups suddenly claimed the spotlight. Most of these "white" vocal groups came from tough Italian city neighborhoods: Brooklyn, the Bronx, Manhattan's Lower East Side.

"There was something about the sight of four Italians, decked out in city slicker clothes, snapping their fingers acting like Negroes," Dion DiMucci recalled in his autobiography, *The Wanderer*. "We were kind of exotic, which, back then, meant foreign, and that, in turn, meant dangerous."

I managed to reach Dion, in spite of his agent, Dick Fox, through the head of the National Italian American Foundation, an organization based in Washington, D.C.

I asked him where they got the inspiration for "I Wonder Why"—from the bass to the melody.

"That was all Louis Prima, man," Dion said to me, speaking in a gravelly voice that still carried the thick accents of the Bronx. "He was rock and roll, man. Prima would have been the first guy inducted into the Rock and Roll Hall of Fame if he didn't sing in Italian."

Dion DiMucci grew up on the top floor of a two-story building in the Italian neighborhood of the Bronx called Belmont, from which the group took its name. Belmont's main street is Arthur Avenue, which is now the better-known name of the neighborhood near Fordham University in the northwest Bronx. DiMucci's grandparents had emigrated from Calabria, Abruzzi, and Apulia. His father went from job to job, working briefly in a millinery making hats (as did my grandfather). He was "a dreamer," according to Dion, and he often worked the marionettes at Italian theaters. Dion remembers his father crafting the faces of his puppets from plaster of Paris. Whatever he was doing, his father struggled to come up with the thirty-six-dollar monthly rent for the family's apartment.

In describing his neighborhood, Dion mentions Our Lady of Mount Carmel Church—"the parish cathedral and the hub in the wheel of my little kingdom." It was there that his family worshipped—most often his father, who attended not for religious reasons, but to listen to the organ. "After the organist died, we never went back." Dion stopped going to church at age eight.

The DiMuccis grew up poor in the Bronx, and yet Dion remembers his father taking him on his shoulders through the Metropolitan Museum, introducing him to things artistic (in Dion's Bronx-speak, "artistic" sounds like "autistic").

Dion's memories are not that different from those of other Italians of his generation—from my father's, for instance. Dion would accompany his grandmother shopping. She would pick out chickens from a pen, "making sure that their eyes weren't cloudy or anything." She would do the same thing at the fishmonger's, studying the fish swimming in a tank before she selected one.

Dion's paternal grandfather, Tony, played a big role in Dion's young life.

"I consider it a blessing that my grandfather would take me to see opera," Dion said. "The first one—at the Windsor on Fordham Road and Grand Concourse—was *Pagliacci.*" This was the opera that Enrico Caruso had made popular in America, about a scorned lover's revenge.

His grandfather would sing popular Italian songs whenever the family got together. Nevertheless, there was an Italian neighborhood element that Dion didn't like. "I remember these guys on the corner—let's say *Sopranos*-like guys." They were thugs, he recalled, and they weren't terribly bright.

Combine that with a cloistered Italian neighborhood, and, Dion reflected, "You know, I was kind of embarrassed to be Italian." Music served as an escape—for Dion it would be the blues guitars of Robert Johnson, John Lee Hooker, and Jimmy Reed, as well as the faraway cry of Hank Williams. Dion couldn't even conjure where someone with a twang like Williams's could possibly live. But he could relate to the loneliness in Williams's voice. Like opera for Italian men, country music was the only thing that allowed a grown man to cry.

Dion grew up singing Italian songs in neighborhood bars like Ermondo's on Fordham Road. "Because I was Italian, they all wanted me to sound like Vic Damone—someone who sang as if all he did was take voice lessons. No, for me it was the energy of Louis Prima." Dion wanted to rock, not croon.

So Dion incorporated in his music the sound of Louis Prima—along with rhythm and blues, as well as an element of toughness. Dion had known from the neighborhood—and even harmonized with on stoops, on occasion—the boys with whom he would form the Belmonts: Carlo Mastrangelo, Fred Milano, and Angelo D'Aleo. Freddie and Carlo had once been members of the Imperial Hoods. Today, the names of street gangs are just as evocative of the 1950s as the names of vocal groups. In Dion's neighborhood there were the Imperial Hoods, the Italian Berettas, the Golden Guineas, and the Fordham Daggers, which was the gang Dion belonged to before joining the Baldies (a name taken from the bald eagle, which was a fixture at the nearby Bronx Zoo).

They sang in the vestibules of apartment buildings to hear the echoes. They sang on the corners of streets lined with Italian bakeries, pork stores, and cheese shops. They harmonized on the Sixth Avenue D train as it headed downtown. They sang after dark under the Crotona Avenue streetlights, which illuminated the thick air of the humid summer nights.

Dion and the Belmonts took that street-gang toughness to their music, to their collective persona. Most groups incorporated into their shows some sort of unison footwork, stepping back and forth, turning around. "We didn't dance like other groups," Dion explained. "We just snapped our fingers."

As big a song as it was for Dion and the Belmonts, "I Wonder Why" only reached number twenty-two on the pop charts. Nearly a year later, they hit number five with a song called "A Teenager in Love."

"Each night I ask the stars up above," the nineteen-year-old Dion sings, "why must I be a teenager in love?" Perhaps his singing was inspired by a girl who had just moved into the neighborhood—a girl with auburn hair and whose skin was so white there was no mistaking her for Italian. Her name was Susan.

At this time, Dion became friends with Frankie Lymon of the Teenagers. They would hang out together, mostly in Frankie's neighborhood, Washington Heights in northern Manhattan, which offers views of both Manhattan and the Bronx. Directly below them was the Polo Grounds, where the New York Giants baseball team had played; across the river in the Bronx was Yankee Stadium.

There, in the dark and under the stars, Frankie and Dion would transport themselves out of their neighborhood "villages" with the assistance of heroin.

The success of "I Wonder Why," along with "No One Knows" and "Don't Pity Me," prompted music promoters to put the Belmonts on a tour of record hops, where bands went from town to town promoting their records in school gymnasiums or cafeterias, at town fairs or in theaters. Often, the promoter would play the record as the band lip-synched to it.

"It was acceptable back then," Bruce Morrow told me. "We simply didn't have the money or the technology to put on a live show. Everyone knew this; the audience wasn't being tricked."

On one such tour Dion met Bobby Darin, and the two—both Italian, both from the Bronx—quickly formed a bond. "He was only three years older than me at the time, but he was like my father," Dion recalls in his memoir. Darin advised him on how to keep his books and file for tax deductions, useful advice for a kid from the Bronx flush with cash for the first time in his life.

During a three-week "Winter Dance Party" tour in February 1959, Dion played a show in Clear Lake, Iowa, with Buddy Holly, who had broken up the Crickets the year before. The next stop, Fargo, North Dakota, was three hundred miles away, and the bus was freezing cold. Buddy Holly decided that he didn't want to spend another moment on the bus, and besides, if he took a private plane to Fargo, he could do a load of laundry. Two musicians Holly had hired to back him—the guitarist Tommy Allsup and Waylon Jennings, who was playing bass—gave up their seats on the plane for the Big Bopper and Ritchie Valens, the latter of whom had been sick with the flu. Holly offered Dion a seat. The price of a ticket was thirty-six dollars. That was what his father paid for monthly rent. He remembered the fights that came around when rent was due. It seemed an extravagance. He turned down Holly's offer and decided to take the bus instead.

33

"Sixteen Candles"

JOHNNY MAESTRO AND THE CRESTS

Johnny Mastrangelo, before he changed his last name to Maestro, was a seventeen-year-old lead singer looking for a group. He put the word out in the Italian neighborhood on Manhattan's Lower East Side where he had grown up, on Roosevelt Street between Pearl and Madison. Down the street toward the water stood the Alfred E. Smith Houses, a complex of twelve high-rise buildings where many black and Puerto Rican families lived. The street no longer exists— nor does the entire Italian enclave. Roosevelt Street, which was a site of the New York draft riots of 1863, has now been replaced by apartment buildings.

"Each street was its own little town," Maestro told me over the phone in 2008, prior to his death in 2010. He spoke in a soft, measured voice, hardly seeming like the person who fronted one of the biggest doo-wop groups of its time. "Each street had its own cleaners, fruit stand, grocery store, corner newspaper stand."

Mastrangelo, whose grandparents had come from Calabria and Basilicata, had grown up listening to Italian pop songs on the radio. His grandfather listened to Phil Brito sing "Mama," and Johnny listened to Frankie Laine and to Johnnie Ray, who had a hit with "Cry."

Then, when Alan Freed came on the airwaves as "Moondog" with his R&B music programs in the early 1950s, Mastrangelo was introduced to the harmonies of the Moonglows, the Harptones, and the Flamingos—"it was their vocals that really interested me."

Wanting to sing with a group, he auditioned several kids from his neighborhood, but none of them had the chops he was looking for—none of them could sing like the Moonglows. Word had gotten around to the Al Smith projects, and one day three young men—two blacks, one Puerto Rican—approached him. They had been singing gospel together, but they needed a lead singer.

And thus in 1957 the Crests were formed, becoming one of the first interracial vocal groups.

Trying to get a new sound, the group brought in a woman to sing first tenor. Her name was Patricia Vandross, and her younger brother Luther would hang out listening to the band. Luther Vandross would become a popular R&B singer in the 1980s. ("I like to think that we might have influenced him," Maestro said.)

"J. T. Carter sang bass, Harold Torres sang baritone, Talmadge Gough sang second tenor, and Patricia sang first tenor," Maestro told me. The group's lead singer had by then changed his last name.

The group would rehearse in the IRT subway station at Park Place across from City Hall, as Maestro explained, "in order to find an echo."

It was there that the wife of an orchestra leader named Al Browne heard them. When she got home, she told Browne, who soon signed the group for his small Brooklyn label, Joyce Records. The Crests' first two singles were "My Juanita" and "Sweetest One," released in 1957. The latter song just squeaked onto *Billboard*'s Top 100, at number eighty-six.

At this time, the group began going on record-hop tours, and Patricia, who was only fifteen, was forbidden by her parents to join.

The next year the Crests made two more records. One of them hit big: "Sixteen Candles"—which reached number two in 1958.

"Happy birthday, baby," Maestro opens at the top of his range. With his voice hitting the main beats of the triplet-based doo-wop rhythm, you can easily picture the swinging, swaying, finger-snapping moves of the group onstage.

To be sure, Italians, blacks, and Puerto Ricans didn't always get along in New York, but it wasn't until the group began touring outside the Northeast that they experienced true institutional segregation.

"It was in Baltimore," Maestro explained. "It was our first record hop, and the night before we stopped off at a diner. After a while, I realized we were the only table that hadn't been served."

He got up to ask the manager, who, looking at the table, responded, "We don't serve colored." They got up and left the restaurant.

I once saw a videotape of a conference at the John D. Calandra Institute, a part of the City University of New York devoted to the study of Italian and Italian American issues, where a group of old-time doo-wop singers recalled what it was like leaving their New York neighborhoods for the South.

"When we got on the bus down there," joked Vito Picone, the lead singer of the Elegants, "we didn't know which part of the bus to sit in—we were Sicilians!"

With the Elegants, who came from Staten Island, Picone wrote and sang "Little Star," based on "Twinkle, Twinkle Little Star." The list of Italian doo-wop groups is endless: the Brooklyn group the Mystics sang "Hushabye"; the Passions, from Red Hook, Brooklyn, sang "Just to Be with You"; the Capris, from Queens, sang "There's a Moon Out Tonight"; the Regents came out with "Barbara-Ann," which a couple of years later would be a hit for the Beach Boys, the Regents' member Ernie Maresca wrote "The Wanderer" and "Runaround Sue" for Dion; Vito & the Salutations (Vito Balsamo, not Picone) sang their post-doo-wop version of "Unchained Melody"; there was Teddy Randazzo and the Three Chuckles, and Joe Villa and the Three Friends. Joe Villa would team up with Bob Gaudio to form the Royal Teens and record the irrepressible novelty record "Short Shorts." Bob Gaudio would later become the final member of the Four Seasons.

There were even a few Italian girl groups.

"Connie Francis was one of the only girls singing rock and roll," said Mary Reparata, who sang with the Delrons. "It's just not something parents would push their daughter to do."

Most of the girl singers formed their groups at their local church. Mary Reparata's Delrons got together in St. Brendan's Church in Brooklyn, while the Carmelettes, with Angela LaPrete, was formed by members of the choir at Our Lady of Mount Carmel Church in Jersey City.

In the mid-1960s, Johnny Maestro would join the Del Satins. They would become, with the inclusion of a seven-piece band, Johnny Maestro and the Brooklyn Bridge, and they would revive the first song the Crests recorded: "My Juanita."

34

"Mack the Knife"

BOBBY DARIN

With the snap of his fingers, the style of Bobby Darin went from teen idol to saloon singer.

Your foot begins to tap with the pluck of the strings of a stand-up bass—and then Darin comes in, singing about a shark.

That shark, he explains, "has such teeth, dear. And he shows them pearly white." Darin himself oozes such confidence, such cool. You feel his command of the song, the band, the entire audience.

The song, "Mack the Knife," came from Kurt Weill's *Threepenny Opera*, written in 1928. Before Darin's version, most knew the song through Louis Armstrong, who recorded it in 1956 and played it with a Dixieland rhythm during hundreds of concerts.

Darin's 1959 version is different, ironic—made so by his hip addition of the word "babe" to the opening line about the shark. The band joins in, and Bobby Darin swings with the tune. Darin was just twenty-two when he released the song—only eight months had passed since his hit with "Splish Splash."

Darin knew that rock and roll wouldn't get him in the Copa, so just as Connie Francis had done, Darin, once he had earned rock-and-roll fans, looked back at the pop standards. It worked. Teens and adults alike were listening to his music.

"Mack the Knife" was released on his first full-length album, *That's All*, which comprised pop standards: Sigmund Romberg and Oscar Hammerstein II's "Softly, as in a Morning Sunrise"; George and Ira Gershwin's "It Ain't Necessarily So"; and Bob Haymes's "That's All," among others.

Also on the album—and on the flip side of the "Mack the Knife" single—was a traditional French song, "La Mer," adapted by the singer and composer Charles Trenet. Rewritten in English by Jack Lawrence, it became "Beyond the Sea." That song swings even more than "Mack"; yet it's also a song a couple can dance close together to. Muted trumpets open the song to a Nelson Riddle–like arrangement—a bed of strings punctuated by brass. As he sings "Somewhere beyond the sea, somewhere waiting for me," Darin controls the lyric as well as even Sinatra could have done.

"What can I say?" Sammy Davis Jr. quipped in a telegram to Darin, upon hearing the songs on the new album. "They're so good I hate you!"

He continues: "I think the album's another step in a career I feel will last a long time . . . I dig it."

On November 29, 1959, Darin was awarded a Grammy for Best New Artist, while Sinatra was awarded Best Male Vocalist and Best Album for *Come Dance with Me!*

Just after the awards, Bobby Darin was walking through the lobby of the Beverly Hilton when a United Press International reporter caught up with him. He asked Darin, "Do you want to be bigger than Frank Sinatra?" Darin was offended by the question: "Why would you ask me that? We are a different generation. All I want to do is be the biggest and best Bobby Darin I can be."

The headline that ran in thousands of papers across the country: "Darin Wants to Be Bigger Than Sinatra."

From that point on, for better or worse, Darin would be compared to Sinatra.

The next year was a momentous one: in June 1960, when he opened at the Copacabana, the lines of people waiting to get in night after night were even longer than those for Sinatra, and the dance floor was filled with additional tables and seats to accommodate the crowd.

Bobby Darin played a part in breaking the notorious color code at the Copa, insisting that the black comedians Richard Pryor, George Kirby, and Flip Wilson be allowed to perform on his bill.

Darin would truly travel beyond the sea when he appeared in *Come September* with Rock Hudson, Gina Lollobrigida, and an eighteen-year-old blond American actress named Sandra Dee. In the movie, Darin plays a rebellious though funny Italian American kid who falls in love with a prep-school girl.

Soon after filming, Sandra Dee and Bobby Darin married; also, he and Connie Francis reunited professionally to sing a duet on *The Ed Sullivan Show*. That year, *American Bandstand* named Connie Francis the year's best female vocalist and Bobby Darin the best male vocalist.

35

"It's Now or Never"

ELVIS PRESLEY

It all came together for me while I was walking through Graceland.

As a kid, I had been a big fan of Elvis Presley. Huge. I owned dozens of his records, and I even saw him in concert—twice. The first time was in 1976, the second in 1977, just a few weeks before he died.

For that first concert, my best friend and I pulled up to the stadium in St. Petersburg, Florida, in a brand-new white Cadillac convertible. He sat in the front seat with his parents; I was sandwiched in the backseat with mine. I was nine years old.

It was only some thirty years after that concert that I made my pilgrimage to Graceland. I have to admit that upon first arriving at Graceland and seeing the lines of people similar to those at Disney World—as well as the mall-sized gift stores and the fleets of shuttle buses—I was crushed. I felt overwhelmed by the crowds; but perhaps, like attending his concerts, this is simply how one experiences Elvis—publicly.

The tour of the old Sun Records studios in downtown Memphis was much smaller but immensely more moving. Here was where the songs—the art—of Elvis Presley, Johnny Cash, and Jerry Lee Lewis were first recorded. I could stand at the microphone that Elvis used to record "That's All Right." (At least that's what they told us, and I was only too eager to believe.) A charming and sassy young woman with strawberry blond hair led a group of twenty people through the upstairs museum, then downstairs to the studio, control room, and back office. She had "Honky Tonk Angel" tattooed across the top of her chest.

A couple of days later I took a trip to the Stax Museum of American Soul Music, which had just reopened in the old recording studios, where Stax's founders, Jim Stewart and Estelle Axton, recorded dozens of black R&B hits with the racially mixed backing band Booker T. and the MG's. The self-guided tour began at a hundred-year-old one-room church that had been moved from somewhere in the Mississippi Delta and rebuilt inside the museum; Memphis soul—Otis Redding, Isaac Hayes, Sam & Dave—was the soundtrack for the rest of the tour. The fact that the tour was self-guided allowed for contemplation—an intimate interaction between you, the many artifacts, and the music.

But at Graceland, I felt crowded in by other tourists and "pilgrims." There was an audio tour, which made a point of mentioning all the King's crazy furniture. The decor was indeed tacky—exactly how you would think a poor southern boy who suddenly became wealthy might decorate. But that didn't bother me as much as the claustrophobia of being herded throughout this house, a house that I believe Elvis would have preferred not to have opened to his legions of fans. Perhaps I'm wrong.

One man in his sixties or seventies said, "Wow, Elvis was a little odd." Indeed, some of his rooms were disturbing, in particular one with green shag carpeting covering the walls and ceilings. But it seemed to me that Elvis wasn't so much odd as struggling.

It wasn't until I got downstairs that I was able to break away from the crowd. I found myself looking into a relatively small room where Elvis would listen to music. His headphones sat on a table next to a turntable. On shelves above was a small record collection. The one record that was facing out was by Mario Lanza—*For the First Time*, which included popular Neapolitan songs from Lanza's last movie. I can't remember if it was the narrator on my headset that explained the record, or whether I went back to read about it—but I learned that records by Mario Lanza were some of the few that Elvis listened to often.

The tour eventually led us outside to a separate building that was Elvis's recording studio. Aside from the recording equipment were couches, a small platform-like stage, and photographs of him onstage. Along the walls, glass cases displayed his costumes—many studded, and some with capes.

Having seen the Mario Lanza album and now Elvis's costumes, I filtered them through my memories of his concerts. His presence onstage was bigger than anything I could remember, or any performer I have experienced since.

And then it occurred to me. For Elvis, each concert was an opera.

From his costumes to the brassy flourishes that opened his concerts, Elvis Presley was about the spectacle. And his performances throughout the late 1960s and 1970s included a range of songs that were full of emotional highs and lows: humor, love, and tragedy.

I went back to the biographies by Peter Guralnick and read that as a boy Elvis had listened to opera and Enrico Caruso on his parents' radio in Tupelo, Mississippi. When he was young, the local radio stations played whatever was popular. There could be an opera aria, right after a country song, followed by a Tommy Dorsey big-band number. As strange and fascinating as the music of the rural South must have seemed to Tommy DeVito, Joni James, and Dion, Italian opera must have seemed to Elvis.

In the late 1950s and early 1960s, when Elvis was making movie after movie in Hollywood, Deana Martin, Dean's daughter, remembers Elvis circling Dean's house at 601 Mountain Drive on his motorcycle. Deana idolized Elvis, but when the two finally met on a lot at Paramount studios, Elvis told her, "You know, your father is the king of cool."

Elvis was most likely inspired by Martin's version of "I Don't Care if the Sun Don't Shine." Listen to "Love Me Tender" or "Don't" or "Are You Lonesome Tonight?" and you can hear the influence of Martin: the deep, warm baritone voice scooping up to the note in an easy, devil-may-care manner (though with an earnestness not heard in Martin).

He was also a big fan of Frankie Laine's and, in fact, recorded songs that Laine was known for, such as "I Believe" and "Lord, You Gave Me a Mountain."

Looking at Elvis, you could have sworn he was Italian. He had Martin's jet-black hair, Sinatra's swagger, Lanza's and Caruso's love of operatic staging, and Louis Prima's gyrating hips. Keely Smith, singer and wife of Louis Prima, maintains that the King of Rock and Roll got his moves from the King of the Swingers. "Elvis's hips—that was all Louis Prima."

In 1958, already a star, Elvis was inducted into the Army and served two years, during which his mother, Gladys, died. "Elvis died in the Army," John Lennon famously said, and upon his discharge in 1960 the King of Rock and Roll came back a crooner.

As he had blended country and blues in the Sun recordings, he now threw in elements of Italian balladry and opera.

"It's now or never," sings Elvis, opening the song of that name in an operatic tenor voice. "Come hold me tight." And then he's crooning, serenading a girl.

"It's Now or Never," of course, was "O sole mio"—first recorded by Enrico Caruso in 1916 on Victor, which later became RCA Victor, the label for which Elvis recorded his Americanized version, one of his bestselling records.

Frank Sinatra loathed rock and roll. "[It] smells phony and false . . . and was played and written for the most part by cretinous goons," he said.

But in March 1960, the Chairman of the Board invited the King of Rock and Roll on his television show to welcome him back from the Army.

"Looking back, I'm struck with the realization that you didn't miss much after all," said Sinatra, by way of introducing Elvis. "As a matter of fact, all you seemed to have lost are your sideburns."

The girls in the audience could hardly contain themselves. On the video, the camera flashes to Elvis coming out of the wings, wearing a slim-fitting tux, out of respect for Sinatra, who always performed in formal wear. The rockabilly rebel had become a southern gentleman (the black crossover tie he wore hinted at both). His hair is slicked back at the sides, a puffy pompadour bouncing on top of his head with every movement. He signals a four-piece combo and then croons a song called "Fame and Fortune" to the rhythm of a slow two-step. He then loosens up a bit as he sings his next number, "Stuck on You." He shakes his hips, but seems to keep himself in check—all the sexual energy appears to exit through the jiggling mound of hair atop his head.

Sinatra and the comedian Joey Bishop join Presley when he finishes singing.

"Wow, I never heard a woman scream at a male singer before," Bishop quips. Sinatra flinches in mock anger.

"I'd like to do one of your songs," says Elvis. Sinatra shoots him a look.

"I wonder if I would have recorded 'Love Me Tender' if it would have made any difference," says Sinatra.

"I think about two million records less," Bishop says.

Sinatra and Elvis sing a duet, a swinging medley of "Witchcraft" and "Love Me Tender," with each singing the lyrics of the other's song.

Sinatra swings his shoulders as Presley genteelly gyrates his tuxedoed hips.

"We work the same way," Sinatra jokes. "Only different areas." At the end of the song, they put their arms on each other's shoulders. Frank Sinatra ruled the stage, and Elvis paid court to him.

In his heart, Elvis Presley was really a crooner.

36

"The Wanderer"

DION

By 1960, Dion and the Belmonts had broken up. There were arguments over money—how much each should make—and, as Dion explains in his biography, because of Bobby Darin's financial advice, Dion had been able to spend his money more shrewdly than his bandmates. Of course, the biggest reason for the band's split was Dion's heroin addiction.

In Dion's mind at the time, though, things couldn't have been better. He was still with his girlfriend, Susan, and in 1961 he hired another vocal group to back him: the Del Satins, made up of Stan Ziska, Les Cauchi, Fred and Tom Ferrara, and Keith Koestner. Together they recorded a song Dion had written with Ernie Maresca, a friend from Belmont. The song was "Runaround Sue," and it charted at number one.

After the initial croon from Dion ("Here's my story, it's sad but true"), the song breaks into a fast, jumpy rhythm similar to the one on "Quarter to Three," a hit that year for a friend of Dion's named Gary U.S. Bonds. I asked Dion the inspiration for the song.

"That was Sam Butera," Dion said proudly. "In my head I heard the rhythm of Sammy's sax."

Just two months after "Runaround Sue," Dion brought out the song with which he would become most closely associated—"The Wanderer."

It's a kind of anthem for the disenfranchised at the time—the hoodlums and the directionless kids wanting to break away from the strict social norms of the Eisenhower 1950s. I think of Marlon Brando in *The Wild One* ("What are you rebelling against?" a girl asks Brando, to which he casually responds, "What've you got?")

Dion brought to the song his tough street-gang edge. "The song is black music filtered through an Italian neighborhood that comes out with attitude," he told me. It was his version, he says, of Muddy Waters's "Hoochie Coochie Man."

Dion brags about all the girls he's been with, and when asked which one he likes best, he tears open his shirt and shows a tattoo of "Rosie on my chest."

Although the song sounds happy and upbeat, it's really about being an angry guy who's got "two fists of iron but I'm going nowhere."

Italian attitudes and sentiment ran strong in Dion's music, and the next year he released a song called "Little Diane."

"Down deep inside I cry, Diane," Dion sings as if he's indeed crying, all above the song's dissonant melody. Then a kazoo blares. You don't know whether you should laugh at it or be haunted by the eerie, out-of-place sound.

Every time I hear it, I think back to Dion seeing the opera *Pagliacci*, in which the main character takes revenge and kills his unfaithful wife. Then I think of the folk songs of the small Italian villages that a man, cuckolded by his girlfriend or wife (perhaps by something as simple as a glance at another man), might sing aloud throughout the streets and alleys in order to take revenge on the girl by tarnishing her name.

"I wanna spread the news that you're untrue," Dion sings, his sadness turning to anger.

One year later, in September 1963, Dion had a hit with a much tamer, more upbeat song, "Donna the Prima Donna." It was about a girl who "had a pair of roving eyes" and who "tried to make a fool out of me"—the ultimate insult for an Italian man, to be cheated on.

The record was a huge hit in Italy, and Dion's manager thought it might be a good idea for him to sing the song in Italian and re-release it in Italy.

They sent a translation along with phonetic spelling to Dion, who spoke a few words of dialect at best. He brought it to his grandfather, who helped him with the pronunciation.

He was invited to Rome to appear on Italian state TV, after which the show's producer congratulated him while they were driven to supper in a limo. Dion retold the story to me, quoting the promoter in Italian-accented English.

"Dion, you're a big success here!" the promoter said. "They love your song. I especially like when you sing the part where the IRS comes to the house and Donna gets on her knees and says, 'Don't take-a the house; I'll do anything.' I love that part the best."

Dion, who had a part in writing many of his songs, was taken aback: "I had no idea what I was singing; and my grandfather, who probably didn't understand the lyrics of my song in English, couldn't tell me that it was something different than what I had written."

During the late 1960s and early 1970s, Dion experienced a couple of life-altering events. In early 1968, his old friend Frankie Lymon died of a heroin overdose—after getting high with Dion.

"It's been forty years since that day," Dion said, "that I've been clean and sober." A few months later, Bobby Kennedy was shot.

Dion, who had been a supporter of Kennedy, was devastated. He changed his musical style and wrote a folk song called "Abraham, Martin, and John"—a tribute to Abraham Lincoln, Martin Luther King Jr., and Bobby and John F. Kennedy. As it happened, that year Bobby Darin was also touring in support of the Kennedy presidential campaign, and he too made the switch to folk music with "If I Were a Carpenter."

In the early 1970s, as Dion tells it, someone had given him the book *Blood of My Blood* by the sociologist Richard Gambino. In it, Gambino describes and explains the mentality of close, private Italian American communities.

"I'll tell you one thing," Dion said. "It changed my life, because I had thought of Italians as ignorant buffoons. I read the book and my mind exploded." The book had explained Italian ritual as sophisticated.

Dion traveled to Italy, this time as an explorer, not as an entertainer, but only to Rome and points north. Then he returned to Belmont in the Bronx. He stopped off in his old church, Mount Carmel, and sat with his childhood pastor, on whom he had turned his back as a youth. He re-embraced his Catholic faith.

"I had fallen in love with the Italians, with art and poetry, with the old neighborhood," Dion said. "And then I fell in love with the Church."

37

"Walk Like a Man"

FRANKIE VALLI AND THE FOUR SEASONS

The Four Seasons' sound, the high-pitched voice of Frankie Valli over a solid three-part harmony, was the sound of the streets of urban New York and New Jersey. It was the sound of the projects of Newark and the poor Italian neighborhoods of Belleville. The tight living quarters brought the singers out onto the street, where they competed with the sounds of pedestrians, taxis, buses, and trains. Their songs were sharp and quick—just as you had to be in the rough parts of town.

Their sound was the perfect blend of doo-wop, rock and roll, and the croon.

On the surface, the Seasons looked like nice, clean-cut boys; but they struggled with the realities of living in tough neighborhoods—the fighting, the petty crime, the jail time. While so many other groups of the time projected a street-tough, edgy image, the Four Seasons cleaned themselves up to break out of the neighborhood and land in the living rooms of mainstream America.

"On the way to church you could stumble over three or four crap games," Tommy DeVito recalled. Sitting in the Waldorf hotel in a polo shirt and leather loafers, he was setting the scene, describing Belleville in the 1950s, when he, his brother Nick, and a friend named Nick Massi first formed a trio called the Variatones. "We used to perform in dives and pool halls."

"The neighborhood was tough, but you never had to lock the door," DeVito said in a raspy voice, commenting on the neighborhood's ability to rule itself—and the presence of the Mob.

DeVito soon met a singer named Francis Castelluccio, who was going to various bars trying to land gigs. Already on the track to fame, Castelluccio had changed his name to Frankie Valli. When Tommy's brother dropped out, the band was introduced to a tall, thin, contemplative guy from the New Jersey suburb of Bergenfield named Bob Gaudio. Originally from the Bronx, the precocious Gaudio had already, at age fifteen, written the hit "Short Shorts," which he made up while driving with friends along the main drag in Bergenfield. With DeVito on guitar, Massi on bass, the voice of Valli and the songwriting and keyboard playing of Gaudio, the Variatones became the Four Lovers before becoming the Four Seasons.

Driving through Stephen Crane Village—one of Newark's first projects, built in the 1940s—you notice that its current occupants are mostly black. Alleys wind throughout the complex. The two-story brick buildings still open up to long front yards, though now those yards are enclosed by chain-link fences. There are still clotheslines in front of the houses, and you can still picture the shirts, pants, and sheets that would have been held by the same wooden clothespins.

This is where Frankie Valli grew up, and it was in his family's tiny kitchen—when they weren't on the street corners—that the newly formed band would get together and practice late at night over cups of coffee, eggs, and fresh-baked bread, their voices echoing off the linoleum floors and metal kitchen table.

"There are a lot of reasons why Newark will always be special to me," Frankie Valli said to me, speaking in a voice that is powerful though soft in volume. "There was a place called the Adams Theater where I used to hear so much great music." A wry smile expanded beneath his cheekbones. He is dressed in a tailored sport coat and a cashmere sweater, and his gestures are understated. He acknowledges you with a nod, or simply a look.

Valli was unsure of his chances in the music business and had been studying to become a hairstylist, a more contemporary take on the Italian barber. He went knocking on the doors of music producers in the Brill Building in midtown Manhattan with Gaudio. It was by chance and with luck that they ran into a producer and songwriter named Bob Crewe, who was from Belleville himself and who had worked with Valli before. In time Crewe would match his lyrics with Gaudio's music, and would produce several of the Four Seasons' records.

Although the group had a producer, they had yet to have a hit. They continued to play various clubs around Belleville and Newark—but before things got better, they got worse.

"We had auditioned for a gig at a bowling alley and cocktail lounge in Union—and were turned down," Valli said, explaining how they came up with the name of the band. "As we were leaving, we looked up at the name of the place, the Four Seasons." Perhaps taking the name from a place that had rejected them was a sign both of their hardscrabble background and of their optimism.

Finally, in 1962, the Seasons managed to get a show at the Sea Breeze, a nightclub in Point Pleasant on the Jersey Shore. They had just finished their last song, and the crowd wouldn't let them off the stage.

"They had run out of their songs, but then Frankie picks up some maracas and does a great imitation of 1940s singer Rose Murphy in a falsetto," Bob Crewe recalled. "It was so clear, so crisp." That night Bob Gaudio went home and wrote a song with that falsetto in mind. "Sherry" took all of fifteen minutes to write. Released weeks later, it jumped onto the charts, hitting number one.

Gaudio and Valli knew there was a match between them—the songwriting with the voice. And from then on the two agreed to work together, each having a financial interest in the other's success.

"I have a relationship with Gaudio that's based on words we had with each other," said Valli.

"We were fifty-fifty partners on a handshake," Gaudio said later.

The Four Seasons have often been discussed in the same breath as the two other harmony-based groups of the time, the Beatles and the Beach Boys. The three bands vied for chart position throughout the 1960s. The Seasons represented the East Coast, the Beach Boys the West, and the Beatles, well, they were out of this world.

The Four Seasons recorded for Vee-Jay, a predominantly black R&B label. In fact, upon first listening to the Seasons, many people thought they were black. "Many of the songs from that record were first picked up by black DJs," Bob Crewe told me. The Beatles, too, had released some of their first songs on Vee-Jay in America, and in 1963 the label's executives came up with a double-LP package called *The Beatles vs. the Four Seasons*, which pitted songs such as "Please Please Me" and "I Saw Her Standing There" against "Walk Like a Man" and "Sherry."

Even those of us who didn't grow up with these bands have a visual image of the Beatles and the Beach Boys. John Lennon is singing into a mic while Paul and George are facing each other, singing harmony. Ringo is happily shaking his head of what was then considered long hair back and forth to the rhythm. We see countless images of Mike Love, Brian Wilson, and the rest of the Beach Boys lining up on the length of a surfboard with Southern California's sunny beaches in the background.

But the Four Seasons? Unless you were a teen in the early 1960s, you might have only known that they wore suits. Or did they? Did they play their own instruments? We know their songs, at least many of them, yet are surprised when we hear that along with "Big Girls Don't Cry" they sang "Dawn," "Rag Doll," "Let's Hang On," "Working My Way Back to You," or that Valli had solo hits with "My Eyes Adored You" and "Can't Take My Eyes off You."

Those songs are all classics, every one. But few people today have a solid image of the Seasons. "No one—not *Rolling Stone* magazine—really wrote about us like they did other bands," said Gaudio.

We hear the girls scream at Beatles concerts, and can picture blond guys and girls "cruising the strip" or "shooting the curl" while listening to the carefree Beach Boys songs. But who listened to the Four Seasons? Rick Elice, who along with Marshall Brickman wrote the book for *Jersey Boys*, the 2005 Broadway show based on the band, explains: "They were the factory workers, the truck drivers. The kids pumping gas, flipping burgers. The pretty girl with circles under her eyes behind the counter at the diner."

As the follow-up to "Sherry," the Four Seasons released "Walk Like a Man."

Valli sings in a boy's falsetto, recalling his father's advice. "No woman's worth crawling on the earth."

It's the cold, practical advice an Italian father would give to his son, a boy the father—who was once a young romantic himself—wants to help make a man.

Part Three

Las Vegas

38

"Nice 'n' Easy"

FRANK SINATRA AND THE RAT PACK

"Frank Sinatra is one of the most delightful, violent, dramatic, sad and sometimes downright terrifying personalities now on public view," a writer remarked in *Time* in 1955. In other words, he was, for the magazine, the quintessential Italian.

Musically, Sinatra was coming out with some of his best songs—most of them arranged by Nelson Riddle.

Yet he was still the guy you could pull up a stool next to at a bar—at two in the morning. There's a drizzle outside, and you're much more comfortable inside the bar, drink in hand, with people you don't know. Talking anonymously gives you freedom.

His 1958 album *Only the Lonely* sets that tone of urban anonymity. He's got the world on a string—at least on the outside, that is; on the inside he can be just as lonely as the next guy.

The piano plinks in the background. It's a lonely night. Then somber strings warm the tone. And when he sings "One for My Baby," toasting the girl who just left, it's a conversation between him and the bartender.

It's the perfect saloon song. "And when I'm gloomy, won't you listen to me till it's talked away." Listening to him, you feel as if you're listening to a best friend—one who's telling you that, no matter what, you will survive. Maybe your girlfriend left you for another man. Maybe your wife has been diagnosed with cancer. Sinatra once famously said: "I'm for whatever gets you through the night."

They referred to themselves and to their nightclub gigs as the Summit; others called them the Clan. But to everyone, they became known as the Rat Pack.

Credit for the term goes to Lauren Bacall, who first used it to refer to her husband Humphrey Bogart, who would hang out with other actors—including Errol Flynn, Mickey Rooney, Cesar Romero, and eventually Frank Sinatra—in their houses in the Holmby Hills section of Los Angeles. However, it was upon seeing this group all gathered in a casino in Las Vegas that Bacall said: "You all look like a goddam rat pack."

Journalists took to the term so much that the name followed Sinatra from that group of guys to this one. The core of the Rat Pack we know was Frank Sinatra, Dean Martin, and Sammy Davis Jr. (Peter Lawford and the comedian Joey Bishop were part of the group for only a short time). They sang to the men, loved their women, gambled, drank, had fun. Theirs was the ultimate neverending boys' night out. They played golf after lunch, then lounged in Jacuzzis and saunas to relax. In the evening they put on their tuxes, roamed the casinos, took turns tossing some dice. Dean might elbow out the dealer at the poker table and take his place for a couple of hands. They sang two sets, ate dinner, then drank into the early-morning hours. They woke up at 1:00 p.m. and began the day again.

When we look back at the late 1950s and early 1960s, this is an image we all carry of how men enjoyed themselves. This was before Beatlemania conquered America, before the hippies came to Woodstock—unshaved, uncut, undressed, unshowered. Frank, Dean, and Sammy were clean, cool, smooth. There was sex, sure, but most of their exploits were performed with clothes on—smart, snazzy, hand-tailored clothes.

And their Summit was the Copa Room at the Sands Hotel in Las Vegas.

In 1958, Frank Sinatra became a 9 percent owner of the Sands, with Dean Martin buying in for a 1 percent share. (A syndicate of over a dozen investors owned the Sands, led by Jack Entratter with 16 percent.)

The year 1960 marked the real beginning of the Rat Pack, brought together to film a Las Vegas heist movie called *Ocean's 11*. Frank, Dean, and Sammy were joined by the comedian Joey Bishop, who wrote many of the jokes, and the English actor Peter Lawford, who married a Kennedy, and was therefore in good standing with Sinatra, who was campaigning for JFK. At times, Marilyn Monroe, Shirley MacLaine, Angie Dickinson, and Juliet Prowse all hung around with the men; they were sometimes referred to as the mascots.

In the film, a gang of ex-GIs, each with his own skills and led by Danny Ocean (played by Sinatra), scheme to raid five hotels. The deadline is the stroke of midnight on New Year's Eve, and their planned hits are the great hotels of Las Vegas—the Sahara, the Flamingo, the Riviera, the Desert Inn, the Sands.

During the five weeks of filming, the actors were fixtures in Las Vegas, filming the movie during the day and performing at the Sands at night.

The unofficial opening of the Summit was February 7, 1960, when John F. Kennedy came to town and was introduced by Frank Sinatra. Kennedy sat at a cocktail table with his brother Ted near the front of the stage.

I watched a video on YouTube of a performance by Frank Sinatra, Dean Martin, and Sammy Davis Jr. at the Copa Room in 1963. A thirty-piece orchestra takes up most of the stage, leaving what seems to be a narrow, cramped strip for the singers, about thirty feet long and maybe ten feet deep.

"Ladies and gentlemen," the announcer says over the PA system. "For your enjoyment, Mrs. Sinatra, Mrs. Martin, and Mrs. Davis present their sons—the drunk singers. And the first drunkard, direct from the bar, Dean Martin!"

Dean enters the stage from a curtain behind the orchestra. Dressed in a tux and carrying a lowball glass in his hand, he stumbles to the microphone.

"Drink to me, always," he sings, slurring the lyric. "That's all I axe . . . ask."

The audience laughs. The music continues, but Dean walks to the side of the stage, sways back and forth, and takes a drink. After a couple of measures, he glances up at the audience, feigns surprise and says, "How long I been on?"

He grabs the microphone with his left hand, his large fingers, like those of a boxer, dwarfing his pinky ring. "When you're drinking," he continues singing, "the show looks good to you."

After another number, "Lady Is a Tramp," he bows and leaves the stage. Then Sammy Davis Jr. is announced.

He's dressed in a suit, uncharacteristic for anyone performing with Frank Sinatra, who always demanded that singers wear a tuxedo. In complete juxtaposition to Martin, Davis, wearing black-framed glasses, is a ball of energy. Just as he's about to sing, Sinatra interrupts him over the PA.

"The Yiddish are coming, the Yiddish are coming," Sinatra says, referring to Davis's religion. Sammy bends over in laughter.

"Hey," Martin says. "He's smoking a white cigarette."

Without missing a beat, Davis responds: "I was smoking a brown one and almost got arrested."

Sinatra then ribs Davis for wearing a suit, in a way that you're not convinced is entirely in jest.

Davis sits on a stool and sings a song Frank Sinatra had made popular, "One for My Baby," in a voice that, if your eyes were closed, you'd bet was Sinatra's. Thus begins a stream of impressions, from Nat "King" Cole, to Vaughn Monroe, to Billy Eckstine. During his imitation of Tony Bennett singing—all bombastic—Sinatra and

Martin wheel onstage a service cart, covered by a white tablecloth. When they get to Sammy, they pull off the cover to reveal a full bar setup—bottles of liquor, ice bucket and shaker—and toss the tablecloth onto Davis.

"All right, folks, put on a sheet and let's have a meeting," Martin says, referring to the KKK.

Davis begins to stomp offstage in mock anger.

"There he is, the African queen," Martin says. The audience is right there with them in laughter.

A few skits later, Sinatra takes the microphone. The air in the room suddenly changes. The audience is very quiet. Sinatra, who is not a natural comedian, tells a joke, then looks out with those steely blue eyes. The audience laughs, out of deference to him, out of respect, but perhaps also out of fear of some sort of retribution.

He then sings "A Foggy Day (in London Town)" and "Embraceable You." It's one of the few times onstage that any of the three sings a song straight through. He segues into "Lady Is a Tramp," and as he does, Davis begins tap-dancing and gliding, with jazz moves across the floor. All eyes focus on him instead.

Then Davis sings "Me and My Shadow." Sinatra is standing behind him, and Martin is just two steps behind Sinatra.

"How does it feel to be standing at the back of the bus now, Dean?" Davis says.

Each formed the perfect foil for the others. Dean was the carefree guy, just passing time, enjoying everything for the moment. Frank commanded the show with a hint of sardonic wit. And Sammy alternated between playing the role of the "black man" and bringing the house down with his exuberant tap-dancing and singing.

The Rat Pack lasted only a thousand days—about the length of John F. Kennedy's presidency. Although Frank, Dean, and Sammy would perform together intermittently in the years to follow, the party fizzled out in 1963.

For many people, the Rat Pack was their first time seeing a black person onstage with white people—joking around, insulting one another, and having a blast.

In 1962, Frank Sinatra contributed an article to *Music Journal* magazine (a version of which originally appeared in *Ebony* in July 1958) for a series on prejudice, in which he stressed the importance of battling bigotry. "Because some of my good friends happen to be Negroes it has been suggested that I have a preference for colored people, that I 'like' them. The fact is that I don't 'like' Negroes any more than I 'like' Jews or Moslems or Italians or any other group. I don't *like* according to the color of a man's skin or his place of worship."

"I believe an entertainer's function is to entertain," he declared. But the entertainer has the same "obligations as the next man. When an entertainer shirks his duty . . . he is as much to be criticized as anyone else." In this regard, Frank was his mother's son, recalling her work in neighborhood organizations and her fights for justice in Hoboken.

Yet no matter what their success, in the eyes of many Americans, Frank and Dino were Italians, and Sammy was a Negro.

In the same article, Sinatra recalled a recent experience he had had while sitting alone at a table. A woman walked up and sat next to him. He could tell she had already had a few drinks. At one point, showing no reluctance about speaking to a star at the top of his game, she told Sinatra, "Do you know what we call you at home? The 'wop singer.'"

In 1960, Frank Sinatra started his own record label, Reprise. He wanted artistic freedom, and the artists who recorded on his label would enjoy freedom too—singers, musicians, and comedians like Sammy Davis Jr., Dean Martin, Bing Crosby, Jo Stafford, Rosemary Clooney, and Redd Foxx, and later, either on the label or distributed by it, Joni Mitchell, Neil Young, the Kinks, Frank Zappa, Gram Parsons, Emmylou Harris, and Richard Pryor, among dozens more.

One of the last songs Sinatra recorded for Capitol, though, seems to symbolize the Rat Pack ethos.

This is "Nice 'n' Easy," and Sinatra shows what it means to take it easy from the very first line. There's a pianist tickling the ivories under dotted rhythms from the brass; the feel is that of a stroll on the beach. Even the strings—playing whole notes—seem to be taking their time. No matter where they were, what they were doing, Sammy, Dean, and Frank all seemed to be taking it easy—drink and cigarette in one hand, broad or poker chips in the other. "Hey, baby, what's your hurry, relax and don't you worry." It was as if Frank and Dean had converted Italian concern with a graceful image into American-style confidence. Within the Rat Pack was an Italian flair—that of the *bella figura*, or cutting a good image—that had come to define what it meant to be "cool" as an American.

39

"Bye Bye Blackbird"

SAMMY DAVIS JR.

"I'm black, Puerto Rican, and Jewish—whenever I move into a neighborhood, everyone moves out."

So said Sammy Davis Jr., repeating a version of a line from his nightclub act. Hanging out with Martin and Sinatra, Sammy Davis Jr. was, in ways, an honorary Italian. He was a decade younger than Frank and Dean, and even Frank Sinatra said he was the greatest entertainer. Sammy gave the Rat Pack its flash.

Because he was black, he was the object of jokes—both his own and Frank's and Dean's.

One bit involved Dean Martin carrying Sammy Davis Jr. onstage, presenting him to Sinatra as "a gift from the NAACP."

The jokes were off-color and offensive (and all very rehearsed), but despite it all the humor diffused the tension and allowed blacks and whites to perform together in a way that was still uncommon.

In one televised performance at the Kiel Opera House in St. Louis, Sammy, Dean, and Frank are onstage, with Johnny Carson filling in for Joey Bishop. Sammy's at the microphone, setting up his signature song, "Birth of the Blues."

As he talks, Frank keeps goosing him.

Sammy turns to Dean and says, "When was the last time you've seen an Italian cut?" At first you think he's referring to a style of suit, but then he points to Frank standing behind him and says, "I'm gonna cut him if he touches me one more time."

The audience roars with laughter—who would ever dare say that to Frank Sinatra, even during a comedy skit on national TV?

In 1962, Sammy Davis Jr. was a Grammy nominee for both Record of the Year and Male Solo Performance for his rendition of "What Kind of Fool Am I?" which came from the hit musical *Stop the World—I Want to Get Off*.

Davis had been performing onstage since he was a kid, and in 1956 he appeared in his first Broadway show, *Mr. Wonderful*, in the role of a struggling entertainer named Charlie Welch, supported by song-and-dance routines with the Will Mastin Trio.

In 1964, he landed a leading role in the musical *Golden Boy*.

Golden Boy, adapted from a 1937 play by Clifford Odets, tells the story of a twenty-one-year-old Italian American violinist named Joe Bonaparte who becomes a boxer in the hopes of making a better living. His father, Italian-born Joe senior, who runs a grocery on the ground floor of an apartment building, wants nothing more than for his son to play violin. But Joe nevertheless finds himself a manager, Tom Moody, and then falls in love with Tom's girlfriend, Lorna Moon.

The play is full of prewar social realism, focusing on the plight of immigrant Italians struggling to make a living and assimilate in their new country in pursuit of the American dream. After a successful run in New York City, it was adapted as a movie in 1939, with a young William Holden starring as Joe Bonaparte and Barbara Stanwyck playing Lorna Moon.

The film opens with Joe Bonaparte walking into Moody's office and demanding that he manage him. We learn that Moody's star prizefighter had broken his arm while sparring that afternoon and will not be able to fight that night. As it turns out, Joe was his sparring partner, and he tells Moody that he can fill in for the injured boxer. Lorna Moon, impressed with Joe's forthrightness, encourages Moody to give him a chance. At one point Moody looks at Joe and makes fun of his curly hair: "Everyone will laugh at you once you step into that ring."

The next scene is set at Joe senior's grocery store, where he's playing chess with a Jewish neighbor. Joe senior has saved up a substantial amount of money, and with it he has bought his son a very expensive violin, which he plans to give him for his birthday the next day.

Joe junior enters and tells his father he has just won his first fight, and that soon he will be making a lot of money. Joe senior, nearly breaking down in tears, says that he doesn't want his son to be a millionaire; he just wants him to make music.

"Money? We've got heart, soul! And we've got to take care of them," cries Joe senior. Most of all, he worries that his son will break his hand and never play violin again.

Toward the end of the movie, before the big fight that would solidify Joe as a world contender, Joe cuts off his Italian curls. He asks his father if he likes the new look. His father, seeing how his son has changed, shrugs his shoulders and says, "It'll grow back."

The night of the big fight, Joe senior sits in his son's training room waiting for the bout to be over. Joe comes in—a winner by a knockout—but with a broken hand. Moments later the referee enters the room to say his opponent, a black fighter nicknamed Chocolate Drop, has died, killed by one of Joe's punches.

Odets rewrote the play to feature Sammy Davis Jr. in the lead role—renamed Joe Wellington—and to address the struggles of African Americans in the civil rights era. The play was reworked as a musical with the help of Lee Adams and Charles Strouse.

The day it opened—October 20, 1964—many of Sammy's friends took out ads in *Variety*, the film and stage industry magazine, wishing him luck: Sam Butera, Richard Burton, Elizabeth Taylor,

Sam Cooke, Duke Ellington, Ira Gershwin, Harold Arlen, Robert Goulet, Nat "King" Cole, and Joe E. Lewis.

Davis thrived in the role of Joe Wellington; in the song "Night Song," he sang, "Who do you fight when you wanna break out, but your skin is your cage?" and the question resounded across America. As in the play, Joe falls in love with Lorna Moon. In the musical's most controversial moment, Joe and Lorna kissed; it was thought to be the first time a black man had kissed a white woman on a Broadway stage. In his own life, in 1960, Davis himself had married a white woman, a Swedish actress named May Britt, which infuriated white and black folks alike (interracial marriage was still illegal in many states). The musical's depiction of interracial relationships caused so much anger among whites that Davis received hate mail throughout the run of the production.

The show was a hit, running for 568 performances, and Davis was nominated for a Tony Award for Best Actor in a musical.

Life magazine devoted a fourteen-page spread to him:

> As Sammy Davis Jr., he has—due to his extraordinary talents—just made the show into a Broadway hit. It was a sweet desperately achieved triumph for Davis, a performer who can sing as well as Frank Sinatra, dance as gracefully as Fred Astaire, do impersonations better than anyone, who can do anything from vaudeville to Shakespeare.

To use a boxing phrase: pound for pound, Sammy Davis Jr. was the world's greatest entertainer.

Davis put out one of his best albums in 1961. *The Wham of Sam* was an early record released on Frank Sinatra's Reprise label.

One number that I think highlights Davis's singing at its best is "Bye Bye Blackbird," an old standard first recorded by Gene Austin in 1926, with a popular version of the song released later that year by the singer and guitarist Nick Lucas. Davis, who usually puts over each phrase emphatically, is subtle here.

A solo upright bass walks the rhythm, then Davis sings that he's packing up all his woe and he's swinging low. He begins snapping his fingers.

Then we hear the light tapping of a high-hat cymbal and the raps of a snare drum. Sammy sings, "No one here can love and understand me, oh, what hard luck stories they all hand me." And as a black man who claimed to be part Puerto Rican (although his mother was actually Cuban), who converted to Judaism, and who palled around with a couple of Italians, he was indeed very much misunderstood. Blacks accused him of being an Uncle Tom; whites still saw him as colored.

Then full orchestra with brass—strong, though nevertheless restrained—accompanies Davis singing a reprise of the opening verse. This time he's emphatic, almost triumphant. He may be misunderstood, but he's doing all that he wants to do.

40

"Fly Me to the Moon"

FRANK SINATRA

"When the Beatles came, we all struggled with our jobs," said Jerry Vale. "Just like that, music changed."

Vito Picone, lead singer for the Elegants, cast the change in light of doo-wop and rock and roll: "Before the Beatles, kids created music on the street corners; afterward, they formed bands in garages and basements."

In 1964, as the Beatles were leading the British Invasion, the baby boomers had just reached record-buying age. Suddenly, for them, the songs of the crooners were what their parents listened to.

But it didn't mean the death of the Italian saloon singers.

Dean Martin had his first Top 40 hit since "Volare" in 1958, with "Everybody Loves Somebody." It went all the way to number one; in fact, it knocked the Beatles' "Hard Day's Night" from the top spot.

After the Beatles arrived, Tony Bennett never had another Top 10 hit. But in 1962 he was as popular as he had ever been, having released the song for which he would become best known—"I Left My Heart in San Francisco."

He sang it live at what would become a landmark event for Bennett, a performance at Carnegie Hall on June 9, 1962, which was recorded and soon released. Along with his new hit, he sang "Anything Goes," followed by "Blue Velvet."

"I guess everybody knows what this is by now," Tony Bennett said to the audience at Carnegie Hall as he sat on a stool center stage, remarking on the two songs he had just sung. "You know what this is? It's an Italian singing stool—Frank Sinatra and Perry Como." He was referring to the songs that each of these Italian singers had made famous.

Three years later, Frank Sinatra paid Tony Bennett the highest of compliments: "Tony Bennett is the best singer in the business; he's the best saloon singer."

That year, 1965, after six years of debate, Congress finally eliminated the restrictions that had been placed on immigrants from eastern and southern Europe in 1911, 1917, and 1924, which had drastically reduced the number of Italians entering the country. For the first time since the age of Enrico Caruso, America opened its gates to a new wave of immigrants from Italy.

Eighty percent of Italians born in America in the 1960s would marry non-Italians—an indication that by this time, Italians had assimilated.

As more Italian Americans moved to the suburbs during the 1960s, their music changed. At this time, the second, third, and fourth generations of Italian American singers take center stage; their voices and their ethnicity—as their Italian lineage has been mixed with that of other nationalities—have blended into the American patchwork.

In 1966, a band from New Jersey called the Rascals (previously Young Rascals) had incorporated the sounds of Motown and Memphis soul into their music. The Rascals—Felix Cavaliere, Eddie Brigati, Dino Danelli, and Gene Cornish—had hits with "Good Lovin' " and "Groovin'," and their music, coming from a band comprised mostly of brown-eyed Italians, came to be called blue-eyed soul.

Frank Zappa was born in Baltimore in 1940 to Francis Vincent Zappa, who emigrated from Sicily at a young age and worked as a chemist and mathematician, and Rose Marie Colimore, who was three-quarters Italian and one-quarter French. His music throughout the mid-1960s with his band, the Mothers of Invention, is noted for experimentation. In 1968, Zappa released an album called *Cruising with Ruben and the Jets*, which was inspired by 1950s doo-wop, the music he came of age to.

From South Philadelphia—the same area as Lanza, Martino, Rydell, Fabian, and Avalon—came folk guitarist and balladeer Jim Croce. In 1972 he released *You Don't Mess Around with Jim*, which included his hit songs "Time in a Bottle" and "Operator."

In 1973, Bruce Springsteen released his first album, *Greetings from Asbury Park*, and two years later a record that would solidify his position in the pantheon of great musicians, *Born to Run*. He had grown up in Freehold, New Jersey, the son of a bus driver father, Douglas, of Dutch and Irish extraction, and Adele Ann Zirilli, a legal secretary whose parents had emigrated from a village outside of Naples. He was raised Catholic and working-class, like his fellow New Jerseyan Frank Sinatra, but came of age at a time when it was acceptable to embrace one's working-class background. Steve Van Zandt joined Springsteen's E Street Band in 1975, and was instrumental in writing "Born to Run." He grew up in New Jersey as Steven Lento.

Steven Tallarico from Boston formed a band called Aerosmith, and in 1975, as Steven Tyler, he and the band released their third album, *Toys in the Attic*, which included one of their biggest songs, "Walk This Way."

Then, in 1983, Jon Bon Jovi from Sayreville, New Jersey, formed a band with Richie Sambora, David Bryan, Tico Torres, and Alec John Such and went on to sing "Keep the Faith" and "Livin' on a Prayer." In fact, the theme of prayer and confession figured largely in the music of Madonna Louise Ciccone, who as Madonna sang "Like a Prayer" and released an album called *Confessions on a Dance Floor*.

She was from the suburbs of Detroit, and turned the (typically Italian) trope of virgin-whore on its head in "Like a Virgin" in 1984. Eschewing overt sexuality, the Buffalo-born Ani DiFranco brought feminist ideals to her music. Prince, who was one-quarter Italian and grew up in Saint Paul, Minnesota, crossed all kinds of borders with *Purple Rain* in 1984.

In the 1990s, a blond woman named Gwen Stefani sang with No Doubt before going solo; in some ways, she carried on Madonna's virgin-whore flame.

Now, as the first decade of the twenty-first century comes to a close, an Italian American singer named Stefani Joanne Angelina Germanotta, born in 1986 in New York City, puts on pop shows of operatic proportions—as far as costumes go, anyway—as Lady Gaga.

When the New York Yankees won the World Series in 2009, the song "Empire State of Mind" (an echo of Billy Joel's "New York State of Mind") was heard coming out of delis and cars throughout the streets of New York and New Jersey. It was sung by the rapper Jay-Z along with Alicia Keys, originally Alicia Augello Cook, who was born in New York in 1981 and was of Italian, Irish, and Jamaican descent. She originally attended Columbia University but left to pursue her singing career and eventually recorded hits such as "Fallin'" in 2001 and "Diary" and "You Don't Know My Name" in 2003.

It didn't go unnoticed by me that the only two nonblacks Jay-Z mentioned in his song were Italian Americans—Robert De Niro and Frank Sinatra.

With no false modesty, Jay-Z sings: "I'm the new Sinatra. And since I made it here, I can make it anywhere."

In other words . . .

Frank Sinatra sang "Fly Me to the Moon" triumphantly, in an arrangement by Quincy Jones and accompanied on piano by Count Basie in 1964. Let him play among the stars, he says, wanting to know how spring feels, say, on Jupiter and Mars.

There's the light tap-tapping of a muted snare, the thumping of a bass, and a lone flute riding above it all. The song swings in all its optimism. Everything seems possible. It became the anthem for the astronauts on the 1969 Apollo 10 and 11 missions to the moon.

His was the voice of the Italian singers reaching their dreams in America. And while it wasn't actually the moon they had reached, for them it might as well have been.

"Fill my heart with song. Let me sing for ever more."

"Fly Me to the Moon" (Reprise)

TONY BENNETT, SEPTEMBER 2001

It was the second of two sold-out shows at Radio City Music Hall—nearly a century after Enrico Caruso first performed at the Metropolitan Opera House. Tony Bennett and k. d. lang strode onstage to a standing ovation—he wore a tailored indigo suit with a red pocket square; she was barefoot in a black suit. From the balcony, I could see Bennett's full head of silver and black hair, which framed a prominent nose and a broad smile. The applause nearly drowned out their opening number, "I've Got the World on a String." At seventy-five, Tony Bennett still commanded the hall—one of the last of the Italian American singers who helped shape American popular music.

After a few numbers, lang bowed and left the stage. Bennett kicked in with an up-tempo "Summer Wind," backed by a bright four-piece jazz combo. The music swung; Bennett's full, raspy baritone voice rose above the applause.

The plush hall felt intimate, despite its size. Outside, however, dust had settled over the city, and trucks were hauling debris along the West Side Highway out of Manhattan. It was September 29,

2001, just over two weeks after the Twin Towers were destroyed. For days following, concerts had been canceled, baseball games rescheduled, and even the National Football League had recoiled in shock, rescheduling the second week of games. The world had its eyes glued to the TV.

But Tony Bennett went on with the show—and his fans had packed the hall. At a time when everyone was offering their thoughts, beliefs, and condolences, Tony Bennett didn't mention the World Trade Center attack at all. I was expecting at any moment for him to say something—and I knew the entire audience was waiting as well.

At one point, after singing "That's My Home," he paused and said, "I'm from a little town called Astoria." The audience was silent, full of anticipation.

"You know," he continued. "I gotta tell you . . . I love this city." The crowd erupted in applause and cheers. And that was all he said. All he had to say. He knew that no words could take back what had happened; nothing he said could fully capture the horror, the pain. Tony Bennett knew why he was there—he had been doing it for decades. He was there to entertain. He was there to make people forget about their daily lives, to transport them someplace else.

Toward the end of the concert, Bennett paused after an up-tempo number, "It Don't Mean a Thing If It Ain't Got That Swing." He thanked his band and said to the audience, "You know, they don't make theaters like this anymore." He looked up at the control booth and spoke to the eaves: "Hey, Jimmy, can you do me a favor and kill the sound."

Bennett then walked up to the front of the stage—without amplification, without accompaniment—and sang the saddest, the most yearning version of "Fly Me to the Moon" I had ever heard.

It was as if he were standing on the piazza of his Calabrese town for all of the villagers to hear.

Notes

Bibliography

Acknowledgments

Index

Notes

Most of the sources I've relied on are listed in the bibliography; each of them has informed some aspect of my research and writing. Included here are books and articles on which I've relied more heavily, or from which I have borrowed quotations. If a chapter is not in the notes, it means that its source material has been mentioned previously. In some cases, when singers appear throughout the book, such as Frank Sinatra, the source material is listed in the first chapter in which that person appears. I've also mentioned when a chapter was informed by interviews I've conducted. Two books I felt were invaluable as general reference works were *The Italian American Heritage: A Companion to Literature and Arts*, a collection of articles edited by Pellegrino D'Acierno, and *The Italian American Experience*, edited by Salvatore J. LaGumina, Frank J. Cavaioli, Salvatore Primeggia, and Joseph A. Varacalli.

1. "I HAVE BUT ONE HEART": FRANK SINATRA AND VIC DAMONE

Much of the information in this chapter and in chapter 14 came from two interviews with Vic Damone.

5 Nearly seven million Americans of Italian descent: 1950 U.S. Census.

2. "VESTI LA GIUBBA": ENRICO CARUSO

Much of the information here came from interviews with Aldo Mancusi, director of the Enrico Caruso Museum in Brooklyn. For information on Caruso, I found particularly helpful two books by Howard Greenfeld, *Caruso* and *Caruso: An Illustrated Life*, as well as Michael Scott's *The Great Caruso*.

15 "By God, if this young Neapolitan": Greenfeld, *Caruso*, p. 65.

16 The press butchered him: Greenfeld, *Caruso: An Illustrated Life*, p. 45.

16 "I'll only come back": Greenfeld, *Caruso*, p. 69.

17 "Forti iusi fô": Alan Lomax, in "Folk Song Style" and in the liner notes for the Italian Treasury series, offers insightful comments on Italian folk music.

18 "Eh, c'aimm' a coce": For additional information on Italian folk songs, refer to the liner notes for *Italian Folk Songs* by Carla Bianco and Anne Lomax, Alan's daughter.

18 The voices of *cantastorie*: Del Giudice in *Italian Traditional Song* is particularly insightful on southern Italian ways of life and how they manifest themselves in the region's folk music.

19 "Come and sit": ibid., p. 109.

22 "Because I pass": Branco and Lomax.

23 "Who sent you?": Greenfeld, *Caruso*, p. 38.

3. "CORE 'NGRATO": EDUARDO MIGLIACCIO AND GILDA MIGNONETTE

Jerre Mangione and Ben Morreale offer a comprehensive history of Italian art and culture in America in *La Storia: Five Centuries of the Italian American Experience*. Emelise Aleandri deftly focuses on those subjects, as well as on the performer Eduardo Migliaccio, in *The Italian-American Immigrant Theatre of New York City*. Much of the information on popular Italian songs composed in New York's Little Italy came from an article I wrote for *The New York Sun* (Nov. 22, 2004) and came out of interviews with Joseph Sciorra as well as with Luigi and Ernie Rossi.

27 By 1911, 340,000: 1910 U.S. Census.

29 Migliaccio studied design: Aleandri, *Italian-American Immigrant Theatre*, p. 88.

29 as in "Ammore all 'americana": Aleandri, *Italian-American Immigrant Theatre*, p. 95; Mangione and Morreale, *La Storia*, p. 7.

31 changed her name: Carlo Avvisati, "Mignonette, Gilda," in LaGumina et al., *Italian American Experience*.

4. "O SOLE MIO": ENRICO CARUSO

38 "He indulged frequently": Greenfeld, *Caruso*, p. 59.

41 "New Yorkers are no longer opera mad": Greenfeld, *Caruso*, p. 71, quotes W. J. Henderson in *The New York Sun*.

5. "TIP-TOE THROUGH THE TULIPS": NICK LUCAS

Michael Pitts and Frank Hoffman offer succinct histories of the early crooners in *The Rise of the Crooners: Gene Austin, Russ Columbo, Bing Crosby, Nick Lucas, Johnny Marvin, and Rudy Vallee*. Also, William Perkins has shared information with me both via e-mail and through his website, www.nicklucas.com.

44 "Frank would drag me along": Perkins, www.nicklucas.com.

49 "If you disk jockeys": Pitts and Hoffman, *Rise of the Crooners*, p. 140.

6. "YOU CALL IT MADNESS (BUT I CALL IT LOVE)": RUSS COLUMBO

Lou Miano offers comprehensive details of Columbo's life in *Russ Columbo: The Amazing Life and Mysterious Death of a Hollywood Singing Legend*, as do Joseph Lanza and Dennis Penna in *Russ Columbo and the Crooner Mystique*.

52 The curtains opened behind: Miano related this story to me over the phone, as witnessed by his own father.

7. "SING, SING, SING": LOUIS PRIMA

For many details on Prima's life, I referred to Garry Boulard's *Louis Prima*, as well as the film *The Wildest!* The late Joseph Maselli, who wrote *Italians in New Orleans* with Dominic Candeloro and who founded the American Italian Museum in New Orleans, gave me a tour of Italian New Orleans.

61 Storyville section: Brothers, *Louis Armstrong's New Orleans*.

61 "the white and colored musicians": Boulard, *Louis Prima*, p. 9.

62 About 250: Maselli and Candeloro, *Italians in New Orleans*, p. 35.

62 "one of the toughest honky-tonks in black Storyville": Teachout, *Pops*.

62 "The things he said": Berrett, *Louis Armstrong Companion*, p. 27.

63 "I got a solo": Ibid.

64 "more piercing": Guy Lombardo, *Auld Acquaintance*, p. 166.

65 I saw a grainy film: From *The Wildest!*

8. "ALL OR NOTHING AT ALL": FRANK SINATRA

On Frank Sinatra, I relied on Richard Havers's *Sinatra* and Nancy Sinatra's *Frank Sinatra* for their supremely useful chronology of his life; J. Randy Taraborrelli's *Sinatra* for its thorough, descriptive narrative; Will Friedwald's *Sinatra! The Song Is You* for its marvelous music assessment; and Pete Hamill's *Why Sinatra Matters*, which sets Sinatra's life in a larger context in a fantastic biography and personal memoir.

67 "I'm going to make it": Taraborrelli, *Sinatra*, p. 38.

67 "I felt the hairs": Havers, *Sinatra*, p. 43.

68 "You want the voice": Lahr, *Sinatra*, p. 17, and quoted in many other places with slight differences in recollections.

68 "Although he learned Italian first": Busch, "Joe DiMaggio."

69 "Someday, that's gonna be me": Havers, *Sinatra*, p. 36; Hamill, *Why Sinatra Matters*, p. 100.

72 "You can't sing": Havers, *Sinatra*, p. 38.

73 "The thing that influenced me": Friedwald, *Sinatra! The Song Is You*, p. 86; Granata, Sessions with Sinatra, p. 9.

73 "He came on": Havers, *Sinatra*, p. 62.

9. "NIGHT AND DAY": FRANK SINATRA

74 "What the hell was that?": Friedwald, *Sinatra! The Song Is You*, p. 124.

75 "He weighed 120 pounds": Friedwald, *Sinatra! The Song Is You*, p. 124.

76 "not since Rudolph Valentino": *Time*, July 1943.

76 "Mr. Sinatra's baritone": *New York Times*, Aug. 4, 1943.

10. "ANGELINA": LOUIS PRIMA

79 "I'm not worried": Mangione and Morreale, *La Storia*, p. 25.

80 Italians were rounded up in Montreal: Duliani, *City Without Women*, pp. xi, 15.

81 *capicia* was dialect of *capisce*: *Life*, Aug. 20, 1945.

82 "Hello, Daddy": Boulard, *Louis Prima*, p. 63.

11. "I'M GONNA LOVE THAT GAL (LIKE SHE'S NEVER BEEN LOVED BEFORE)": PERRY COMO

85 "If you decide": Brigstock, "7th Son of a 7th Son," *Band Leaders*, Aug. 1946.

85 "voice, his easy manner": Ibid.

85 "When I look back": Ibid.

86 "Black-haired and black-eyed": *Downbeat,* April 1927.

86 "husky college freshman": *Downbeat,* April 1927.

12. "PRISONER OF LOVE": PERRY COMO

90 Gardner, "The Wildest Saturday Night Fight," Oct. 1955.

13. "MAM'SELLE": FRANK SINATRA

92 "Ladies and gentlemen": Davis, Boyar, and Boyar, *Yes I Can.*

95 "We was all proud of him": Taraborrelli, *Sinatra,* p. 90.

95 "Sinatra is playing": Robert Ruark, *Washington Daily News,* Feb. 20, 1947.

95 "A middle-aged dame": Lee Mortimer, *New York Daily Mirror,* March 30, 1947.

96 "slowly walking down Broadway": Davis, Boyar, and Boyar, *Yes I Can,* p. 116.

14. "YOU'RE BREAKING MY HEART": VIC DAMONE

Much of this chapter is based on interviews with Damone; some stories were rendered differently in his autobiography, *Singing Was the Easy Part.*

100 "Actually, his wife's brother": Pett, "Usher to Gusher."

105 "The people who want to hire popular singers": *New York Herald Tribune,* Jan. 3, 1948.

105 "Mom has a vacuum container": Ibid.

108 "I couldn't concentrate": John S. Wilson, "Vic Set with New Schnoz," *Downbeat,* Aug. 12, 1949.

108 "His new schnozzola": Ibid.

15. "THAT LUCKY OLD SUN": FRANKIE LAINE

Most of this chapter came from a long interview with Laine in 2004, as well as his autobiography with Joseph F. Laredo, *That Lucky Old Son.*

16. "BE MY LOVE": MARIO LANZA

In his book, *Mario Lanza: An American Tragedy,* Armando Cesari painstakingly details the life of the great opera singer and movie star. Also helpful was a documentary called *The American Caruso,* which was narrated by Placido Domingo.

121 "If I am an opera singer": Placido Domingo, in *American Caruso.*

17. "HERE IN MY HEART": AL MARTINO

I tried contacting Martino to talk about the events of his life. His wife, now widow, Judi, very kindly accepted my calls. I managed to speak with Al Martino briefly until he suddenly felt he wasn't yet ready to talk, telling me that he had hoped to save the details for his own book one day.

127 "Martino Missing": United Press International, Nov. 8, 1953.
129 Bennett had once performed at the wedding: Talese, *Honor Thy Father*.
130 "We befriended them": Havers, *Sinatra*, p. 153.

18. "BECAUSE OF YOU": TONY BENNETT

For events in Bennett's life, I found *The Good Life*, written with Will Friedwald, to be very helpful. Unless otherwise stated, the quotations come from this book. Mitch Miller, who graciously agreed to an interview, was also insightful on Bennett and many of the other Italian American singers whose songs he produced.

135 "that's the only music": Unpublished interview with Tony Bennett conducted by David Berreby.

19. "YOUR CHEATIN' HEART": JONI JAMES

Most of the information in this chapter was the result of two interviews with James.

20. "THAT'S AMORE": DEAN MARTIN

For facts on Martin's life, as well as Italian American life in general at the time, I relied on the wonderfully engaging *Dino* by Nick Tosches and on *Memories Are Made of This* by Martin's daughter Deana Martin.

147 "I fought twelve fights": Tosches, *Dino*, p. 57.
148 "Dean looks a lot": Lee Mortimer, *New York Daily Mirror*, Sept. 24, 1943.
149 The popularity of pizza began growing: Helstosky, *Pizza*, p. 6.
149 "Booming Popularity": Owen, "Food News: Mozzarella."
149 "Americans see Italian films": Nickerson, "Taste for Things Italian."

21. "EH, CUMPARI!": JULIUS LA ROSA

Much of this chapter came from an interview with La Rosa.

22. "DARKTOWN STRUTTERS' BALL (ITALIAN-STYLE)": LOU MONTE

The background on Monte's life largely came from www.loumonte.com, a website maintained by his son Ray Monte.

23. "(THE GANG THAT SANG) HEART OF MY HEART":
DON CORNELL AND JOHNNY DESMOND

Cornell's widow, Iris, agreed to talk with me on the phone about his career and life. Some good information came from a website devoted to him, and maintained by Mrs. Cornell, www.doncornell.com.

24. "SWEET AND GENTLE": ALAN DALE

Dale's memoir, *The Spider and the Marionettes*, offered incredible insight into the mind of a performer. A fan site devoted to him, www.members.tripod.com/frasuer/, is maintained by Suzanne Frasuer, who was also helpful via e-mail correspondence.

168 Spurned Suitor": *Journal-American*, May 19, 1958.
168 A photograph from the tabloid: *Confidential*, May 19, 1958.

25. "I'VE GOT THE WORLD ON A STRING": FRANK SINATRA

170 "Hell, you go into show business": Taraborrelli, *Sinatra*, p. 128.
176 "You don't have to sing loud": *Metronome*, Dec. 1953.

26. "JUST A GIGOLO": LOUIS PRIMA

180 "I didn't know what to do": *The Wildest!*
180 "Until Prima had Sam": Ibid.

27. "INNAMORATA": JERRY VALE

Many of the details from Vale's life were related to me during an interview with Vale and his wife, Rita. Also helpful was *Jerry Vale: A Singer's Life* by Richard Grudens. For details on Jimmy Roselli, I referred to *Making the Wiseguys Weep* by David Evanier.

189 "I didn't have the know-how": Grudens, *Jerry Vale*, p. 49.

28. "VOLARE": DEAN MARTIN

192 "The swarthy, mop-headed Sicilian": "Blue Nell Rides Again."
195 "I didn't know Dean very well": Tosches, *Dino*, p. 257.

29. "MAMA": CONNIE FRANCIS

Francis was very forthcoming about her life during an interview. To help tie together the details of her life story, I relied on her autobiography, *Who's Sorry Now?* as well as biographies of Bobby Darin by David Evanier (*Roman Candle*) and Michael Starr (*Bobby Darin*).

196 "Belleville, huh?": Francis, *Who's Sorry Now?*, p. 32.

30. "DREAM LOVER": BOBBY DARIN

Again, David Evanier's *Roman Candle* proved entertaining and helpful, as did Michael Starr's *Bobby Darin* and Francis's *Who's Sorry Now?*.

204 "Someday we'll be the Italian": Starr, *Bobby Darin*, p. 25.

31. "LIGHTNIN' STRIKES": LOU CHRISTIE

Much of this chapter came out of a couple of wonderful dinners with Christie, as well as subsequent phone calls.

32. "I WONDER WHY": DION AND THE BELMONTS

It took two years for me to track him down, but Dion finally agreed to let me interview him, and more than once. For other details, I relied on his memoir, *The Wanderer*. A remarkably useful history of doo-wop can be found in Bobby Hyde's liner notes to Rhino's *Doo Wop* CD box set, as well as *The Complete Book of Doo-Wop* by Anthony J. Gribin and Matthew M. Schiff. Particularly insightful information on doo-wop and early rock and roll came out of an interview I did with "Cousin Brucie" Morrow.

33. "SIXTEEN CANDLES": JOHNNY MAESTRO AND THE CRESTS

Maestro spoke with me twice at length about the formation of the Crests and early vocal harmonization. A recording of a doo-wop symposium by the Calandra Institute proved to be very helpful.

34. "MACK THE KNIFE": BOBBY DARIN

226 "Why would you": Evanier, *Roman Candle*, p. 89.

35. "IT'S NOW OR NEVER": ELVIS PRESLEY

231 "Elvis's hips": *The Wildest!*
231 "[It] smells phony and false": *Western World*, Oct. 1957.

36. "THE WANDERER": DION

234 It was his version: *Rolling Stone*, Jan. 10, 2006.

37. "WALK LIKE A MAN": FRANKIE VALLI AND THE FOUR SEASONS

This story comes out of an article I wrote for *The New York Times* (Oct. 2, 2005), and was informed by interviews with Frankie Valli, Bob Gaudio, Tommy DeVito, and Bob Crewe, as well as the writers of the Broadway musical *Jersey Boys*, Marshall Brickman and Rick Elice.

38. "NICE 'N' EASY": FRANK SINATRA AND THE RAT PACK

Some of the footage I describe of the Rat Pack shows came from the DVDs *Live and Swingin': The Ultimate Rat Pack Collection* and *The Rat Pack*.

245 "Frank Sinatra is one of the most delightful": Havers, *Time*, 1955.
249 The Rat Pack lasted: Per the movie *The Rat Pack*.
250 "I believe an entertainer's function": Frank Sinatra, "Musicians Must Fight Prejudice."

39. "BYE BYE BLACKBIRD": SAMMY DAVIS JR.

For information on Davis, I read his autobiographies *Yes I Can* and *Sammy*, written with Burt and Jane Boyar, as well as *In Black and White* by Wil Haygood. Over the course of several conversations and e-mail exchanges, Burt Boyar generously addressed many of my questions regarding Davis.

40. "FLY ME TO THE MOON": FRANK SINATRA

258 Eighty percent of Italians: Stanislao G. Pugliese in *The Italian American Heritage*, p. 691.

Bibliography

Abissogno, Bruno. *La canzone napoletana: Antologia dal 1920 al 1970, storia e testi.* 2 vols. Naples: Rossi, n.d.

Adams, Val. "Como to Continue TV's 'Music Hall.'" *New York Times,* March 17, 1961.

Aleandri, Emelise. "Cordiferro, Riccardo." In *The Italian American Experience: An Encyclopedia.* New York: Garland, 2000.

——. *The Italian-American Immigrant Theatre of New York City.* Charleston, S.C.: Arcadia, 1999.

Alexander, Shana. "I Want to Be a Legend by 25." *Life,* Jan. 11, 1960.

Armstrong, Louis. *Satchmo: My Life in New Orleans.* New York: Da Capo, 1986.

"Back on Top." *Time,* May 10, 1958.

Bennett, Tony, with Will Friedwald. *The Good Life.* New York: Pocket, 1998.

Berrett, Joshua. *The Louis Armstrong Companion.* New York: Schirmer, 1999.

"Blue Nell Rides Again." *Time,* Aug. 25, 1958.

Boulard, Garry. *Louis Prima.* Urbana: University of Illinois Press, 2002.

Brigstock, Dorothy. "7th Son of a 7th Son." *Band Leaders,* April 1946.

Brodsky, Alyn. *The Great Mayor: Fiorello La Guardia and the Making of the City of New York.* New York: St. Martin's, 2003.

Bronson, Fred. *The Billboard Book of Number One Hits.* New York: Billboard, 2003.

Brothers, Thomas. *Louis Armstrong's New Orleans.* New York: Norton, 2007.

Brunn, O. H. *The Story of the Original Dixieland Jazz Band.* Baton Rouge: Louisiana State University Press, 1960.

Busch, Noel F. "Joe DiMaggio." *Life*, May 1, 1939.

Cannistraro, Philip V., ed. *The Italians of New York: Five Centuries of Struggle and Achievement*. New York: New-York Historical Society, 1999.

Caruso, Enrico, Jr., and Andrew Farkas. *Enrico Caruso: My Father and My Family*. Portland, Ore.: Amadeus, 1997.

Cesari, Armando. *Mario Lanza: An American Tragedy*. Fort Worth, Tex.: Baskerville, 2003.

Coleman, Mark. *Playback: From the Victrola to MP3, 100 Years of Music, Machines, and Money*. New York: Da Capo, 2003.

Copquin, Claudia Gryvatz. *The Neighborhoods of Queens*. New Haven, Conn.: Yale University Press, 2007.

Cramer, Richard Ben. *Joe DiMaggio: The Hero's Life*. New York: Simon and Schuster, 2000.

Crawford, Richard. *America's Musical Life*. New York: Norton, 2001.

Cross, Milton. *Complete Stories of the Great Operas*. New York: Doubleday, 1957.

D'Acierno, Pellegrino. *The Italian American Heritage: A Companion to Literature and Arts*. New York: Garland, 1999.

Dal Cerro, Bill, and David Anthony Witter. "Bebop, Swing and Bella Musica." *Primo*, Sept.–Oct. 2004.

Dale, Alan. *The Spider and the Marionettes*. New York: Lyle Stuart, 1965.

Damone, Vic. *Singing Was the Easy Part*. New York: St. Martin's, 2009.

Davis, Sammy, Jr., Burt Boyar, and Jane Boyar. *Sammy: The Autobiography of Sammy Davis, Jr.* New York: Farrar, Straus and Giroux, 2000.

———. *Yes I Can: The Story of Sammy Davis, Jr.* New York: Farrar, Straus and Giroux, 1990.

Del Giudice, Luisa. *Italian Traditional Song*. Los Angeles: Istituto Italiano di Cultura, 1995.

———, ed. *Studies in Italian American Folklore*. Logan: Utah State University Press, 1993.

De Simone, Roberto. *Disordinata storia della canzone napoletana*. Ischia, Italy: Valentino, 1994.

Di Donato, Pietro. *Christ in Concrete*. New York: Bobbs-Merrill, 1939.

Di Franco, Philip. *The Italian American Experience*. New York: Tom Doherty Associates. 1988.

DiMaggio, Joe. "It's Great to Be Back." *Life*, Aug. 1, 1949.

DiMucci, Dion, with Davin Seay. *The Wanderer: Dion's Story*. New York: Beech Tree, 1988.

DiStasi, Lawrence. *Una Storia Segreta: The Secret History of Italian American Evacuation and Internment During World War II*. Berkeley, Calif.: Heyday, 2001.

Duliani, Mario. *The City Without Women*. Translated by Antonio Mazza. Oakville, Ont.: Mosaic, 1994.

Engel, Edward R. *White & Still All Right! A Collection of "White Group" Histories of the 50s and early 60s*. Scarsdale, N.Y.: Edward R. Engel, 1980.

Evanier, David. *Making the Wiseguys Weep: The Jimmy Roselli Story.* New York: Farrar, Straus and Giroux, 1998.

———. *Roman Candle: The Life of Bobby Darin.* New York: Rodale, 2004.

Fante, John. *Ask the Dust.* New York: HarperPerennial, 2002.

———. *Wait Until Spring, Bandini.* New York: HarperPerennial, 2002.

"Fast Flight to Fame." *Life,* Jan. 1, 1958.

Ferlinghetti, Lawrence. *A Far Rockaway of the Heart.* New York: New Directions, 1968.

Francis, Connie. *Who's Sorry Now?* New York: St. Martin's, 1984.

Friedwald, Will. *Jazz Singing: America's Great Voices from Bessie Smith to Bebop and Beyond.* New York: Da Capo, 1996.

———. *Sinatra! The Song Is You.* New York: Da Capo, 1997.

Gabaccia, Donna R. *Italy's Many Diasporas.* Seattle: University of Washington Press, 2000.

Gambino, Richard. *Blood of My Blood.* Toronto: Guernica, 1998.

Gardaphé, Fred L. *Italian Signs, American Streets: The Evolution of Italian American Narrative.* Durham, N.C.: Duke University Press, 1996.

Gardner, Hy. "The Wildest Saturday Night Fight." *TV and Radio Magazine,* Oct. 1955.

Giddins, Gary. *Bing Crosby: A Pocketful of Dreams: The Early Years, 1903–1940.* Boston: Back Bay, 2001.

Granata, Charles L. *Sessions with Sinatra.* Chicago: A Capella, 1999.

Greenfeld, Howard. *Caruso.* New York: Putnam, 1983.

———. *Caruso: An Illustrated Life.* London: Collins and Brown, 1991.

Gribin, Anthony J., and Matthew M. Schiff. *The Complete Book of Doo-Wop.* Iola, Wis.: Krause, 2000.

Grudens, Richard. *Jerry Vale: A Singer's Life.* Stony Brook, N.Y.: Celebrity Profiles, 2000.

Guglielmo, Jennifer, and Salvatore Salerno. *Are Italians White? How Race Is Made in America.* New York: Routledge, 2003.

Guralnick, Peter. *Careless Love: The Unmaking of Elvis Presley.* Boston: Back Bay, 1999.

———. *Last Train to Memphis.* Boston: Little, Brown, 1994.

Hajdu, David. *Heroes and Villains.* New York: Da Capo, 2009.

Halberstam, David. *The Fifties.* New York: Fawcett Columbine, 1993.

Hamill, Pete. *Why Sinatra Matters.* Boston: Little, Brown, 1998.

Hauser, Thomas, and Stephen Brunt. *The Italian Stallions: Heroes of Boxing's Glory Days.* Toronto: Sport Classic Books, 2003.

Havers, Richard. *Sinatra.* New York: DK, 2004.

Haygood, Wil. *In Black and White: The Life of Sammy Davis Jr.* New York: Knopf, 2003.

Helstosky, Carol. *Pizza: A Global History.* London: Reaktion, 2008.

Hemming, Roy, and David Hajdu. *Discovering Great Singers of Classic Pop.* New York: Newmarket, 1991.

"Hit in the Dark." *Metronome,* Aug. 19, 1947.

Horn, John. "Perry Como's Road Show." *New York Herald Tribune*, May 27, 1965.

Huey, Steve. "Al Martino." Yahoo! Music, music.uk.launch.yahoo.com/ar-256474-bio—Al-Martino (accessed April 17, 2005).

Hyde, Bob. *The Doo Wop Box*. Rhino Records, 1993.

Jackson, Kenneth T., and John B. Manbeck, eds. *The Neighborhoods of Brooklyn*. New Haven, Conn.: Yale University Press, 2004.

Jeffers, H. Paul. *The Napoleon of New York: Mayor Fiorello La Guardia*. New York: Wiley, 2002.

Jennings, Dean. "That Lucky Old Laine." *Collier's*, Aug, 12, 1950.

Kelley, Kitty. *His Way: The Unauthorized Biography of Frank Sinatra*. New York: Bantam, 1986.

Kuntz, Tom, and Phil Kuntz, eds. *The Sinatra Files: The Life of an American Icon Under Government Surveillance*. New York: Three Rivers, 2000.

LaGumina, Salvatore J., Frank J. Cavaioli, Salvatore Primeggia, and Joseph A. Varacalli, eds. *The Italian American Experience: An Encyclopedia*. New York: Garland, 2000.

Lahr, John. *Sinatra: The Artist and the Man*. New York: Random House, 1997.

Laine, Frankie, and Joseph F. Laredo. *That Lucky Old Son: The Autobiography of Frankie Laine*. Ventura, Calif.: Pathfinder, 1993.

Lanza, Joseph, and Dennis Penna. *Russ Columbo and the Crooner Mystique*. Los Angeles: Feral House, 2002.

Larkin, Colin. *The Virgin Encyclopedia of 50s Music*. London: Virgin, 2002.

Leahy, Jack. "The Second Time Around." *Sunday News*, Sept. 1, 1963.

Leider, Emily W. *Dark Lover: The Life and Death of Rudolph Valentino*. New York: Farrar, Straus and Giroux, 2003.

Levinson, Peter J. *September in the Rain: The Life of Nelson Riddle*. New York: Billboard, 2001.

———. *Tommy Dorsey: Living in a Great Big Way*. New York: Da Capo, 2005.

Levy, Shawn. *Rat Pack Confidential: Frank, Dean, Sammy, Peter, Joey, and the Last Great Showbiz Party*. New York: Doubleday, 1998.

Lewis, Jerry, and James Kaplan. *Dean & Me (a Love Story)*. New York: Doubleday, 2005.

Live and Swingin': The Ultimate Rat Pack Collection. Reprise Records, 2003.

Lomax, Alan. "Folk Song Style." *American Anthropologist* 61, no. 6 (Dec. 1959).

———. *Italian Treasury: Calabria*. Rounder Records, 1999.

Lomax, Anne, and Carla Bianco. *Italian Folk Songs, Volume 1*. Folkways Records, 1965.

Lombardo, Guy, with Jack Altshul. *Auld Acquaintance: An Autobiography*. New York: Doubleday, 1975.

Louis Prima: The Wildest! Directed by Don McGlynn. Blue Sea Productions, 1999.

Mangione, Jerre, and Ben Morreale. *La Storia: Five Centuries of the Italian American Experience*. New York: HarperCollins, 1992.

Mario Lanza: The American Caruso. Narrated by Placido Domingo. Kultur Video, 1995.

Martin, Deana. *Memories Are Made of This: Dean Martin Through His Daughter's Eyes.* New York: Harmony, 2004.

Martinez, Raymond J. *Portraits of New Orleans Jazz: Its People and Places.* Jefferson, La.: Hope, 1971.

Maselli, Joseph, and Dominic Candeloro. *Italians in New Orleans.* Charleston, S.C.: Arcadia, 2005.

McCarthy, Albert. *The Dance Band Era: The Dancing Decades from Ragtime to Swing, 1910–1950.* Radnor, Pa.: Chilton, 1982.

Miano, Lou. *Russ Columbo: The Amazing Life and Mysterious Death of a Hollywood Singing Legend.* New York: Silver Tone, 2001.

Miller, Jim, ed. *The Rolling Stone Illustrated History of Rock and Roll: A New Edition of the Best and Most Complete History Brought Up-to-Date and Expanded.* New York: Random House/Rolling Stone Press, 1980.

Moliterno, Gino, ed. *Encyclopedia of Contemporary Italian Culture.* New York: Routledge, 2000.

Nickerson, Jane. "The Taste for Things Italian." *New York Times,* Sept. 2, 1956.

O'Brien, Geoffrey. *Sonata for Jukebox: Pop Music, Memory, and the Imagined Life.* New York: Counterpoint, 2004.

Orsi, Robert A. *The Madonna of 115th Street: Faith and Community in Italian Harlem, 1880–1950.* New Haven, Conn.: Yale University Press, 2002.

Owen, June. "Food News: Mozzarella." *New York Times,* Feb. 24, 1958.

Petacco, Arrigo. *Joe Petrosino.* New York: Macmillan, 1974.

Petkov, Steven, and Leonard Mustazza, eds. *The Frank Sinatra Reader.* New York: Oxford University Press, 1995.

Pett, Saul. "Usher to Gusher." Associated Press, Jan. 18, 1948.

Pignone, Charles. *The Sinatra Treasures: Intimate Photos, Mementos, and Music from the Sinatra Family Collection.* New York: Bulfinch, 2004.

Pitts, Michael, and Frank Hoffman. *The Rise of the Crooners: Gene Austin, Russ Columbo, Bing Crosby, Nick Lucas, Johnny Marvin, and Rudy Vallee.* Lanham, Md.: Scarecrow, 2002.

Pleasants, Henry. *The Great American Popular Singers.* New York: Simon and Schuster, 1974.

Podell-Raber, Mickey, with Charles Pignone. *The Copa: Jules Podell and the Hottest Club North of Havana.* New York: Collins, 2007.

Primeggia, Salvatore. "Comedy." In *The Italian American Experience: An Encyclopedia.* New York: Garland, 2000.

Pugliese, Stanislao G., ed. *Frank Sinatra: History, Identity, and Italian American Culture.* New York: Palgrave Macmillan, 2004.

Puzo, Mario. *The Fortunate Pilgrim.* New York: Fawcett Columbine, 1964.

Rat Pack's Las Vegas. White Star Productions, 2002.

Reid, Cornelius L. *Bel Canto: Principles and Practices.* New York: Joseph Patelson Music House, 1950.

Romeyn, Esther. "Performing High, Performing Low: Enrico Caruso and Eduardo Migliaccio." *Differentia,* nos. 6–7 (Spring/Autumn 1994).

Sadie, Stanley. *The Billboard Encyclopedia of Classical Music.* New York: Billboard, 2004.

Schoell, William. *Martini Man: The Life of Dean Martin.* New York: Cooper Square, 2003.

Sciorra, Joseph. "Who Put the Wop in Doo-Wop?" *Voices in Italian Americana* 13, no. 1 (2002).

Scott, Michael. *The Great Caruso.* New York: Knopf, 1988.

Shaw, Arnold. *52nd Street: The Street of Jazz.* New York: Da Capo, 1971.

Simon, George T. *The Big Bands.* New York: Schirmer, 1967.

Sinatra, Frank. "Musicians Must Fight Prejudice." *Music Journal,* Feb. 1962.

Sinatra, Nancy. *Frank Sinatra: An American Legend.* Santa Monica, Calif.: General Publishing Group, 1998.

Smith, Bill. "Sinatra Thrills Copa with Mature Brilliance." *Billboard,* Jan. 1, 1955.

Smith, Tim. *The Crescent City Lynchings.* Guilford, Conn.: Lyons, 2007.

Starr, Michael. *Bobby Darin: A Life.* Dallas: Taylor, 2004.

Stewart, Jack. *Funerals with Music in New Orleans.* New Orleans: Save Our Cemeteries, 2004.

Sudhalter, Richard M. *Lost Chords: White Musicians and Their Contributions to Jazz, 1915–1945.* New York: Oxford University Press, 1999.

Summers, Anthony, and Robbyn Swan. *Sinatra: The Life.* New York: Knopf, 2005.

Talese, Gay. *Honor Thy Father.* New York: Ballantine, 1971.

———. *Unto the Sons.* New York: Ivy, 1993.

———. "Frank Sinatra Has a Cold." *Esquire,* 1966.

Taraborrelli, J. Randy. *Sinatra: Behind the Legend.* Secaucus, N.J.: Birch Lane, 1997.

Teachout, Terry. *Pops: A Life of Louis Armstrong.* New York: Houghton Mifflin Harcourt, 2009.

Thomas, Tony. *Harry Warren and the Hollywood Musical.* Secaucus, N.J.: Citadel, 1975.

Thompson, Howard. "Como Returns Tonight in 'Winter Show.'" *New York Times,* Dec. 14, 1973.

Thompson, Thomas. "A Five-Month Ordeal, with a Whole Career at Stake." *Life,* Nov. 13, 1964.

Tosches, Nick. *Dino: Living High in the Dirty Business of Dreams.* New York: Delta, 1992.

Turgeon, Charlotte. "Something Fit to Eat." *New York Times,* Nov. 16, 1958.

Turner, John Frayn. *Frank Sinatra.* Dallas: Taylor, 2004.

Van Horne, Harriet. "Perry Como, a Barber Shop Star, Slated for Big Time Build-Up." *New York World-Telegram,* June 22, 1943.

"Vic Damone Still a Family Boy Despite Fame." *New York Herald Tribune,* Jan. 30, 1948.

Walker, Leo. *The Wonderful Era of the Great Dance Bands.* New York: Doubleday, 1972.

Ward, Geoffrey C., and Ken Burns. *Jazz: A History of America's Music.* New York: Knopf, 2000.

Whitburn, Joel. *The Billboard Book of Top 40 Hits, 1955–2000.* New York: Billboard, 2000.

———. *Billboard Pop Hits, Singles, and Albums, 1940–1954.* Menomonee Falls, Wis.: Record Research, 2002.

———. *Pop Memories, 1890–1954: The History of American Popular Music.* Menomonee Falls, Wis.: Record Research, 1986.

Wilson, Earl. *Sinatra: An Unauthorized Biography.* New York: Macmillan, 1976.

Wilson, John S. "Vic Set with New Schnoz." *Downbeat,* Aug. 12, 1949.

Zehme, Bill. *The Way You Wear Your Hat: Frank Sinatra and the Lost Art of Livin'.* New York: HarperCollins, 1997.

Acknowledgments

The liner notes for this album must begin with the stories of my parents and my grandparents, who themselves assimilated into American culture at the turn of the twentieth century. So I must first thank my mother and father for sharing their stories with me.

I first encountered Italian American song as a boy at my family's dining room table; I eventually found myself in the living rooms and kitchens of many of the singers whose stories are told in this book. To those (and their spouses) who so graciously opened their doors to me, invited me to their dinner tables, gave me driving tours, or simply picked up the phone, I am indebted: they are Bob Crewe, Lou Christie, Iris Cornell, Vic Damone, Tommy DeVito, Dion DiMucci, Connie Francis, Bob Gaudio, Joni James, Frankie Laine, Julius La Rosa, Johnny Maestro, Jerry Vale, and Frankie Valli.

Two guides offered unparalleled help. My friend Joseph Sciorra at the John D. Calandra Italian American Institute, Queens College, City University of New York, gave me a foundation in Italian folk music and popular song, and, as an academic impresario, made introductions to people I could not have encountered otherwise. And Danny Stiles, New York's own Vicar of Vintage, still active on AM radio after more than fifty years, spent much time with me discussing the music of his time and earlier times.

Aldo Mancusi, the founder of the Enrico Caruso Museum of America in Brooklyn, spent several hours with me, gave me two private tours of the museum, and offered insights for various chapters of my book. The late Joseph Maselli of the American Italian Renaissance Foundation in New Orleans, a born storyteller, gave me a most enjoyable and enlightening tour of Italian New Orleans.

Mitch Miller spent an afternoon with me, recollecting the record business of the 1950s; the Sammy Davis Jr. biographer Burt Boyar offered valuable comments on various chapters through the prism of the world's greatest entertainer. And there were those who spoke with me on various subjects and assisted in research: Charles Alexander; Joshua Berrett; Wancy Cho; Marty Cooper, formerly of Colony Records; Jim Cummins; Will Friedwald; Jonathan Hiam at the New York Public Library's Library for the Performing Arts; Michael Hittman at Long Island University; Tom Kelly; Wolf Knapp; Lou Miano; Peter Michel, director of special collections at the Lied Library of the University of Nevada, Las Vegas; Robert Perkins; Stephanie Romeo; Joe and Sal Scognamillo of Patsy's Italian restaurant; Bill Tonelli; and Mike Viola.

There are those who read drafts of the text and offered invaluable commentary. Floyd Skloot was a most generous, thoughtful, and honest reader, poetic in his evaluation; Louisa Ermelino, my boss at *PW*, who has always been more than supportive, told me where I was on- and offtrack; Stan Pugliese managed to send comments between his teaching gigs at Hofstra and Harvard; and Natalie Danford and Paolo Pierleoni looked over my Italian and dialect translations and spellings. As a fact-checker, my good friend Stan Friedman took a fine-toothed comb to the manuscript.

I am grateful beyond words for the generosity of the folks at Getty Images: Katie Calhoun, Katie Walker, and Mitch Blank. This book wouldn't be complete without the evocative images they provided.

I thank the team at Farrar, Straus and Giroux for supporting my second book with them: Jonathan Galassi; Jeff Seroy, Sarita Varma, Kathy Daneman, and Stephen Weil in publicity; Susan Mitchell, Jennifer Carrow, and Abby Kagan for the spot-on design and jacket; managing editor Debra Helfand, who worked hard to make sure it all made sense; and Karen Maine, who stayed on top of it all.

I am grateful to Columbia University for arranging the assistance of Josh Garrett-Davis through its Hertog Fellowship; and to John Marino, John S. Salomone, and Elissa Ruffino of the National Italian American Foundation for their interest and support, and for the grant they provided.

A big thank-you goes to my good friends David and Wendy Kidd for providing me wth a Los Angeles home; to my childhood friend Jorge Vidal and his parents, Jorge senior and Adela Vidal, for providing me a writing refuge in St. Petersburg, Florida; to my brother-in-law Jimmy Valenti; and to my sister, Michelle, who, even as she ribs me, never seems to lose faith in me.

I raise a glass to my friends, who offered immense support, guidance, and ears for my frustration during the rough spots of this trip: David Hajdu, Rebecca Skloot, Rebecca Miller, Steven Kuchuck, Dana Jennings, David Prete, Nathan Ward, and Jonathan Segura. And I raise another one to the guys who have provided me with years of great BBQ, poker, and friendship: Gerry Gallagher, Thomas Jackson, Stephen Morrow, Charles Nix, Ian Schoenherr, George Scott, and Carl Zimmer. Salut'.

My agent, Maria Massie, patiently supported me through this prolonged journey, offering helpful encouragement along the way. She was even-keeled and upbeat and refused to let me be anything but.

Paul Elie, my editor and good friend, was, if I may evoke a great Italian American, a Vince Lombardi to me. He patiently read several drafts of this book, guiding me to my true voice. He was tough when he needed to be, at times when I was least prepared for it. Taking an editorial turn on a Lombardi phrase, Paul might as well have said, "Making art isn't everything; it's the only thing."

Finally, this book would have never been written without the patience, love, and encouragement of my wife, Martha, with whom, during the course of writing this book, I became a parent twice over. Her ear for music informed my own.

Index